Reel Families

ARTS AND POLITICS OF THE EVERYDAY

Patricia Mellencamp, Meaghan Morris, Andrew Ross,
series editors

REEL FAMILIES

A Social History of Amateur Film

Patricia R. Zimmermann

Indiana University Press

Bloomington and Indianapolis

The paper used in this publication meets the minimum requirements of
American National Standard for Information Sciences—Permanence of
Paper for Printed Library Materials, ANSI Z39.48-1984.

♾™

Manufactured in the United States of America

Library of Congress Cataloging-in-Publication Data

Zimmermann, Patricia Rodden.
Reel families : a social history of amateur film
/ Patricia R. Zimmermann.
p.   cm. — (Arts and Politics of the Everyday)
Includes bibliographical references and index.
ISBN 0-253-36876-6 (cl : acid-free paper). — ISBN 0-253-20944-7
(pa : acid-free paper)
1. Amateur films—History and criticism.   I. Title.
PN1995.8.Z56   1995
791.43'0222—dc20   94-22840

1 2 3 4 5 00 99 98 97 96 95

For Stewart and Sean

Contents

Preface

ON ANY SUN-DRENCHED, humid August day in Washington, D.C., tourists cruise the mall, hauling popcorn, kids, and cameras. Fathers pose their children in front of the African elephant grandly inhabiting the rotunda of the National Museum of Natural History. The kids assault the phones that play pre-recorded descriptions of this stuffed behemoth. Fathers survey their children's mischief with camcorders like FBI agents at a demonstration. The kids lash their tongues out at their fathers, contort their faces, and defiantly perform for the camera.

These seemingly innocuous representations of the American family devouring its leisure and travel time like flies zooming in on hamburgers at a picnic float through all of our family albums and home-movie collections. During their leisure time, these parents direct the most important and consuming narrative of all—the grand, happy epic of nuclear family life. However visually primitive home movies may appear textually, their historical and discursive structures present much more complexity. These images are the confluence of the unstable intersection of family history, state iconography, and consumer technology. Amateur film occupies one of the central contradictions of communications in the twentieth century: on the one hand, domination and consumption; on the other, resistance and hope.

In 1974 Hans Magnus Enzensberger interrogated the mass media's alteration of social relations. He argues in his book *The Consciousness Industry* that contemporary use of mass-media technologies may actually inhibit meaningful communication, because these media operate almost exclusively as one-way transmitters. However, he notes the untapped potential of these technologies to facilitate the expression of diverse opinions. For Enzensberger, vigorous public expression constitutes a basic democratic right, a central component for freedom.[1] Thus, the proliferation and subsequent derailing of amateur-media technologies to consumer markets defuse amateur film's democratic potential by reconstituting it as an irrelevant pastime with limited social, political, or aesthetic consequences.

While Enzensberger envisions a more democratic public sphere facilitated by access to amateur media, he does not explain the concrete historical processes that chiseled away at the emancipatory potential of amateur-media technologies. Analyzing how social, economic, aesthetic, and political discourses have historically defined amateur film can chart how dominant media formations marginalized and stabilized the potential, but latent, political disruptions of amateur film.

Amateur film occupies the unsightly, sprawling underside of more traditional commercial-film histories. The deficit of historical study on amateur film boldly underscores the power of "professional" film and film studies' enamoration with it to marginalize the aberrant, the primitive, and the undeveloped phenomenon of amateur film and its corollaries. To study amateur film means detouring from the analysis of textuality into the power relations of discursive contexts, a much less-finite pursuit. This book invites readers to relocate to a different, more private terrain of cultural production.

This previously unexplored, subterranean territory of film history is located in consumers, everyday life, popular magazines, and camera manufacturers. The history of amateur film parallels, imitates, circumvents, and occasionally disrupts traditional film history. The investigation into a subjugated film history—a term deployed by historian Michel Foucault to designate historical contents submerged by more dominant, coherent knowledge—portrays a scattered, incomplete, and amorphous discourse.[2] From 1897 to 1962 amateur-film discourse incrementally relocated amateur filmmaking within a romanticized vision of the bourgeois nuclear family, thereby amputating its more resistant economic and political potential for critique. This book analyzes how that public discourse positioned amateur film within specific economic, aesthetic, social, and political processes. Mired in twentieth-century patterns of leisure-time commodity consumption, amateur filmmaking is always defined as a hobby rather than as a job. I use *amateur film* in this book as a covering term for the complex power relations defining amateur filmmaking, whereas I employ *home movies* as a descriptive term for actual films produced by families.

A few anthropologists, photographic critics, and avant-garde filmmakers have ventured into amateur-film territory. Although methodologically disparate, these writers all aim to decode home photographs and home movies to uncover larger, more complex, and universal cultural meanings. They feel the snapshot or home movie functions simultaneously as a cultural artifact and as a mediator between the social and linguistic rules of a given culture.

All of these writers identify amateur film and photographs through their unintentionality, lack of deliberate formal and textural codes, circulation within the leisure and affective systems of participants, and social distance from commercial forms of media production. For example, anthropologist Richard Chalfen defines home-mode imagery as

conceptually and pragmatically distinct from the professionally produced forms seen in advertising, photojournalism, art or museum exhibitions, feature films, education, film festivals, and the like . . . generally produced by nonprofessional photographers using inexpensive, mass produced cameras.[3]

His position extends Sol Worth and John Adair's research on Navajo filmmaking.[4] Other anthropologists decipher larger cultural codes, regularities, and patterns in nonprofessional visual communication, a form that forsakes professional visual standards because it is excised from professional economic relations.[5] However, all of this work remains text bound and ahistorical.

Photographic critic Julia Hirsch in *Family Photographs: Content, Meaning and Effect* distinguishes professional from home-mode photography through lack of intention and transcendent revelations into specificities of the human condition.[6] Hirsch presumes amateur image-making operates in a purified, ahistorical, aesthetic vacuum. Removed from the visual regimes of more commercial media, "candid photography" unselfconsciously discloses a priori truths.

In contrast, Susan Sontag in her *On Photography* maintains amateur photography constitutes a social rather than an artistic process:

Photography has become almost as widely practiced an amusement as sex and dancing—which means that, like every mass art form, photography is not practiced by most people as an art. It is mainly a social rite, a defense against anxiety, and a tool of power.[7]

For Sontag, amateur photography replaced "authentic bonds" at the time when industrialization reconfigured the family. For historian Michael Lesy, amateur photography's mistakes, geographic sensibility, and individuality render it an intriguing oddity.[8] Art photographers have appropriated the imaginary spontaneity and freedom of amateurism to unlock "revealing moments" and "visual truths" through adoption of nonintervention.[9] For example, the work of Emmet Gowin and the *Aperture* Snapshot Collection exhibit how the so-called spontaneous and unencumbered language of the amateur elevates the everyday to the metaphysical.[10]

Some historians and critics of avant-garde film connect available, inexpensive filmmaking equipment to the development of experimental film. In *Movie Journal* Jonas Mekas imagines an emergent film utopia: "The day is close when the 8mm home movie footage will be collected and appreciated as beautiful folk art, like songs and lyric poetry, that was created by the people."[11] Mekas collapses amateur film into the avant-garde. Later in the book he reproduces George Kuchar's optimistic 8mm manifesto: "[The] 8mm is a tool of defense in this society of mechanized corruption because through 8mm and its puny size, we come closer to the dimensions of the atom."[12] Mekas and Kuchar recast amateur technology as resistance, forecasting its emancipatory potential.

However, most of this previous work insulates amateur film and photography from other more dominant forms of representation. A political definition of amateur film is located more specifically within its social relations to dominant cinematic practices, ideologies, and economic structures rather than in its presumed textual innocence. Additionally, amateur film hinges on the ideological function of leisure time to insert commodities into the nuclear family. This book poses a different question from that of the art critics and anthropologists: How were consumer technologies like movie cameras drafted into an idealization of the family rather than developed as a means to critique social and political structures?

These anthropologists, art historians, and avant-garde filmmakers privilege amateur films and amateur filmmakers, betraying a text-centered approach mired in authorial innocence. Amateur film, however, is a socially and politically constructed discourse. How has Hollywood film, as represented by the photographic press, family press, and popular press, intersected with amateur filmmaking? Rather than probing home movies as mysterious, transcendent textual systems, this book analyzes discursive practices—defined by Foucault as language practiced with its own rules of operation and with specific relationships to politics, culture, economics, and social institutions[13]—that continually reconstitute amateur film.

Reel Families argues that amateur film enacts continually realigning social relations and discursive presuppositions—relations functioning in a complex dynamic to professional filmmaking. Thus, not only do economic, aesthetic, political, and familial power relations construct the category of amateur film but a negative, compensatory relation to professional film also inscribes its discourse. Historically, amateur film's trajectory transformed from an economic to a social category: from a participation in entrepreneurial myths to a popularization of professional equipment as consumer items and, finally, to a professionalization of leisure time.

Amateur film cannot be fixed as an agent, event, or situation; it is simultaneously a discursive construct and a category of producers and productions. The interrogation of the development of amateur film requires a historical method that can explain shifting social structures and categories. The reorganization of different discourses and power relationships spurs historical transformations in amateur film. As Hubert Dreyfus and Paul Rabinow have shown, Foucault's concept of discursive practices questions the formation of statements: Who produces statements and from what site?[14]

In *The Archaeology of Knowledge*, Michel Foucault rejects the history of events and unities, describing discursive formations as "a system of dispersion, whenever, between objects, types of statements, concepts, or thematic choices, one can

define a regularity (an order, correlations, positions, and functions, transformations)."[15] Discursive formations reroute historiography from linear events toward an analysis of relations between discourse and events. Foucault's historical method explains the significance of statements, such as "madness," or the
epistemological suppositions of the medical science of prisons. He analyzes not
only their intricate relationships to economic and political formations and their
particular articulation of power but also their discursive dispositions locating
choice, direction, and selection. For Foucault "events" emerge as "ruptures, dis-
continuities"—breaks within discursive formations.[16]

In *Foucault, Marxism and Critique*, Barry Smart further distinguishes discourses from nondiscursive practices. He explains that Foucault defines discourse as "systems of formal statements about the world." The nondiscursive
would then span social, institutional, and economic practices. By investigating
how the formations of practice and discourse intertwine, Foucault's deployment
of discourse deflects traditional Marxist historiographic claims of the economic
base determining superstructures.[17] *Reel Families* defines this rather slippery
term *discourse* as a system of statements locating a specific territory in language—in this case, amateur film. Institutional and social relationships, on the
other hand, constitute practices. Amateur aesthetic advice expresses discursive
relations, while the economic structures of the amateur-film manufacturing industry, equipment, designs, and political context chart the more material relations of the nondiscursive.

Reel Families, then, analyzes amateur-film history as a constant reorganizing
of aesthetic, economic, and political formations, not as a linear history of particular amateur-film producers, film circles, or films. For the most part, this book
examines the public discourse that continually revamped the roles, functions,
and purposes of amateur film, along with its relationship to industrial, marketing, and technological formations. How do dominant institutional formations
like familialism, camera magazines, and corporate equipment manufacturers
define amateur film? How do we explain definitional transformations? What
discursive and nondiscursive strategies negotiate between professional and
amateur film? What democratic possibilities for media access does amateur film
offer historically?

Any discussion of discourse raises questions of practice; the two terms are
inextricably linked, each suggesting the contours and problems of the other.
This analysis of amateur-film discourse raises the inevitable question of just
how much the discourse of advice columns and camera manufacturers overdetermined the actual practices of amateur filmmakers. It would be theoretically
foolish to presume a one-to-one correspondence between discourse and practice. Were amateur filmmakers willing to ascribe to Hollywood norms without

deviation? Or did amateur filmmakers simply continue with their own skewed, shaky imaging of the world, undeterred by aesthetic advice? Or did amateurs openly resist Hollywood indoctrination? The complexities of the relationship between discourse, which often presents itself as even, uninterrupted, and organized, and practice, which is much more multiple, unruly, and contradictory, erupt when we consider the myriad of relations between amateur-film discourse and actual amateur filmmaking. While these theoretical issues are tempting to analyze, their empirical answer is bound by the availability of amateur film.

While the major thrust of this book is oriented toward an examination of the written discourse that positions and defines amateur film, actual amateur productions are also discussed. Very few film archives—until recently—collected amateur film. To my knowledge, films from the early period of amateurism, from 1897 to 1923, are not widely available due to the variety of technological formats. More amateur films are available from 1923 to 1962 simply because the 16mm format was standardized. The discussion of actual amateur films in this book is limited to films available in the Wisconsin Historical Society and the Smithsonian Institution, and even then, the choice of particular works is rather arbitrary. For the most part, films were selected to illustrate a salient theoretical or historical issue during a period rather than for their textual interest.

To analyze the definitional and structural transformations of amateur film, a long time frame is necessary to compare separate and distinct historical periods. In an essay entitled "History and the Social Sciences: The Long Term," Ferdinand Braudel explains the centrality of temporality for all historians, whether measuring historical time by events or by cycles. Not only do social structures change very slowly, but other historical phenomena, such as science and technology, often transform at different rates than the economic or the social.[18] Long-term histories exchange dramatic, causal narrative for structural analysis. According to Gregor McLennon, Braudel's long-term history analyzes slow transformations rather than rapid changes precipitated by events, situating the economic and the social in a reciprocal rather than a causal relationship.[19]

Charles Lemert and Garth Gillan locate Foucault's historiography as an intervention into the Braudelian structural explanation of events.[20] For Foucault, historical change is uneven, migrating between discourses and practices at different velocities. Historical description and explanation pivot on the reorganization of aesthetic, cultural, economic, political, technological, and social formations. Michel Foucault designates this synchronous, conjunctural type of historical analysis archaeology: "Its model [is] neither the purely logical schema of simultaneities; nor a linear succession of events, but . . . [it] tries to show the intersection between necessarily successive relations and others that are not so."[21] By deciphering the shifting relationships among the economic, political, social, and aesthetic, *Reel Families* interprets the power relations marginalizing amateur film as an insignificant media discourse and practice during its first sixty-five years and develops a history of the relationship between the bourgeois nuclear family and consumer technology.

Amateur film is not simply an inert designation of inferior film practice and ideology but rather is a historical process of social control over representation.[22] The periodization of this book is important for an understanding of the significance of the various changes that have transformed amateur film. This study extends from the initial forays into amateur technology and concludes in the early 1960s when 8mm and super-8mm film technology began to dominate the family consumer market. By the early 1960s amateur film had become firmly ensconced within the patriarchal bourgeois nuclear family, signaling the end of discursive contestation over its definition and placement. The chapter periodization is based on significant shifts and changes in film technology. Although one might argue that this periodization strategy suggests technological determinism, I have utilized technological change and innovation as an organizing device and as a locus for the analysis of social, political, and aesthetic maneuvers. Chapter 1 traces the theoretical and historical origins of amateurism, while chapter 2 examines its initial technological development from 1897 through 1923. Chapter 3 analyzes the institution of dominant aesthetic paradigms from 1923 through 1940, and chapter 4 looks at the massive transformations and professionalization of amateur film during World War II. Chapter 5 investigates the emphasis on the nuclear family from 1950 to 1962. The final chapter maps some contemporary articulations of amateur media.

Each chapter not only retrieves amateur-film history from the garbage dump of film and cultural studies but also examines how different periods elaborated amateur film within extremely different articulations: technological, aesthetic, political, and social. This trajectory reveals a systematic stripping of the democratic, participatory, and public potential of amateur film and its marginalization within the much more privatized, isolated, and denuded domains of the nuclear family. On perhaps a less analytical and more polemical level, *Reel Families* is, if anything, a recycling project: it hopes to rescue amateur film and home movies from the trash and to rehabilitate these vehicles as an integral part of a suppressed and discarded film history.[23]

Acknowledgments

T HIS SOCIAL HISTORY of the public discourse on amateur film represents the confluence of veritable material conditions of theory, practice, and passion. In Oskar Negt's graduate seminar at the University of Wisconsin–Madison, I studied German critical theory and the Frankfurt School's latent pessimism over the domination of the mass media. During that time, I also screened my parents' home movies. This project began to take shape with that strange contradictory intersection. In these amateur films I imagined an archive of my own personal history and memories and an intellectually invisible, vast, and unmined history of film. I deduced a cheap, if not eccentric, way to produce films. And I realized that amateur film was very much feminized within women's cultural practice and neutralized within the family. Those family images unspooled in my scholarly research and in the film theory classes that I taught as examples of innovative, inexpensive ways to make films and to excavate family ideology. I began to ferret out the political and social frameworks that disenfranchised and obscured this most democratic of media-making practices.

Along the rocky, winding road to becoming a book, this project has collected many friends. Jane Shattuc, Diane Waldman, Richard Herskowitz, Gina Marchetti, Jeanne Allen, Tino Balio, Wendy Shay, and Jake Homiak encouraged, critiqued, and patiently listened to my obsessions. Patricia Mellencamp and Meaghan Morris provided incisive suggestions in the final stages of manuscript preparation, serving in effect as *Reel Families'* midwives. My running partners, Zillah Eisenstein and Carla Golden, conditioned my mind as well as my body, blurring the binary opposition between the two. My incredibly energetic and supportive brother, Byron Zimmermann, coached me in personal computing and pushed me into twentieth-century technology. Stewart Auyash provided sustenance, encouragement, love, and the intellectual space to work. Thank you for dinners cooked, lawns mowed, day-care drop-offs and pick-ups, encouragement, and love.

Some portions of this book have been previously published as journal articles, although the research and arguments in the initial essays have been greatly revised and expanded: "Amateurs, the Avant-Garde, and Ideologies of Art," *Journal of Film and Video* (Summer/Fall 1986): 63–85; "Filming Adventures in Beauty: Pictorialism, Amateur Cinematography, and the Filmic Pleasures of the Nuclear Family from 1897 to 1924," *Afterimage* (December 1986): 8–11; "Entrepreneurs, Engineers, and Hobbyists: The Formation of a Definition of Amateur Film, 1897–1923," *Current Research in Film*, vol. 3, ed. Bruce Austin (Norwood, N.J.: Ablex, 1987), 163–88; "Hollywood, Home Movies, and Common Sense: Amateur Film as Aesthetic Dissemination and Social Control, 1950–1962," *Cinema Journal* 27, no. 4 (Summer 1988): 23–44; "Professional Results with Amateur Ease: The Formation of Amateur Filmmaking Aesthetics, 1923–1940," *Film History* 2, no. 3 (1988): 22–36; "Trading Up: Amateur Film Technology in the 1950s," *Screen* (Summer 1988): 17–29; "Fighting with Film: 16mm Amateur Film, World War II, and Participatory Realism," *Current Research in Film*, vol. 5, ed. Bruce Austin (Norwood, N.J.: Ablex, 1990), 142–73; and "Our Trip to Africa: Home Movies as the Eyes of the Empire," *Afterimage* 17, no. 8 (March 1990): 4–7.

Historical work depends on the labor, generosity, and enthusiasm of many archivists and librarians. The wonderful librarians and archivists at the Bell and Howell Company, Cornell University, Eastman House, the Smithsonian Institution, Harvard University, Ithaca College, Northwestern University, the Wisconsin State Historical Society, the Center for Creative Photography, the University of Arizona, the University of Wisconsin–Madison, the British Film Institute, and Northeast Historic Film deserve special Academy Awards for their professional support of amateurism.

An anonymous group of people buried in history need to be recognized: the millions of people who have produced amateur films since 1897. While I only know the work of filmmakers in the Smithsonian Institution in any depth, I hope that these unnamed and as yet unknown films, if not the memory and names of their makers, will be housed in more archives in the future. Preservation of these amateur films could balance out, reinvigorate, and challenge the more traditional history of commercial cinema.

Beyond labor, historical work requires financial backing. Grants and fellowships from the Smithsonian Institution, the National Endowment for the Humanities, the Kaltenborn Foundation, the Ithaca College Summer Research Fund, and the Ithaca College Small Grants Program supported many trips to various collections, archives, and libraries. In particular, without my fellowship with the Human Studies Film Archive of the National Museum of Natural History of the Smithsonian Institution, it would have been impossible to screen any existing amateur films. Wendy Shay, Jake Homiak, and Pam Wintle—the excellent and tireless curatorial staff of the Human Studies Film Archive—energized and exhausted me with their enthusiasm for this project, their probing critical questions, their debate, and their gleaning of an amazingly accessible, rare, and extensive collection of amateur film.

Unfortunately, computers have not completely erased the physical and mental labor of producing a manuscript. Karen Wheeler and Karen Brown typed the words *amateurism* and *home movies* more times than any mortal should be compelled to execute in a lifetime. Dorothy Owens's incredible editing, syntactical precision, grammatical rigor, hawklike eye for mistakes and inconsistencies, amazing deftness at the computer, and infectious optimism whipped the final manuscript into shape. Patricia St. John-Doolin honed the final manuscript with her deft copyediting; I thank her for her precision and care.

The dissecting queries of my students in the Department of Cinema and Photography at Ithaca College into my enchantment with home movies invigorated my arguments and propelled me to implement these theories in my teaching. Warm thanks goes to my unflagging research assistants over the years who toiled in the library stacks checking references for me: Christine Angland, Monica Digilio, Beth Herren, Karl Wiedemann, Bridget Lalley, Diana Meo, Lenore diPaoli, Ann Estorov, and William Hooper.

Finally, for their encouragement of my intellectual pursuits and writing, for their unswerving support through sometimes excruciatingly difficult times, and for their precious home movies, I lovingly thank my parents, Alice Rodden Zimmermann and Byron Zimmermann.

1

Pleasure or Money

Professionalism and the Economy

MOST SIMPLY, PROFESSIONALISM suggests performing a task for financial return, and amateurism indicates doing something for pleasure, for the sheer love of it, as its Latin root—*amare*—denotes. However, these rather value-laden, popular distinctions conceal much more complex social relations: while the professional conducts activities for work, an amateur labors away from work, in free time or leisure time. In amateurism as a social and historical phenomenon, work and free time are not locked into simple binary oppositions; rather, the absence of one defines and imbricates the other.

The theoretical debate surrounding the public sphere (traditionally defined as the realm of economics and politics) and its relationship to the private sphere (positioned by most theorists as the realm of the family and personal life) has recently been reinvigorated by such diverse writers as Jurgen Habermas, Peter Hohendahl, Eli Zaretsky, Oskar Negt, Eberhard Knodler-Bunte, and Arthur Brittan. In its classical phase, active participation in the politics, law, and morality of the state comprised the public sphere, whereas the household defined the private sphere.[1] As nation states and the economy developed, these distinctions became more complex. The public sphere emerged as the site of political and economic power and discussions of law, rationality, and morality; the private sphere became increasingly identified with women, the family, personal sentiment, and feeling.

Jürgen Habermas argues that the public sphere—"the realm of our social life in which something approaching public opinion can be formed"[2]—developed as a distinct social formation from the private sphere after the rise of the bourgeoisie in the eighteenth century. Before this period, the public sphere was linked directly to the public display of sovereign power symbolized in the body of the prince, king, or ruler. The location of rational discussion within the public sphere paralleled the rise of private property; private individuals could transmit "rational authority" to the state via the public sphere.[3] The public sphere interceded between fragmented individuals and the political power of the state. Interestingly, Habermas observes that modern communication systems (such as print media and newspapers) further mediated between private individuals and the liberal, quasi-participatory public sphere typical of advanced industrialized countries.

Habermas explains that the public sphere functions as both a normative and historically descriptive category. As a normative construct, the public sphere insures individuals equality in access and in freedom to express ideas and opinions. Mass media composes the public sphere in the twentieth century and contains this possibility.

Many theorists have analyzed the intricate relationship between the public sphere and the role of experts. Professionalism and amateurism traverse this dichotomy between the public sphere of the economy and the private sphere of the home and personal life in very specific ways. Several critics have shown, for example, that as communication and economic systems expand into more elaborate structures, social divisions between experts and nonexperts escalate.

Raymond Williams connects this technical specialization with the appearance of more layered, differentiated social constructs than those contained in a traditional Marxist class analysis. He explains that

> as a culture becomes richer and more complex, involving many more artistic techniques developed to a high degree of specialization, the social distance of many practices becomes much greater, and there is a virtually inevitable if always complex set of divisions between participants and spectators in various acts.[4]

The difference between professional film and amateur film, then, marks a social distance sustained through the specialization of technique. Habermas argues that these specializations manifest a positivist, scientific mentality that controls the public sphere, redefined almost exclusively by economic and political relations rather than by rationality. These instrumental actions depend on technical rules, skills acquisition, extension of market control, and power.[5]

For Habermas, the rise of "experts" precipitates the gradual destruction of the normative public sphere: technical rules replace equal access to participation in public discussion. Political problems formerly discussed by groups transform into technical dysfunctions repaired by individual experts. Scientific paradigms and epistemologies gradually dominate the public sphere, and in particular, the economy, diminishing access and equality.[6] Observation, codification, and expertise function as deterrents to access to a severely truncated and economically circumscribed public sphere. As an objective and replicable set of rules and standards, science increasingly defines the economy.[7] Expertise—based on appropriating scientific methods of observation, standardization, and regularity—circumscribes the public sphere of political discussion; its emphasis on the acquisition of technical skills promotes stratification, thus diminishing equal access.

Professionalism, then, can be explicated as a system of technical rules insuring access to the economy for only a qualified and privileged few. Professional film's "codes of expertise"—narrative paradigms, capital-intensive production, division of labor, and market control—determine access to the market economy. Williams observes that "the market is still, by its nature, profoundly reproductive of both known demand . . . and of known priorities."[8] Because professionalism incorporates rational rules and the reproduction of known qualities, to invoke Habermas's formulation, it operates within a more public domain. On the other hand, because amateurism structurally rejects these rational modes, it is marginalized within the private sphere of personal life, outside wage labor and economic relations, and operates almost exclusively as consumption.

Professionalism depends on the standardization and interchangeability of skills. Professionalism eradicates autonomous individual or collective access to the economy; it signifies the smooth coordination of technical rules and procedures within complex, stratified organizations. With their enormous financial resources and professional experts, only bureaucracies have access to the economic and political public sphere. Professionalized categories of technical skill isolate workers, inhibit them from producing independently, and fragment access. Professionalism, then, is congruent with market operations. In addition, capital-intensive productions form a significant barrier to entry. For example, Hollywood film depends on elaborate financial resources, a division of labor, specialized technical expertise, and access to national markets. Professionalism revolves around two separate interlocking constructs. On the one hand, professionalism articulates scientific norms; on the other hand, this incorporation of standards differentiates the professional, insuring a limited amount of control over a small sector of the economy.[9]

Amateurism and the Private Sphere

The private sphere—traditionally defined as the realm of family and personal life—developed as the site for the resuscitation of all those needs that instrumental actions cannot satisfy. This contradiction between alienated wage labor and what Adolfo Vazquez has termed the "creative essence"—the need for fulfilling, integrated, meaningful work, assumed to be latent in all individuals[10]—is dispersed into the social categories of professionalism and amateurism.

Eli Zaretsky's *Capitalism, the Family and Personal Life* charts the historical development of the split between the private and public spheres.[11] The rise of industrial commodity production severed the family from economic and social production. Because capitalism depended on rationality and control, the family, in contrast, acquired greater significance as the site of happiness, love, freedom, creativity, personal relations, feeling, and the subjectivity denied in productive labor. Subjectivity simultaneously reinforces and threatens capitalist relations: the ideology of individualism put forth by liberalism supports the needs of production for skilled, creative workers, while the freedom for self-expression may exceed, and perhaps undermine, productive modes. The private sphere sustains an important category of analysis for investigating leisure-time goods, such as amateur-film equipment. Amateur film simultaneously reinforces the market as a consumer commodity and presents the possibility for creativity to middle-class consumers. Habermas has elaborated on the private sphere as the location for the more fully integrated needs and activities excised from the rationalized structure of the economy.[12]

Artistic endeavors, including amateur film, evolve into depositories for all these more subjective needs not satisfied in public wage-labor situations. In a similar vein, Vazquez argues that while wage labor conforms to the demands of the market, artistic labor depends upon freedom, creativity, and spontaneity—values challenging standardized rules.[13] Amateurism safeguards these ideals of artistic labor while simultaneously functioning outside economic relations. The division between professionalism and amateurism hierarchically balances the contradiction between rationalized wage labor and more integrated creative labor. The public discourse on amateur film functions as a form of social control, because it harnesses subjectivity, imagination, and spontaneity within the more privatized contexts of leisure and family life.

Professionalism and amateurism operate together in multiple articulations: dependency, dominance, subordination, and/or resistance. Labor parallels divisions between the public and private sphere: wage labor and professionalism are defined by rational control, while artistic labor and amateurism are inscribed by freedom.

In *The Rise of Professionalism*, Magali Sarfatti Larson proposes that professionalism exemplifies a tendency toward monopolization of status and work in order to maintain social hierarchies.[14] Formalized paradigms protect this monopoly. They standardize not only procedures but also producers. They depend on codifying knowledge to depersonalize producers and to offer reliable, predictable control of services.[15] This unequal access to specialized knowledge increases the power of professionals.

Within these theoretical contours, more historically specific questions loom. How did Hollywood become linked with the epitome of professional film production? How did this ideology of Hollywood infiltrate writing on amateur film? The popular discursive construct of Hollywood exhibits the structures of professionalism through its division of labor in production, its development of formalized paradigms of narrative construction and composition, and its control and dominance of the motion picture market through distribution and exhibition. Hollywood professionalism consolidates three trajectories: division of labor, formal paradigms of aesthetic standards and conventions, and market control and monopolization through access to national distribution because of technological standardization. The division of production labor into camera, director, and other technical skills, as well as the division of aesthetic material into reproducible narrative parts (e.g., the close-up and cutaway), made film production more efficient.[16] Professional filmmaking, then, mirrors rationalized, scientific management. As early as 1908 the Motion Picture Patents Company, a consortium of producers and camera manufacturers who controlled not only technology but also distribution, monopolized markets and patents to diminish competition.[17] Further, professional 35mm film equipment not only produces more elaborate and larger images but also standardizes production, distribution, and exhibition, erecting a powerful barrier of entry as it bolsters the dominant ideologies of consumption, nuclear familialism, and liberal pluralism.[18] Discursively, professional film and amateur film diffuse a potentially explosive contradiction: professional film signifies rationalized, specialized wage-labor and economic control, whereas amateur film represents marginalized, yet integrated, production wedged within the private sphere.

Public discourse constructs amateur film as a safeguard to the economic stultification of professional film; it functions simultaneously as an illusory ideal of democratic freedom and as a potential market for disseminating inferior consumer versions of professional tools. Amateurism materializes as a cultural reservoir for the liberal pluralist ideals of freedom, competition, fluidity among classes, upward mobility, and inalienable and creative labor—social relations dislodged from the economic by scientism, the division of labor, and the cult of expertise.

The social formations and ideologies of professionalism and amateurism emerged in tandem in early nineteenth-century America. The period between 1840 and 1887 marked the most rapid growth of the modern professions—clerical, medical, and law—in the United States. Reflecting tremendous alterations in the American economy, this early period witnessed a qualitative leap in communications with the development of railroads, the telegraph, newspapers and periodicals, a population shift from rural areas to the cities, and the rise of manufacturing.[19]

During this increasing nationalization of the American economy in the 1880s, the significance of professionalism and amateurism escalated. In *The In-*

corporation of America, Alan Trachtenberg observes that the rise of American corporations during the latter half of the nineteenth century encouraged both science and professionalism to increase productivity and efficiency.[20] However, during the 1880s and 1890s, disputes between labor and management, as well as the perpetuation of a popular entrepreneurial mythology about captains of industry like Thomas Edison, obscured the migration of these new social processes into corporate bureaucracies.[21] Interestingly, the social concept of amateurism developed at this time, probably as a result of urbanization and the rise of leisure time.[22]

The symbiotic relationship between professionalism and amateurism mitigates this split between work and freedom. The economy controls and fragments wage labor. On the other side, amateur labor retains transmuted vestiges of total individual control and freedom within private life. Outside of market relations, it is immunized, so to speak, from class and expertise constraints. The imaginary fluidity between professionals and amateurs thus supports the myth of personal fulfillment.

Historical Origins of the Dynamic between Professionalism and Amateurism

Magali Sarfatti Larson argues that professionalization reflected the rise of the middle class, resulting from the corporate concentration of industries and their monopolization of technical knowledge.[23] Older occupations such as medicine and law professionalized in the early nineteenth century to insure monopoly market control and occupational status. Modern professionalization dating from the late nineteenth century however functioned differently; it became dependent on scientific control by experts. This structural shift of professionalization corresponds with the gradual transformation in the American economy from the competitive capitalism of small entrepreneurs into the corporate capitalism of large bureaucratic production units.[24] This more modern professionalization and its "new middle class" reacted to bureaucratic subordination: the ethics of individual advancement disguised class interests within an aura of objective professional standards and access to higher class status.[25]

The promulgation of experts and professionals solidifies Taylorism, which first emerged in the teens of the twentieth century. Developed by engineer Frederick Taylor, this system promoted scientific management of labor through time and motion studies as the most efficient way to control production costs and profit margins. Utilizing scientific principles of observation and quantification, Taylorism signified the further incorporation of rationality in order to control workplace relations. Taylorism legitimated the social importance of the professional and expert, who implemented its discourse.[26] Large bureaucratic organizations and professional occupations insulated themselves against class interests. For example, as a result of national markets after 1870, the numbers of production workers decreased, while the number of service and distribution workers increased.[27] Jobs shifted from production and manual labor to the more abstract, cognitive skills of professionals.

With industrial expansion and the nationalization of culture, engineers, teachers, doctors, and social workers increasingly relinquished their individual, heterogeneous, disconnected, autonomous, community-oriented character and transformed themselves into bourgeois professionals with standards, national organizations, and educational credentials.[28]

Professionalism epitomized the organizational logic of industrial capitalism that worked to control labor through the institution of work standards, the white collar corollary to standardized parts and Taylorized assembly line work. The professional—drilled, disciplined, methodical, dependable, and knowledgeable—embodied capitalist production methods. In *America by Design*, David Noble has interpreted the professionalization of engineers during this period as a reaction against the loss of labor control resulting from management attempts to proletarianize craft workers with Taylorized middle management.[29]

On the cultural level, retrieval of control and autonomy dispersed into amateurism. A writer in a 1901 *Atlantic* magazine piece titled "The Amateur Spirit" invoked the amateur spirit to temper, expand, and invigorate the professional "to keep him from hardening into a machine."[30] The writer professed that professionalism even extended into imperialism:

> Ours must be not a "nation of amateurs," but a nation of professionals, if it is to hold its own in the coming struggles—struggles not merely for commercial dominance, but for supremacy of political and moral ideas.[31]

Amateurism, then, emerged between 1880 and 1920 as the cultural inversion to the development of economic professionalization. With labor increasingly rationalized and craftspersons and inventors subsumed into corporate organizations, professionalism reproduced highly trained individuals as efficiently as mass production standardized interchangeable machine gun parts. In contrast, amateurism was not perceived as being standardized or interchangeable, yet it was clearly identified with upper- and middle-class leisure. Amateurism postured as the aesthetic antidote to the total stagnation of the professional.

From approximately 1880 to 1915, the discursive structure of amateurism synthesized two contradictory movements. On the one hand, popular magazines equated the amateur with depth, breadth, and freedom, signifying the survival of heterogeneity and the more humane virtues of a rural America. For example, amateur photography was aligned with women in advertisements for the Kodak hand camera. The image of the woman naturalized and humanized the technology. On the other hand, initiative, enthusiasm, and adventurousness—attributes of the entrepreneur and self-made "man," the new pioneer of economic and technological frontiers—were identified with amateurism. Amateurism functioned as a residual site for nineteenth-century American male economic prowess:

> Never has this restless, inventive, querying, accomplishing type of American manhood lost its prominence in our political and social structure. The self-made man is still, perhaps, our most representative man. Native shrewdness and energy and practical capacity—qualities such as the amateur may possess in a high degree—continue to carry a man very far.[32]

Not confined to a profession, to one track of operations, the amateur's versatility functioned to enforce an idea of class mobility, mental agility, personal freedom, and daring.

Amateurism mediated two different historical articulations of the self-made man. John Cawelti has noted that the ideology of the self-made man stressing individualism, achievement, success, economic enterprise, and self-education was most prevalent between approximately 1820 and 1850, when the United States experienced a surge of economic and geographic expansion.[33] By the 1880s, Cawelti argues these earlier notions of self-improvement transformed into an almost exclusive emphasis on the acquisition of wealth.[34] In popular middle-class magazines, amateurism connected nostalgia for the self-made man with a resistance to corporate and professional domination.[35] Not enervated by routine nor stagnated by standardized methods, amateurs, as delineated by popular-magazine essay writers at the turn of the century, epitomized the consummate inventor whose fresh vision and unfettered spontaneity fueled the best capitalist competitive edge. Symbolically and culturally, this scientized corporate system recognized its own trajectory toward embolism and deflected innovation into an individualized, stochastic sector—amateurism. For example, an anonymous writer in a 1911 edition of *Living Age* remarked:

> Generally speaking, the work of the latter [the professionals] is outstanding, but that of the former [the amateurs] is brilliant. It is as if those inside the ring possessed, like the interior of a circle, no independent capacity of motion, but inertia. Only the application of outside forces can produce any velocity in the system.[36]

In leisure time, undisciplined personal passion replaced the rationalized rigors of work. The same writer heralds Charles Darwin as the penultimate amateur: a self-taught intellectual marginal to traditional academia, who rattled the scientific establishment with his theory of evolution and changed the course of science.[37] However, the rupture posed by amateurism was effectively rerouted into ideological support for the further expansion of the capitalist economic system.

In this early period professionalism and amateurism complemented each other: the professional embodied the logic of scientized work, while the amateur constituted spontaneity. Amateurism was simultaneously marginalized to contain its potential disruptions and invoked as a vehicle of upward mobility, success, and the freewheeling, boundless freedom unavailable in industry.

At this time a variety of magazines published fictional pieces about amateur entrepreneurs, musicians, and actors.[38] Most of these short pieces described the adventures of a male amateur who tries to cross into professionalism, fails, and happily resigns himself to the joys of amateurism. As lessons on the futility of upward mobility, these stories ironically employed the myth of upward mobility as a narrative. For example, an 1893 *Scribner's Magazine* story, entitled "An Amateur Gamble," described the adventures of a young amateur musician from the "east" who travels "west" to fulfill his lifelong dream—investing in the sponsorship of the performance of a symphony orchestra.[39] He ends up in a western town where he speculates for gold and communicates with cowboys in saloons. Finally, he earns enough money panning for gold to finance a symphonic performance, but he realizes he cannot continue and returns east, content once more in his meager clerking job.

This short story synthesizes entrepreneurial effort and artistic, personal fulfillment. The young man certainly does go west to find his fortune, but he uses his newfound fortune to experience the vestiges of ruling-class patronage of the arts. His quick, lucky success panning for gold does not require disciplined work. As an amateur the young man operates outside the rationale of work and therefore can pursue his fantasies to join the ruling class. This story signals how amateurism merged entrepreneurial capitalism with illusions of upward mobility.

This ethos of personal fulfillment through amateurism had a much larger social and historical context. In an essay titled "From Salvation to Self-Realization: Advertising and the Therapeutic Roots of the Consumer Culture, 1880–1930," T. J. Jackson Lears observes that the massive social and economic changes of the late nineteenth century shifted the general population's "sense of self." With the development of a mass culture, leisure, corporate organizations, and the dissolution of communities, Lears argues that a "therapeutic ethos" emerged that stressed "bodily vigor, emotional intensity, and a revitalized sense of selfhood." Lears points out that ministers, self-help writers, and mass-market therapists encouraged personal growth through leisure time to energize nerves worn out by industry.[40] In the 1880s and 1890s, amateurism became the social and cultural site where one could revive one's true self, which was invariably vivacious, ambitious, and imaginative. Amateurism infiltrated sports, art, and engineering in particular during this period, where sports emphasized the body, artistic production suggested the untapped potential of individual vision, and engineering proffered mechanical and entrepreneurial ingenuity.

However, despite the propagation of an idea that amateurism protected equality through artistic, economic, or inventive opportunity, on a less-abstract level there remained a hierarchy of those who performed a task for a living and those who engaged in it for the self. Patronage erected class distinctions between the amateur and the professional. As the aristocracy displayed their power over culture through patronage,[41] the term *amateur* may have served as a way to diminish the significance of competitors and thereby maintain status. While upper-class women financed artists, they themselves also practiced art as amateurs, more frequently than not receiving lessons from the artists they sponsored. Although some of these upper-class women had gallery showings, critics who believed true artists lived on the fringes of society without money reviled them.[42] A 1904 editorial published in the *Photo-Miniature* expresses the class distinctions between amateurs and professionals:

> And in photography, we had the old idea of two classes, distinct and separate: the professional who made photographs of men and things for money as a business; and the amateur who photographed for the love of it—con amore as the phrase went—and who was supposed to lose caste if he accepted cash for his work with the camera.[43]

In the period from 1880 to approximately 1910, the cultural construct of professionals as disciplined and amateurs as spontaneous conveyed the logic of rationalized industrial culture. Professional, remunerated artistic production required the discipline and organization of a good corporate manager. In contrast, amateurs were chaotic and unorganized, as expressed in the *Atlantic*:

> As a general rule, the amateur betrays amateurish qualities. He is unskilled because untrained; desultory because incessant devotion to his hobby is both unnecessary and wearisome; ineffective because, after all, it is not a vital matter whether he succeed or fail.[44]

The amateur's lack of fixity, regularity, and coherence disrupted, challenged, and in the end supported the capitalist system of efficiency, repetition, and prediction. The amateur's spontaneity and lack of purpose momentarily interrupted the control of social and labor relations. Amateurism deflected the chaotic, the incoherent, and the spontaneous into leisure and private life so that public time could persist as methodical, controllable, and regulated.

2

Entrepreneurs, Artists, Hobbyists, and Workers

1897–1923

Technological Development and Economic Competition

F ROM 1897 TO 1923 amateur film was defined in economic and technological terms rather than within social, aesthetic, or political relations. With many inventors and entrepreneurs creating new designs and formats in order to circumvent the 35mm film patents held by Thomas Edison and Eastman Kodak, its economic structure was competitive. This competitive atmosphere exhibited two trends. First, on the cultural level these entrepreneurial efforts represented a reinstitution of the residual myth of the individual inventor, a basic component of amateurism. Second, and more importantly, the definition of amateur filmmaking was based on nonconformity to more dominant technological standards. These standards guaranteed professional film access to larger markets. The wide array of camera designs and formats not only fragmented and isolated producers but also prevented them from competing with professionals shooting 35mm stock.

The professional-film industry sustained monopolies through patents on equipment and manufacturing apparatuses. In his *America by Design* David Noble has noted that technology can function as a powerful instrument of corporate consolidation and protection from competition. While patents insure a company monopoly over a product, they also help the company to maintain a large segment of the consumer market. Noble, for example, remarks:

> Technology is thus a social process, it does not simply stimulate social development from outside but, rather, constitutes fundamental social development, in itself: the preparation, mobilization, and habituation of people for new types of productive activity, the reorientation of the pattern of social investment, the restructuring of social institutions, and potentially, the redefinition of social relationships.[1]

In the late nineteenth century, Noble continues, corporations subsumed individual inventors by purchasing their original ideas for corporate patents in exchange for job security and unlimited laboratory resources.

This corporate consolidation of patents to create manufacturing monopolies is evidenced in the development of motion picture cameras and projectors. From 1894 to approximately 1909, numerous inventors worked in a variety of formats to create apparatuses that would project moving images. C. W. Ceram in his *Archeology of the Cinema* writes that most of these camera inventions were "a jumble of true inventions, clever ideas of secondary importance, incomplete devices, imitations and direct plagiarism."[2] Ceram describes how inventors from several different countries—France, England, Germany, and the United States—simultaneously created projection systems: Louis Aime Augustin Le Prince in France in 1888, William Friese-Greene in Germany in 1893, Jean Aime Le Roy in America in 1895, Greg and Otway Latham in America in 1894, Louis and Auguste Lumière in France in 1895.[3] Ceram notes that nearly fifty other inventors were also working at this time. According to film historian Robert Sklar, Thomas Edison contracted with Thomas Armot and C. Francis Jenkins for their film projector in the winter of 1895–96, the same year as Lumière's first screening.[4] Reese Jenkins in *Images and Enterprise* argues that Lumière and Edison controlled production of cameras, projectors, and film stock in order to protect their monopolies. Eastman Kodak limited its manufacturing to cinefilm, commanding 90 percent of the market by 1910. This policy was based on Eastman Kodak's superior manufacturing of celluloid-roll film; it employed continuous drum methods in the production of film base and emulsion coating. Because of its standardization and high quality, Eastman Kodak-produced stock edged out poorer quality foreign competitors like Agfa, Bayer, or Lumière.[5] Although exhibition, distribution, and apparatus and screenplay production were highly competitive with relative ease of entry, Jenkins observes that the manufacture of film stock sustained high barriers to entry because of technological sophistication and excessive capitalization costs.

While this early technologically competitive climate was eventually reduced to a few powerful camera manufacturing companies, it nonetheless contributed to the idea that new inventions could detour the stranglehold of Edison and Eastman Kodak. For example, both Reese Jenkins and Mae D. Huettig suggest that Edison's failure to file patents on his motion picture equipment in Europe encouraged small-time inventors to patent minimal improvements to his existing system.[6] Huettig claims some patents were secured by amateur inventors. Thus, although it erected high barriers to entry with control over patents and manufacturing, the economic structure of the dominant film manufacturing industry may have also provided an incentive to more entrepreneurial, undercapitalized firms and inventors to develop alternative camera systems. Considering the enormous finances required to produce standardized motion picture film, technological invention and innovation had the lowest barriers to entry. The development of amateur motion picture technologies functioned on two levels. First, it provided a way for amateur inventors to enter the apparatus market and avoid patent infringements against Edison or Kodak. Second, it constituted a response to the growing consumer market for leisure-time goods for a growing middle class.

The development of amateur motion picture technology shows how independent inventors' quests for patents spurred technological innovation from outside the major film manufacturing corporations. Professional cameras were patented in Europe or by major manufacturing firms in the United States like Edison. Eastman Kodak controlled 35mm stock patents.[7] Consequently, inventors and other small companies aligned themselves with amateurs to avoid patent infringement. With the exception of Pathé (1921), Eastman Kodak (1923), and Edison (1912), all of whom entered the amateur-cinema market relatively late (note dates) in comparison to other designers, all companies producing and developing amateur filmmaking equipment during this early period were small and entrepreneurial rather than corporate. By patenting different cameras and film gauges, they sought to establish their own monopolies on equipment and thereby gain entry into the expanding entertainment market. The *British Journal of Photography* and the United States Patent Office record over one hundred fifty patents by obscure inventors and firms for amateur filmmaking equipment and modifications during this period.[8] The success of Eastman Kodak's Cine-Kodak machine in 1923 relied not only on its development by a major photographic monopoly but also on Kodak's patents for an entire amateur system—from film, to camera, to projector, to emulsion, to manufacturing equipment.[9] Thus, Kodak's marketing success was the result of its financial resources that were used to develop a complete mass-production system that consolidated economic control over every phase of production and distribution. Unable to capitalize their own factories, amateur inventors concentrated instead on either camera design or film.

The structure of the American film industry at this time further inhibited small-time, undercapitalized, individual entrepreneurs. Most manufacturing concerns were vertically integrated into production: Edison, Pathé, Lumière, American Mutoscope and Biograph. Pathé and Lumière, although based in Europe, distributed films in the United States. Robert Sklar suggests that free-lance camera people existed during the early years of the industry, but he reinforces their essential reliance on corporations for distribution or employment:

In the earliest days of motion pictures the terms "producers" and "film-maker" could almost have been synonymous. Only Edison and Biograph companies were large enough for a division of labor, and that was because they had begun as manufacturers of equipment, expanding into production in order to supply purchasers of their projectors.[10]

These camera-people were usually a rather elite group comprised of technical, electrical, or photographic professionals. Few untrained amateurs crossed this threshold from cinematography as a hobby into cinematography as employment. In addition, the fact that large camera manufacturers were the first to begin extensive film production implies that only they had the adequate financial resources needed to produce and market films in the first place.

This equipment-centric, patent-protected orientation of the early film industry came to a head with the formation of the Motion Pictures Patents Company (MPPC) in 1908. As a trust to pool sixteen patents, the MPPC united the Edison Manufacturing Company, American Mutoscope and Biograph Company, Vitagraph Company of America, and Armat Moving Picture Company. Eastman Kodak was designated the sole supplier of cinefilm. Through patent control on projectors and licensing arrangements, this group controlled distribution and exhibition. The MPPC posed a formidable threat to anyone seeking entry into the film business; its power lay in its patents of motion picture equipment.[11]

The involvement of Albert S. Howell with one of the MPPC members, Essanay Studios of Chicago, as a supplier of standardized motion picture equipment is significant, because Howell's designs for perforators, printers, and cameras established what were to become professional technical standards for the motion picture industry. According to Lewis Jacobs, nearly one hundred fifty competing manufacturers, importers, and exchange men vied for a part of the burgeoning motion picture industry prior to 1909. Edison, Biograph, and Vitagraph held legal right to virtually all the necessary patents, but bootleggers and independents continued to struggle.[12] In 1906 Albert Howell was employed by the Crary Machine Works in Chicago, where he repaired motion picture equipment for the Orpheum Theater circuit and other independent houses. Howell met Don Bell, another equipment entrepreneur, and together they formed Bell and Howell in 1906 to manufacture, job, lease, and repair motion picture equipment.[13]

In 1906 Howell patented a 35mm projector framing device. Between 1907 and 1910 Bell and Howell provided and repaired equipment for independent producers attempting to work outside the purview of the Motion Picture Patents Company.[14] According to corporate documents from this period, Howell reasoned that unless all machinery in the manufacture, production, and exhibition of films was standardized and precisely engineered, it would be impossible to eliminate flicker and produce steady images.[15] Howell patented the 35mm model standard camera in 1909, the 35mm perforator with special perforation designs in 1910, and a continuous hand printer in 1911.[16] These three designs were not only precision engineered, with calibrations on each model, but they also solved the flicker problem. The 2709 Standard Camera, for example, used two pins in the film gate to position and secure the film for exposure. Howell's establishment of longitudinally uniform perforations on film was a substantial improvement over the Edison and Pathé perforation designs.[17] His precise standards eliminated flutter and flicker, not only through engineering but also by increasing the frames per second of motion picture film from eighteen to twenty-four, thus situating Bell and Howell equipment as rendering the highest quality image. While this reputation for image stability contributed to the adoption of the 35mm standard suggested by Bell and Howell, the company's own policy of refusing to repair motion picture equipment that did not correspond to these elaborate technical standards served as another business factor that helped to establish the company's technical specifications as the industry standard by 1910.[18]

In 1907 Essanay licensed Edison camera patents and instructed Bell and Howell to build cameras, perforators, and printers. Along with other licensees, Essanay submitted their Bell and Howell perforation design to Edison for review in 1908; Edison decided that all licensees should adopt the Bell and Howell standard. According to George Spoor, a founder of Essanay Studios, from 1907 to 1917 Bell and Howell built all their professional cameras under a licensing agreement with Edison via Essanay.[19]

After 1910 Essanay and Selig, trust members located in Chicago, purchased nearly all of their equipment from Bell and Howell, but the company, ignoring the prerogatives of the trust, also sold to independents and movie outlaws on the West Coast.[20] By selling to both trust members and independents, Bell and Howell disseminated this standardized equipment to producers working in many different areas. However, it is important to note that the institution of Bell and Howell manufacturing designs as the industry standard was primarily the result of its exclusive relationship to Edison and the Motion Picture Patents Company. Bell and Howell's prominent position in the amateur motion picture camera market in the 1920s emerged from these relationships with the MPPC. Their alliance erected industry standards and squeezed other competing perforation designs and film widths out of the mass-entertainment market.

Unless consumers could afford the licensing fees on equipment or could amass enough financial backing to operate outside the holds of the MPPC, standardized equipment was not readily available. This stranglehold on standardized equipment may have in fact pushed many smaller companies and independent inventors into the amateur market, which operated more competitively, because it did not yield the financial returns of professional film. Even more importantly, the development of these smaller film gauges and cameras also offered an uncharted area for the development of new patents.

Even when independent producers instituted the star system to cut into the power of the MPPC, they did so with economic clout far beyond the reach of the so-called amateur or consumer. Some established stage celebrities were offered as much as $3,000 per week, for example.[21] In addition, the impulse to legitimate film as an art led to narrative forms that served as formalized professional paradigms.[22] This appropriation of literary devices provided a platform for stars and increased the amount of personnel necessary to produce a film. Although free-lance camera operators between 1900 and 1925 could string documentaries to major distributors,[23] the prospects for amateur-narrative productions were limited because of the increasing codification of expensive stylistic devices, such as match cutting and continuity, and by the large crews demanded for professional narrative production. Thus, even if the diffusion of amateur equipment could have cracked the oligopoly of the film industry from 1897 to 1923 by creating a more competitive market (several 35mm amateur cameras, for instance, were available at this time), standardization and consolidation of equipment protected the established manufacturers who retained patent rights and insured control of the market.

If amateur cameras were available between 1897 and 1923 and entry into the professional film business was so limited, in what cultural sphere did information about them circulate? Where can we locate the articulation and formation of the technology of amateur filmmaking? Until 1923 motion picture technology for the amateur failed to gain a clientele outside of the amateur technical journals. From 1897 to 1923 amateur motion pictures were discussed only in popular technical journals such as *Technical World, Science, Illustrated World,* and *Scientific American.* In addition, nearly every photography journal kept up with the developments of motion pictures for the amateur. But publications with broader scope and appeal, such as the *Saturday Evening Post* and *Harper's,* did not run one ad for home-movie cameras.[24] From the disposition of documentary evidence from this period, amateur-film equipment seems to have been a technical oddity for hobbyists to follow rather than a large social practice or art involving great numbers of people. After the standardization of the 16mm format and the mass marketing of amateur equipment in 1923, the complexion of amateur information changed and became more available in mass-circulation magazines.

These popular technical journals exhibited some peculiar tendencies that help to decipher the characteristics of the amateur motion picture market, albeit with circumstantial evidence. Neither photography nor technical journals emphasized the commercial value of cinematography. At best the camera was positioned as a device that recorded the family in the same manner that commercial directors filmed stories. At worst the camera was viewed as a mechanical gadget to be investigated and probed. Photography journals addressed amateur motion picture equipment as new machinery to be patented, emphasizing the camera.[25] Consequently, it appears that amateur-film technology was positioned more as an entrepreneurial patent opportunity than as a means of cinematic expression.

The persistence of this vision of entrepreneurial freedom and success had its roots in a much larger economic context than just amateur film. In his study *The Rise of Big Business, 1860–1910*, Glenn Porter contends that the rapid expansion of corporations with national markets and administrative hierarchies brought new concerns to American society. One of these concerns, voiced by small businesses driven out of business by combinations and other entrepreneurs, was that these corporate developments were inhibiting opportunity in America. For example, in testimonies before the United States Industrial Commission, a government body whose task it was to monitor concentration in industry, some people worried that the opportunity to use one's own drive, ambition, and resources to create a prosperous business was no longer viable. The huge profits gained by major corporations, according to Porter, threatened individual opportunity.[26] The expression of this fascination with the entrepreneurial nature of film technology may have been a cultural response to the larger economic situation. While the nineteenth-century idea of the self-made man may have gradually deteriorated as a realistic possibility in this period of corporate growth, the concept was being recirculated in hobby magazines. Consequently, the dreams that once motivated one to work may have, during this period, become what fueled "productive" leisure pursuits. The fascination with individual opportunity was dispersed into hobbies, which now presented the possibility of individual fulfillment.

In general popular technical journals, while they kept a cursory tab on recent patents, were essentially geared toward people who invented and played with the construction of machines as a hobby. They catered to the even then outdated notions of the inventor as an entrepreneur, evoking the idea of amateurism as a site for these displaced ideas of individualism and economic democracy. Technical journals served as repositories for the residual ideology of the craftsperson who had sole control over production and distribution of products, while they simultaneously positioned themselves as beacons of technological and industrial progress. Each issue contained many success stories of people who made money by "discovering" such technological wonders as grass cutters attached to shoes, chairs that hung down from a woman's waist under her bustle, and contraptions that did everything from teach people how to swim on a machine on land to machines that would knot ties. These stories about technical inventions demonstrate how far the dominant ideology of scientific rationality extended, testifying to an industrialization of leisure-time reading as well.

In addition these journals were packed with articles describing various gears, gadgets, and constructions of everything from train engines to light bulbs written in a very simplistic, colloquial fashion. One could not garner enough information to rebuild a mechanism or improve it, but one could understand how it worked, and, by extension, participate in the building of the technology of industrial capitalism. Promoting the idea of the inventor, these magazines emphasized that individuals were responsible for innovations during the period of the most intense professionalization of inventors within corporations.[27] These technical journals, then, privileged access to technical trivia and advertised the technology of capitalism.

The photographic and film industries did not overlook this viable amateur market that was fascinated with technology. From 1897 to 1923 the number of amateur motion picture cameras was much greater than the casual observer would suspect. The *Journal of the Society of Motion Picture and Television Engineers* listed forty-two separate cameras and suggested that the list was incomplete.[28] Combined with the cameras not listed, which were described in various technical journals, this figure mounts to nearly seventy. These cameras hold several common characteristics that reflect manufacturing and marketing strategies to preempt the dominance of Edison and Kodak. In addition, these technological features, because they altered or ignored the professional technical standards, helped to diminish the economic impact of amateur-film technologies, since professional exhibition used 35mm film. Consequently, the technical specifications of amateur cameras at this time are critical.

One of the primary features was the film stock itself. The cameras were constructed to adapt to nonstandard film gauges: 17.5mm, 21mm, 22mm, 28mm, 11mm, 9mm, 9.5mm, and even to some 35mm stocks. The prohibitive cost of motion picture celluloid film led many inventors to cost-cutting designs, and the most obvious place to begin was to slit the film in half—thus 17.5mm. Acres of London, the first firm to manufacture this stock, released their special gauge on the market in 1898.[29] Taking Eastman Kodak's simplification and miniaturization of the Kodak as a model, many companies and inventors tried to modify existing camera designs as much as possible. With smaller gauges, the film gate, feed, and take-up spool could be tinier, reducing the size and cost of the camera.

Companies like Victor Animatograph of Iowa, an established professional-camera manufacturer, merely omitted such devices as shutters and pull-down claws in order to decrease costs and to simultaneously adapt their amateur cameras to the standard 35mm film. Smaller-gauge film benefited the manufacturer by reducing the size of the camera, thus slashing manufacturing costs.[30] Amateur-camera design reduced costs by eliminating mechanisms that maintained professional standards.

Another factor influencing this move to substandard film gauges and unusual perforation alignment (perfs were round, square, on one edge, down the middle, and between frames, unlike the standard film, which was double perfed down each side) was the market domination of Eastman Kodak, the largest and virtually the only producer of cinefilm in the world at that time. Although Lumière of France sold professional stock, its poor quality and lack of even distribution of celluloid did not make it competitive in the professional market. By 1910 Kodak held 90 percent of all the international market for cinefilm and virtually all the patents for celluloid and emulsion manufacturing and employed nearly every important scientist doing research in film-related areas.[31] Thus, if a company wanted to break Kodak's monopoly without patent infringement, a new film design had to be created in order to obtain a patent. In addition, by 1909 the Motion Picture Patents Company had entered into a collusive agreement with Kodak whereby 35mm film would be supplied only to trust members.[32]

While 35mm film patents structured both cameras and the patent strategies of manufacturing and entrepreneurial concerns, there were other incentives to promote amateur equipment during this first twenty-six years. With the incredible surge of amateur photographers after the introduction of the hand camera in 1888, many companies and inventors sought to exploit this market. A survey of the seventy cameras available for motion picture amateur production shows that considerably more than half were American-made products. Although technical and marketing data for professional cameras from this period are difficult to obtain (for instance, the *Journal of the Society of Motion Picture Engineers* did not begin publishing until 1916) and are beyond the scope of this study, the character of the American photographic industry during this time provides a useful framework.

European countries, particularly Germany, manufactured superior professional cameras as a result of a long heritage of optical excellence situated within guilds, but the amateur market for still and movie cameras remained open for American competitors.[33] Edison, Vitagraph, and American Mutoscope—significantly large companies employing numerous scientists—manufactured professional cameras for use in the United States. However, it would appear that their entry into the professional market was only a profitable sideline to their patent struggles. Although European cameras and lenses were of superior design and construction, their craft-oriented business structure could not easily adapt to the mass production and bureaucratic organizational structures necessary to generate enough product to capture the large amateur market.[34] Not only did Eastman Kodak hold virtually every patent for the mass production of celluloid, but its immense reserves of surplus capital allowed it to purchase American still-camera companies outright.[35] In that amateur equipment did not require high quality lenses, American firms concentrated on camera bodies. It is interesting to note that educational and phonograph firms, like A. F. Victor for example, moved into the amateur filmmaking market fairly early,[36] no doubt as a consequence of their skills at mass distribution of leisure items. American firms, then, enjoyed two advantages for the production of amateur cameras: access to manufacturing equipment for mass production and expertise in mass-distribution techniques.

While European firms like Pathé and Debrie, major producers of professional motion picture cameras, invented amateur equipment, and small American firms continued to launch new cameras each year, the success of their efforts is questionable due to the fact that there is no evidence of a ground swell of amateur filmmaking during that time period and that figures from firms are unavailable. Once again we can infer that the film itself restricted mass use and public exhibition. Until 1912 the threat of fire inhibited "home" use. Although both the Pathé and Edison home-movie systems used safety film in 1912, all other cameras employed nitrate-based film, a highly inflammable substance that was extremely hazardous for home use. If fire was not enough to limit wide usage, then the expensive negative-positive process certainly contributed to amateur-movie film's limited success. The amateur producer's costs doubled: the individual not only had to buy the film but also had to ship the original negative to a lab for a print.[37] The commercial success and mass distribution of the Cine-Kodak in 1923 resulted from the development of reversal film, whereby, simply speaking, the negative is bleached and reexposed to produce a positive. This process eliminated the extra film required for a print, further reducing costs. Ralfe Tarkington in the *Journal of the Society of Motion Picture Engineers* noted that this system was founded on

> the use of film smaller than that used in the standard camera and the new process for finishing it, the object being to reduce the cost to as low a point as possible. Actually, it was estimated that the new process cut the cost of motion pictures to 1/6 that of the negative-positive method—a very significant saving.[38]

However, this reversal process, which remains the standard for amateur and semiprofessional films today, embodied contradictory effects. While reversal film slashed costs, it was impossible to make prints with it except by very expensive and complicated procedures. This lack of reproducibility cut off distribution and exhibition channels that could have enabled the amateur to compete in a limited way with professionals. Substandard amateur-film technology protected the market for professional-film manufacturers and producers, because the formats and chemical processes did not conform to the dominant industry's technical standards for distribution and exhibition. Although the miniaturization and simplification of cameras and stocks reduced the costs of film production, they nonetheless removed amateur filmmaking from competition with professional producers and stimulated home-consumer use.

During this early period, an array of substandard amateur-camera designs represented the persistence of the entrepreneurial mystique of patent innovation, as well as the transition from filmmaking as a visual oddity to a major industry that needed to control the means of production as a barrier to entry. Consequently, family and leisure-time use inscribed the technological designs of amateur-movie cameras from this period. Although an exact analysis of every amateur camera and projector available from 1897 to 1923 would far exceed the argument of this project, it is possible to selectively group this variety of equipment into five categories: toys, exhibition devices, unusual formats, all-purpose cameras, and substandard designs. The construction of amateur technology excised any possibilities of competition with the 35mm professional format; it thus became firmly embedded in the domain of individual hobbyists or families.

These rather unusual and nonnormative technological designs had their antecedents in eighteenth-century visual toys and magic shows for home use. Visual toys began with hand shadows flashed on cave walls. During the French Revolution, the Phantasmogoria, a device that projected movement by spinning a wheel studded with images, thrilled the French aristocracy. Other types of spinning wheels—like the Fanatascope, Phenavitascope, Stroboscope, and Zoetrope, scientific mechanisms exploited for their recreational value—were popular during the nineteenth century.[39] These devices deposited scientific discoveries in the home as magic; science entertained as a magic trick. Within the home scientific instruments for measuring motion or analyzing visual perception shed their logical and analytical rigor and were instead denuded as nonthreatening. Science postured as a site of wonderment. It is ideologically significant that many amateur cameras copied these early projection devices, because they recall a moment when science was not reorganizing social and economic life as forcefully as it was at the end of the nineteenth century. Many of these early visual toys spun a sequential series of images to create the illusion of motion; the child could manipulate the speed of the illusion. Visual toys evolved into spectacles emanating from the device to the observer, an inversion of photography and cinematography, which, conversely, extends from the observer's manipulation of the device for recordings. For example, analyzing the spread of amateur photography, Helmut Gernsheim exhorted, "For in their hand, the camera became a mere toy and ceased to be a means of expression."[40]

Motion picture toys underlined this cultural obsession with the mechanical gadgetry of science and industry. Amateur film became the domain where one mastered and controlled technology, in contradiction to work where technology and technocracy controlled the worker. A 1910 *Scientific American* article explained how to build a 35mm motion picture camera; a few pieces of wood, cylinders to drive the film, and a lens were all that was needed. Pushpins from a sewing box operated as pull-down claws to secure the film in the gate.[41] A 1917 *Popular Mechanics* article promoted a hand-cranked machine that reflected images spinning on a drum up to a viewing mirror propped on top of the box.[42] Another projection device described in a 1919 issue of *Popular Mechanics* employed a lens mounted on a light box with a pully suspended above the lens. A child could then pull the 35mm film through the gate in strips.[43] Homemade cameras evoked this residual formation of craftspersonship. A 1922 *Popular Mechanics* piece elaborated on a camera, resembling a miniature Diorama, that used a converted cigar box by removing one large side, adding spindles, and a roll of pictures that was wound through.[44] Diagrams and instructions for building a fourteen-by-seven-inch 35mm camera and projector were included in a lengthy 1918 *Popular Mechanics* article.[45] This do-it-yourself ethos reproduced the products and tools of professional production within a residual craft configuration that now presented itself as a tame hobby.

Professional 35mm film could be reduced and redirected toward home consumption by the use of portable projectors and films that could be recycled in either smaller formats or poorer quality equipment. The first home projector, called the 1899 Cinnagraph after the year it was first sold publicly, was smaller and cheaper than the massive theater or nickelodeon machines.[46] Although this outfit was considered the first home projection unit, Oskar Messter, a German inventor responsible for many innovations and refinements in cinematography, offered the Kinetograph and Home Thaummograph, amateur projectors, plus amateur cameras, perforators, processing and printing equipment as early as 1897.[47] From 1913 to 1918 home projecting units became increasingly more prevalent. A 1914 *Scientific American* article describing a home projector observed:

> If the entertainment is a concert a disappointed listener can at least go home and make up the deficiency with his own piano, piano player, or phonograph; or on the other hand, if one has heard something that par-

ticularly strikes his fancy he may purchase the selection and reproduce it to his heart's content at home. In the case of the moving picture show, however, the spectator is obliged to accept a "tabled'hote" program even though prepared for a public whose tastes are absolutely at variance with his own.[48]

Armed with the slogan "Luxuries are becoming necessities to the American people," George R. Webb, an inventor, developed a sound movie system in 1913, which he hoped could be transmitted from some centralized distribution area specifically to individuals, according to a 1913 *Technical World* article.[49] Between 1914 and 1915 the *British Journal of Photography* published patents for six home-movie cinematographs with average dimensions of nine by eleven by eleven inches and weighing less than thirty pounds.[50] Other projectors, such as one that could be taken apart and assembled in five minutes using standard one thousand-foot reels, were also described in a 1914 issue of *Popular Mechanics*.[51] The average cost of a typical machine was approximately one hundred dollars. According to Raymond Fielding's history, by 1922 Pathé began to distribute features to homes by reduction printing their 35mm professional feature films to 9.5mm.[52]

Some amateur-movie camera systems, however, employed technological designs so different from the dominant industry's standard that they could only be used as devices for the hobbyist and thus became technical oddities that were secluded within the obscurity of the die-hard amateur technocrat. Many of these cameras reverted to a design reminiscent of the nineteenth-century Wheels of Life, where images spun through a gate rather than traveling vertically. The earliest model of this type of camera employing glass plates with a sequential series of pictures was the Kammatograph, which appeared in 1900. Using a disc, the twelve-inch diameter plate rotated through the camera at an exposure rate of one fourteenth of a second, compared to the eighteen to twenty-four frames per second utilized in conventional motion pictures.

In 1900 the *British Journal of Photography* claimed that the same camera could be converted into a projector after the amateur developed self-owned positive plates.[53] By 1912 Gianni Bettini, an Italian inventor, improved this disc system by using square plates that were 8.5 by 5.5 inches. Each plate displayed 576 images. This plate system not only eliminated the curling problem of celluloid but also reduced the cost of producing films; each plate cost only four cents compared to a strip of celluloid with the same number of frames that sold at $1.50 in 1912.[54] Later this system changed to flexible discs that could be stored more conveniently. Further reducing the price, discs rendered the cost of motion pictures comparable to that of a phonograph.[55] In a prophetic proclamation, one writer in a 1916 *Scientific American* piece observed that "if the cinematography is to be extended to practically every home, it will be due to the introduction of a cheap substitute for the usual film; in fact, home cinematography will ever have little in common with the standard cinematography, except in ultimate results."[56]

However, while these plate and disc movie formats defined this form of production as distinctly amateur because the multiplicity of their nonstandard designs prevented interchangeability and public exhibition, they nonetheless on an ideological level restored a rather impotent control over production technology to producers, if only within a marginalized amateur status. Similarly, it should be noted that these devices did not fragment the labor process, as was typical of professional film. One could independently shoot, develop, and project the same system without assistance from Kodak or any other large bureaucratic manufacturing concerns. This integration of the labor process in one producer/craftsperson preserved the lost ideal of total control of work.

While some camera designs, like Bettini's, rejected celluloid altogether and used glass plates in order to decrease costs, other manufacturers offered multipurpose cameras that employed the standard 35mm film. Although the cams and drives of these cameras could not rival the precision of professional cameras, their adaptability to a variety of photographic needs was an asset and a selling point to the amateur. The Biokam, manufactured and sold by John Wrench and Sons of England, was an incredible bargain: costing less than the average still hand camera and measuring 9.5 by 5.5 by 3.25 inches, the Biokam functioned as a motion picture camera, snapshot camera, printer, projector, reverse, and an enlarger.[57] Several other cameras resembled the Biokam, among them the La Petite and the Kammatograph, which appeared in 1899 and 1900, respectively.[58] As late as 1923, a multiple-purpose motion picture apparatus whose aperture and shutter could be adjusted to take 35mm still photographs and which used a spring motor drive was available. Operating as a sort of motor drive, the camera enabled the photographer to take sequential photographs at an astounding rate, as noted by a *Popular Mechanics* writer in 1914: "About 200 snapshots can be made in the time consumed in taking six with the ordinary roll film camera."[59]

Amateur-movie film and apparatuses were also employed for still photography. These alternative motion picture formats imitated the Mutoscope, which achieved the illusion of movement by flipping through photographs in succession. Utilizing standard 35mm film exposed on a six-by-seven-by-twelve-inch camera weighing less than ten pounds, the home producer could then cut the celluloid strip into frames and assemble the individual frames into a holder. These films, developed through the direct positive method (an inferior reversal process) eliminated the cost of a projector but also destroyed the projectability of the film, further constraining amateur productions to individual viewings and home use.

With these designs, motion picture production was quite literally fragmented into still images, situating these apparatuses as recording units to produce images rather than to publicly exhibit films. The move to use motion picture cameras and films for still photography became popular, especially since the roll of film—the reel of cinefilm—could take many more pictures than the twenty-four-exposure rolls sold by Kodak. A July 1918 article in *Scientific American* extolled the virtues of this methodology, proclaiming: "In this manner the traveler may take pictures from the beginning to the close of the long tour, keeping them in their proper sequence, and not be obliged to reload the camera nor do developing until his return."[60]

The camera summoned the ideology of amateur spontaneity; one could take as many photographs as possible without interference from the limitations of the apparatus. As a technological compromise that anticipated the Bettini disc/plate multiple-exposure system and the use of movie cameras for still work by advancing the film one frame at a time instead of continually, J. S. Anderson of California created a movie camera in 1909 that "captured the perfect expression." Glass plates moved intermittently through a gate by means of an ingenious system comprised of gears, chains, and a hand crank.[61] While these unusual cameras reduced the amateur's initial production costs, they also limited more commercial distribution possibilities. In fact, the threat of amateur motion picture technology creating a more competitive producing market was subverted by these cameras' designs that straddled the line between still photography and movies.

Lack of standardization among various designs also contributed to their toylike, leisure-time status. The wide array of film gauges and perforation placements prevented any interchangeability among different cameras. While smaller gauges were either hard to come by or were of inferior quality, the cameras themselves instituted some mechanical modifications that designated their amateur rank. A 1913 *Scientific American* article titled "A Cinematograph Hand Camera" describes how one camera eliminated the shutter:

> On the flat side of this disk near its periphery is a window, transparent and circular in shape, the axis of which coincides with the axis of the camera lens, the latter being rigidly secured to the front wall of the camera, and also is in line with the moving film behind.[62]

Lewis Caesar Van Riper of Chicago patented a camera in 1915 that used 17.5mm film with only one row of sprocket holes, and he attached his camera to a clock to drive the film through the gate.[63] The 1913 *Scientific American* article described a 12-by-8.5-by-6.5-inch camera that accepted daylight loading cartridges resembling super-8 magazines and was driven on compressed air. By using cylinders inside the Aeroscope, as the camera was called, the camera could not operate until the pressure reached one hundred pounds, achieved by attaching a pump and stroking it forty-nine times.[64] The time requirement for this procedure restricted the Aeroscope's use to family portraits or other posed situations. Other features common to cameras from the period 1909 to 1923 included fixed focus and exposure.[65]

Although these substandard designs positioned amateur filmmaking outside the commercial-film industry, on an economic level they did allow entrepreneurs to develop amateur cameras and to compete on an extremely limited level with other camera engineers. The development of 16mm reversal film as the standard gauge for amateurs, however, shifted this technologically and economically competitive atmosphere populated with many designs and inventors into an oligopolistic market controlled by Bell and Howell, Victor Animatograph, and Eastman Kodak. The 16mm film presented a significant change in the definition of amateur film: while it standardized the amateur gauge, it also colonized the concept of amateur film as a consumer market controlled by major professional film manufacturing companies. The very design of 16mm film gauge and cameras insured that their use would be confined, at least until World War II, to family leisure activities.

The institution of 16mm as the standardized amateur gauge marks an important turning point in the history of amateur film. Major corporations like Bell and Howell and Eastman Kodak ousted small-time entrepreneurial inventors who lacked the capital and the manufacturing and advertising resources necessary to reach national markets. These large manufacturers redefined amateur film as a consumer commodity; the mainstream press published articles on amateur film and ran Kodak, Bell and Howell, and Victor Animatograph ads. The 16mm amateur gauge formed a filmmaking caste system: 35mm for professionals and 16mm for families.

In 1921 Eastman Kodak and Bell and Howell, the preeminent professional film and camera manufacturers, colluded to standardize amateur-film width at 16mm to discourage amateurs from splitting the standard 35mm film into two strips of 17.5mm stock.[66] Because the highly inflammable nitrate base of professional film limited the amateur market, Eastman Kodak developed an acetate-base stock that employed the reversal process.[67] Kodak, the largest manufacturer of professional film in the world at this time, owned all the manufacturing patents on this amateur stock. Prior to the development of 16mm reversal, 35mm standard film had entailed high shipping and handling costs; the United States

Post Office required that film mailed for processing be packaged in heavy and bulky lead-lined cases. Considering that the film was a negative, many producers screened before printing, thus doubling shipping costs.[68] When Eastman Kodak and the Motion Picture Patents Company entered into agreement in 1908, Eastman Kodak's development of a nonflammable acetate-base film raised the barriers to entry in the motion picture market for independents. However, the higher cost of this film and the lukewarm reception by American producers shelved this innovation until 1921 after two years of unsuccessful marketing.[69]

By 1912 George Eastman had instituted the Eastman Kodak Research Laboratory under the direction of Dr. C. E. Kenneth Mees to undertake research in the photographic process. Insulated from the demands of Eastman Kodak and pursuing pure research, the laboratory focused primarily on film-stock rather than apparatus research. The laboratory's two most significant breakthroughs were the reversal film process and color film, two innovations with considerable impact on the amateur market.[70] The reversal film stock, then, presented several incentives for amateur use: it reduced film cost, it decreased postal costs, and it could be developed promptly and conveniently at several service centers.[71]

Bell and Howell's involvement in amateur filmmaking equipment resulted from its expertise in professional-camera manufacturing. Bell and Howell engineering designs and patents had standardized the professional film industry's equipment, with the company holding patents on the first standardized projector, printer, perforators, splicers, and professional cameras. Most of these designs were used exclusively by the Essanay Film Studios in Chicago, where Bell and Howell was located.[72] Bell and Howell, then, owned factories that were tooled up to manufacture mass-produced, standardized equipment just as Eastman Kodak owned the patents on machines for the mass production of celluloid. Theirs was a formidable alliance.

While many inventors in this early period worked on a variety of formats, Bell and Howell and Eastman Kodak both tried to develop amateur-film systems. Between 1914 and 1920, according to company sources, Eastman Kodak experimented with amateur-movie cameras that utilized short loads of 35mm negative, positive, and reversal film and with cameras that exposed the 35mm stock in two separate run-throughs, which would then be split into 17.5mm.[73] By 1920 Eastman Kodak had developed the 16mm reversal process and prototypical models of cameras.[74] In 1919 Bell and Howell developed a hand-cranked 17.5mm amateur camera. The camera was never marketed however, because the company reasoned that the uncertainty of the availability of 17.5mm film supplies and developing services would deter amateurs. This prototype, called the Filmo, was modified for the 16mm-gauge film at the suggestion of Eastman Kodak. After both companies agreed on the placement of film perforations, Bell and Howell redesigned the camera as a hand-held camera with a spring-driven motor. According to Bell and Howell documents, Eastman Kodak licensed the company's square and round reel mount patent to protect its 16mm reversal film.[75] The agreements between Bell and Howell and Eastman Kodak stretched from patent protection to technical interchangeability.

Bell and Howell had other incentives for entering the amateur-film market, however. In a 1921 letter to the Board of Directors, Bell and Howell president, R. J. Kittredge, commented that three factors had inhibited the development of new product lines: World War I and United States government needs, the company's need for manufacturing improvements, and a huge increase in demand for Bell and Howell apparatuses. Noting that the American economy was in a period of stagnation, Kittredge urged the development of new product lines. Because Bell and Howell had patented narrow-width film, he pushed the engineering department to focus on amateur-camera designs that would utilize this narrow-width film. He wrote, "This development alone, if successful, would assure prospects of the continuation of the Company's expansion and prosperity."[76] Entry into the amateur market would diversify the company.

Bell and Howell's first publicly marketed amateur camera was the Filmo 70, claimed by some to have preceded Kodak's Cine-Kodak, since it was patented in 1921. Unlike previous amateur-movie cameras, the Filmo was designed for easy hand-held operation that designers assumed would appeal to the inexperienced user. Rather than a hand crank, the Filmo worked with a spring-driven motor.[77] Selling at $389, the camera and projector package was so successful it was back-ordered for three years. Two years later in 1923, the innovations of this small, hand-held, spring-driven camera were enlarged in the Bell and Howell Eyemo, a professional 35mm newsreel camera that was constructed with more durable metals.[78] In economic terms, amateur cameras were the site of technological experimentation and innovation for Bell and Howell, a way to test designs for later adaptation to professional gear.

In 1923 Kodak introduced its Cine-Kodak 16mm equipment, assumed by the company to be the first complete amateur system with camera and projector. A writer in *Scientific American* observed that "the diminutive camera weighs only seven pounds and is said to be, relatively at least, as simple in operation as the usual Kodak."[79] The reversal process and smaller film gauge reduced both cost and weight. The Cine-Kodak overwhelmed the photographic industry. The *British Journal of Photography* proclaimed: "The day of the moving picture as a competitor of hand camera photography has been a long time coming, and it looks as though its advent will not be much longer delayed."[80] Dr. C. E. Kenneth Mees, a Kodak research scientist and emulsion wizard, launched an international lecture and demonstration tour to promote the Cine-Kodak. In a two-part series in 1925 in the *British Journal of Photography*, Mees outlined the new system's reversal method, developing improvements, and camera modifications. With a black strip of paper wrapped around the outside edge of the film, daylight loading was also possible, another technical innovation.[81] The Cine-Kodak gained prominence almost overnight as the most efficient, exact, and inexpensive amateur home-movie method and was marketed to middle- and upper-class consumers. Unlike most other camera manufacturers—even Edison, who had patented an unsuccessful home-movie technology in 1912—Kodak had the manufacturing resources and advertising expertise garnered in the amateur still-photography market to distribute amateur cameras for mass consumption beyond the elite group of professionals and avid photography and engineering buffs who toyed with camera innovations and formats in the more competitive period.

Bell and Howell, however, recognized that photo dealers—who had seen many obscure and unconventional amateur-movie systems come and go—were hesitant to launch into amateur-film gear. Under the direction of chairman of the board J. H. McNabb, Bell and Howell targeted an upper-class, luxury market by advertising in exclusive magazines and through direct-selling methods. McNabb himself sold these amateur cameras directly. According to his own account in a 1927 issue of *Sales Management*, McNabb combed local papers for news of wealthy people preparing to depart on world tours. He would go to their offices, give the secretary a wound and running film camera, ask her to give it to her boss, and begin his sales pitch.[82] Three months after the introduction of the Filmo, private camera orders and dealer requests were backlogged for a year for Bell and Howell products. The Filmo, as a luxury item for the upper classes, provided most of Bell and Howell's expansion capital for other ventures at this time: for example, the company built a larger manufacturing plant and developed the first laboratory for motion picture mechanical and engineering research.[83]

The Cine-Kodak process and system firmly situated amateur cinematography as a hobby for the middle and upper classes. If amateur cinematographers ever had the opportunity to enter the film business, create their own businesses, or pose as an opposition to the dominant industry during this period, this process established the realm of 16mm film as distinctly amateur and for private use, cut off from distribution or exhibition outlets that would offer more commercial possibilities. Within months, articles began to appear in photographic journals telling amateurs how to make their films look more like Hollywood narrative films. *Photo-Era* magazine initiated a September to June monthly series on amateur cinematography, stressing how amateurs could imitate and emulate the codes of the feature-film industry. Of course, these 16mm productions, glossy as they might be after advice from one of these magazines, could not be reproduced, distributed, or exhibited beyond other private homes because of the 16mm technology.

However, not all photography writers in this period succumbed to the lure of playing at producing Hollywood-like feature films in the privacy of their homes with this gear. Some writers urged amateur theatrical societies to collectively buy a camera and produce theatrical films about their local communities. As early as 1919, Ernest Dench, writing in the *British Journal of Photography*, encouraged amateur cinematographers to establish a lucrative business filming local events and offering their services to manufacturers and fund-raisers.[84] Others advocated ferreting out local news and spectacles as filler for theatrical film. While amateur-camera equipment became standardized with 16mm, it was quickly commodified into a leisure activity miming the industry.

The overall impact of 16mm film as the standard amateur format was to establish two major professional-film corporations—Bell and Howell and Eastman Kodak—as the dominant manufacturing forces of amateur-film technology. This incorporation of amateur-film technology within two companies and the development of stocks and cameras that limited commercial opportunities had three important consequences: cameras were now mass produced, amateur film emerged as a luxury consumer item, and amateur production was pointed toward the family.

Aesthetic Dimensions of Amateur Filmmaking

Within the aesthetic of pictorialism, residual painterly standards of ideal beauty in nature and pleasing composition were resurrected and linked with amateur photography and then filmmaking. This trend toward pictorialism tended to overemphasize what were fast becoming the values displaced as a result of the bureaucratic tendencies of corporate industrialization—nature, beauty, feeling, family, emotion, higher metaphysical truths. This pattern of aesthetic content determined and judged by "natural" values persisted throughout the history of aesthetic directives to amateur filmmakers, initiating a general trend of amateur-film aesthetics toward idealizing the values of life freed from capitalist rationality that were increasingly deposited within leisure time. This move toward the adoption of pictorialism as an amateur aesthetic standard had its roots in amateur still photography.

From 1880 to 1920 amateur photography posed as the cultural site where control over the image of industrial technology, science, and individual expression could be unified. It strategically intersected both scientific rationality and artistic individualism at a historical conjuncture when the logic of scientific discourse motored dominant corporate, economic relations. Amateur photography promoted the idea that it was the repository for a myriad of scientific and technical skills, from chemistry to math to design. It simultaneously advanced an ideology that its technology was a democratic arsenal of different capitalist technocratic skills. Note how the following writer in an 1889 edition of *Outing*, just one year after the introduction of the Kodak Brownie, connects technical skills and consumer products:

> Those who take up the art of photography will find that it offers a field for the intelligent employment of a varied class of matters constantly occurring in the practical arts and the arts of design. It is quite true that with modern labor saving appliances few things can be more easily learned than how to make a photograph.[85]

By 1900 the amateur still market was immense compared to fifty years earlier. For instance, there was a twentyfold increase in the number of British and American photographic societies.[86] Celluloid-roll films in daylight cartridges and hand cameras were directly responsible for photography's surge of popularity as a leisure-time activity.[87] Nearly every issue of *Photo-Miniature*, a popular photography journal aimed at committed nonprofessionals, contained articles on amateur hand-camera use. Magic lanterns sustained an outlet for plate companies ousted from the larger market when Kodak began to manufacture roll film. Amateur and professional photographers were not distinct groups until the 1888 introduction of the Kodak camera. With the famous advertising slogan "You push the button, we do the rest," Kodak appropriated and controlled the entire process of producing film and photographs. Because photographers had previously mixed their own emulsions on glass plates, amateurism signified loss of control over the production process.

The residual formation of nineteenth-century, individualistic, adventuresome capitalism—components of the more general ideological discourse on amateurism—also infused the relations of amateur photography. For instance, in an 1889 account in *Harper's Magazine*, George Hepworth, in a first-person anecdotal account, described his experiences in buying a hand camera, reading photography manuals, and subsequently photographing the flora and fauna of Cape Cod.[88] This photographic adventure conveyed the pioneering spirit of capitalism, now marooned in leisure time. One writer in an 1896 *Cosmopolitan* article even went so far as to proclaim that the "professional photographer has become an indispensable element in the world's progress."[89] Thus, the amateur and the professional were enjoined in the same quest for "progress."

While classical painting reeked of ruling-class privilege, amateur photography aligned with democratic and middle-class values. Mass produced and simple, it broadened consumption but not control over production. On the discursive level, popular magazines equated mass production with democracy. In nineteenth-century popular discourse, photography facilitated emotional self-development but also displaced this expression into the isolated realm of hobbies. This "democratic" ideology conflated production with consumption; this slippage located amateur photography as an insignificant hobby within private life.

Despite a democratic discourse on amateur photography, this freedom may have operated exclusively on the level of technology itself. The cultural and, by this time, commonsensical distinctions between the amateur as spontaneous and the professional as disciplined emerged in amateur photography from 1888 to 1923 most pervasively on the level of content. Amateurism was associated with "naturalness" and "resemblance," with a distinct lack of posing or studio work, whereas studio portraiture, the pinnacle of posing and manipulation, was identified as the domain of the crasser and less-artistic professional. To create better photographs, photographic columnists advised amateurs to learn the aesthetic principles of "pictorialism," the use of composition that imitated painting to convey an abstract idea that would organize chaotic visual elements to produce an emotional effect in the viewer.

However, these definitions of amateurism and professionalism require some historical qualification. Before the invention of celluloid-roll film for amateurs by Kodak in 1888, the distinctions between the amateur and professional photographer were less acute, inasmuch as both precisely prepared emulsions, plates, and prints. Even after the successful marketing of amateur photography, a cultural class system emerged: those who took photographs as a leisure-time diversion and those serious amateurs who fought for photography as an art. While the general discourse on amateurism linked it with spontaneity, the haphazard, sloppy style of the snapshooter was not tolerated by pictorialists. The pictorialist amateur and art photographer mode demanded concentration, education, and skill; spontaneity was located in the subject or in nature rather than in the shooting style. If anything, the tenets of pictorialism both elevated photography to an art and separated hobbyists from serious amateurs. In this early usage, the term *amateur* insinuated a dedication to art rather than to commercial or industrial values.

As an aesthetic movement, pictorialism may not have had a great impact on the art world, mainly because its insistence on classical, pleasing compositions, idealized nature scenes, and soft-focus or speciality printed images—thought to imitate impressionist paintings—advocated standards that were already nostalgic at the time they were presented, from 1889 to 1920.[90] However, the aesthetic rules argued and established by photographers like P. H. Emerson,

Alfred Stieglitz, and his Photo-Secession had a tremendous influence on both amateur photography and cinematography for many decades after it waned in art-photography circles.

According to Beaumont Newhall's interpretation in his *History of Photography*, pictorialism reacted against "stiffly posed studio scenes and patchwork prints made up of pieces of different negatives."[91] In contrast to this artificiality, P. H. Emerson, a photographer and writer infatuated with the objectivity of science, proposed a photographic aesthetic based on imitating the effects of nature on the eye in a lecture called "Photography, a Pictorial Art" delivered to the Camera Club in London in 1886. Also in that year, he published a collection of his photographs called *Life and Landscape on the Norfolk Broads* (that showed how marsh dwellers lived) in order to illustrate his contentions. In this lecture Emerson claimed that photography was second only to painting in interpreting nature with artistic feeling. He argued that photographers should forego topography and industrial work and follow the artistic precept of finding "truth" in the beauty of form.[92]

In 1889 Emerson published an explanation of his aesthetic principles entitled *Naturalistic Photography for Students of Art*, which created an uproar of controversy in amateur photographic magazines, because it promoted soft focus. In this book Emerson attempted to prove how all great art—from ancient Greek sculpture to Watteau, Rousseau, Millet—employed principles of naturalism. For Emerson, the terms *impressionism* and *naturalism* were interchangeable in that both referred to nature as a standard; Emerson argued that he preferred the term *naturalism*, because it relied less on a single artist's subjectivity. His definition of naturalism hinged on a principle of noninterference:

> By this term we mean the true and natural expression of the impression of nature by an art. Now it will immediately be said that all men see nature differently. Granted. But the artist sees deeper, penetrates more into the beauty and mystery of nature than the commonplace man. *The beauty is there in nature.*[93]

If one concentrated and studied nature long enough, some aspect of it would move one to produce an image. In Emerson's version of art history, the great sculptors and painters interpreted nature in as true a manner as possible and therefore serve as touchstones for photographers. He urged photographers to study these great masters in museums. By imitating painting standards, he legitimated photography.

This emphasis on educating one's artistic tastes based on established high-art masterpieces was elucidated by Emerson in a chapter called "Educated

Sight." Relying on popularized notions of empiricism that foregrounded powers of observation as the absolute verification, Emerson maintained that photographers should study their subjects closely; they should emulate scientific observation so that they could apprehend beautiful forms, arrangements, and lines in the subject. An intensive study of "great art" trained the eye and sensibility of the viewer.[94] The photographer required training and acculturation in the sanctioned and accepted ruling-class artistic styles of composition in order to find them in nature, which was a form of idealism.

By 1891 Emerson had recoiled from his earlier position that photography was an art, admitting that an artist could not manipulate the photographic image enough to demonstrate a subjective interpretation.[95] However, his principles of imitating nature to discover ideal forms and truths attracted many followers who lobbied for photography as an art.

The proponents of pictorialism circulated in amateur photographic societies and amateur magazines in Europe from approximately 1887 to as late as 1910, although pictorialist how-to manuals for beginning amateurs were published in subsequent decades. These amateur photographic societies in England, France, and Germany held exhibitions of art photography exclusively, positioning themselves outside of scientific or technical work. At some exhibitions, painters and sculptors judged the work; at others, photographs were hung with paintings. Indeed, some photographs, particularly those by Robert Demarchy of France, which utilized the gum-bichromate process, resembled paintings in their textural qualities. Attracted to the handwork and control this printing process offered, many pictorialist photographers adopted it to lessen the realism of the photographic image. However, some pictorialists, like Frederick Evans, continued to work in less-manipulated printing styles. This manipulation in the printing stage distinguished snapshooting amateurs from "serious" amateurs interested in artistic practices.[96]

The connection between pictorialism and amateur photographic societies illustrates how a definition of amateurism revolves around a rejection of the modes of industrial society. According to photographic critic Abigail Solomon-Godeau, by 1883 photography emphasized amateurs as artists to differentiate their work from the "increasingly industrialized, standardized, and non-artistic modes of all other photography."[97] Emerson in *Naturalistic Photography for Students of the Art* argued that most photography was practiced for utilitarian rather than for artisanal purposes; he included in his argument scientific work, reproducers, lantern-slide makers, plate makers, enlargers, spotters, printers, retouchers, and those who made scenery images.[98] The arguments about photographic art contributed to the development of the Linked Ring group in England, the

Photo Club de Paris, and various American photographic societies. Art photography was identified as the domain of the amateur; the artist's personal expression was not contaminated by the crassness of commerce.

In the social context of the 1880s and 1890s, amateur photography implied a vocation—not a hobby—dedicated to art. With the prevalence of photographic images in the commercial world and the accessibility and ease of photography after the introduction of Kodak's Brownie camera in 1888, Solomon-Godeau argues that art photography was cornered into a position of differentiating its images as much as possible. By the 1890s art photography, influenced by the pictorialist aesthetic, turned toward manipulated forms of printing such as gum bichromate, bromoil, and glycerine and toward subject matter that reinforced an anti-industrial attitude—landscapes, genre scenes, nudes, tableaux based on historical or mythological themes.[99] In this sense the photographic discourse on amateur photography presented the transference of residual notions and idealizations of past times and nature in order to position amateurs and their images outside of industry. The relationship between amateur and art photography was grounded in idealist conceptions of the artist as being removed and protected from corrupting external influences like society or money.

Alfred Stieglitz, the founder of the Photo-Secession in 1902 and the foremost American proponent of pictorialism, was also closely associated with amateurs. As editor of *American Amateur Photographer* from 1892 and later as editor of *Camera Notes*, he vigorously promoted amateurism as an ideal for art photography and forged its aesthetic with pictorialism. While Stieglitz's exhibitions of pictorial images by such artists as Gertrude Kasebier and Clarence White were not uniformly praised and while he was accused of exerting totalitarian control over his publications and exhibitions, several photographic historians have argued that his influence situated photography increasingly as an art form practiced as a specialized and individual aesthetic with limited access.[100] Although pictorialism was aligned with amateurs, its insistence on the acquisition of nostalgic artistic principles and an artistic education diminished, at least on the discursive level, the democratization of image-making by erecting standards that amateurs had to strive for to become "real artists."

While several different schools of pictorialism—ranging from those who advocated natural scenes to those who manipulated images—vied for control over proper image-making, some general contours of its public dissemination to amateurs surfaced. Pictorialists clung to a Platonic ideal of beauty already rejected by impressionist painters like Claude Monet. The pictorialists adopted a rather skewed version of impressionism that denied the fleeting quality of light that painters embraced, turning instead to more generalizable and less-specific forms.[101] The soft-focus images of some pictorialist photographers transmuted the fuzzy quality of impressionistic paintings for exactly the oppo-site purpose: to render an "ideal." To compose this ideal, pictorialists argued that all photographs should demonstrate a unifying theme, with all other ele-ments in the image as subordinate.

Writing in his book *Artistic Landscape Photography* in 1896, A. H. Wall sug-gested that beginning photographers employ their carefully studied feelings to what they shot. To stimulate a commensurate feeling in the viewer, Wall stipu-lated that nothing in the image should interrupt the presentation of a unified theme:

> A different scale of tones, arrangement of lines, lights, shades, masses, points etc., for a different scene, but for this nothing that does not belong to its pervading sentiment, nothing that will not compose or harmonize therewith and give pictorial effect.[102]

According to Wall, careful use of point of view, a term he employed to describe the combination of an eye-level vanishing point and the thoughts and feelings of the artist, achieved this harmony the best.[103]

In 1910 A. J. Anderson reiterated and expanded these principles in his *Ar-tistic Side of Photography in Theory and Practice*. He promoted the notion that com-position expressed a theme and that this theme should not be "superficial," dis-ruptive, or discordant, but quietly assertive. Achieved through the pictorial essay that suggested the photographer's subjective feelings, the resultant sym-pathy evoked in the viewer should stimulate an emotional exchange. Like many pictorialists, Anderson misinterpreted impressionism: for him it did not capture the changing quality of a specific light but instead revealed subject essence through general values rather than details.[104]

As late as 1923, in his *Principles of Pictorial Photography*, John Wallace Gillies defined pictorial photography as an image that conveyed a feeling or impression through artistic means and that was not merely a reproduction of reality.[105] Gil-lies even offered a history of pictorial photography, asserting that serious ama-teurs were offended by the nonthinking attitudes and behaviors of Kodak snap-shooters.[106] Describing the formation of Clarence White's organization in 1916 called the Pictorial Photographers of America, Gillies implied that the art stan-dard of photography had finally been codified for amateurs. For Gillies, picto-rialism represented the consummate form of art: one that summoned "feeling" and the ethereal spirit rather than aspects of the material self.[107]

These disparate pictorialists invoke common characteristics: a belief in ideal forms, a notion of unified composition, a commitment to subjective re-sponses in both artist and viewer, an imitation of previous artistic standards found in classical painting, and a reinterpretation of impressionist innovations as a naturalist revival.

Pictorial photography's deep entrenchment in outdated, painterly aesthetic standards can be ascertained by comparing its time period of 1889–1920 to other contemporary art movements' time periods. For example, while impressionism captured changing and fleeting movements through light and color, the pictorial photographers appropriated its tenets of intense observation of light to render more classical designs. By the early 1900s fauvism, cubism, expressionism, and futurism had emerged in painting—all aesthetics that challenged representational and imitative art in their own distinct ways: fauvism promoted brilliant and abstract color; cubism emphasized geometric planes; expressionism isolated figures and linear decorative lines; and futurism was fascinated with modern technology and industry. By 1911 constructivism, an aesthetic movement grounded in design, construction, and abstraction, emerged in Russia, while during and after World War I, dadaism, which attacked the concepts of art that advocated coherence, order, and beauty, developed in Germany, France, and America.

While these various art movements represented the avant-garde sector of painting and sculpture, they nonetheless underline pictorial photography's nostalgia for residual representational systems. Indeed, by 1901 some photographers even condemned manipulated printing processes and argued for straight photography that would explore the properties endemic to its own material.[108] In the context of these experimental trends in painting and photography from approximately 1900 to 1920, the association of pictorialism with amateurs excluded them from any kind of formal experimentation or innovation by promoting a visual standard based on classical norms.

Filtering into the aesthetic ideology of amateur photography and cinematography magazines, the precepts of pictorial photography were offered as commonsensical assumptions about composition. According to popular magazine writers, photographic pictorialism required enormous time investment, discipline, and planning. In an 1896 review of amateur photography in *Cosmopolitan*, one writer directed amateur photographers to study great art work, claiming its visual organization would train the amateur to see the world "artistically," that is, according to the principles of the dominant, museum-preserved traditions in art.[109] Some well-to-do amateur photographers even studied with painters to hone this traditional painterly sensibility. Ideologically, this reliance on great paintings conscripted residual artistic formations and steered photography away from more contemporary, unacceptable content—like modern urban life. An 1892 *Cosmopolitan* writer warned that one's work could "not hope to gain appreciation beyond the circle of the immediate family" if one abandoned these aesthetic conventions.[110]

In fact, an 1889 article in *Outing* magazine recommended photographing old European buildings and alpine settings, emphasizing that one might need to enlist the police to restrain passersby from sticking their faces in front of the lens or otherwise cluttering the frame.[111] The representation of the traditional and the residual differentiated serious amateurs from professionals and snapshooters. It deflected cameras, at least on the discursive level, from insertion into the day-to-day world of industrial capitalism.

Everyday images were deemed "amateur" in the nonserious artist's use of the term at this period. In a telling example, the same columnist in *Outing* cited John Ruskin's contention that beauty and pictorialism were located in nature and natural lines. Ruskin, for this particular writer, demonstrated "how these lines [natural lines] are more interesting and valuable to the artist than any machine drawn lines, no matter how interesting and complex."[112] Aesthetically, pictorialism neutralized the potentials of easy-to-operate and lightweight amateur-photography apparatuses; it idealized nature and natural forms at the expense of an exposé of existing social relations, such as industry, factories, immigrant life, or urban culture.

This shift from spontaneous snapshooting toward a planned, disciplined pictorialism simulating the standards of accepted painterly styles prompted a discourse about women as superlative image-makers. Photography magazines considered women "natural" photographers because of their cultural association as cultivators of nature; they possessed, according to this ideology, the patience and time to delve into artistic, pictorial photographs. Asserting that snapshooting failed to satisfy "artistic cravings," Margaret Biskind in an 1890 *Outing* article praising women photographers contended that women were better photographers than men because of their "keenly developed instinct for the decorative and picturesque, their delight in the mere manipulation with their delicate hand of fragile objects, their love of finish in details, their well-known patience."[113] By now, imbued with the pictorialist ideals of patience, higher truths, and art, photography harnessed women to the home even further as an art that reproduced "the more natural" images in a woman's daily life. Symptomatically, F. W. Crane observed in an 1894 edition of *Munsey's* that most serious women photographers photographed their children, nature, interiors, or portraits of their husbands and friends.[114] This aesthetic assumed women retained a closer sympathy with residual cultural values and representations in the home.

This congruence of women with photography is significant for a definition of amateur film, because while it legitimated artistry, it sunk it even further into the isolated sanctuary of the home. However, photography did allow women to develop skills that could remove them from the home as professionals, echoing the movement of amateur actresses, although it is difficult to ascertain how many women did cross the line into professional photography. Women amateur photographers were linked with the technological production of art; as an emblem of the home and bourgeois culture, their presence mediated between industrial technology and traditional art. Women, then, negotiated the contradictions between industrialization and the production of images of everyday life.[115] Margaret Biskind noted in 1890 that women could easily become expert artists or photographers with enough patience and experimentation with the most simple camera. Biskind observed that many women, exiled to foreign countries with husbands relocated by corporations, took photographs and later exhibited them, gaining professional recognition. Amateur photography, then, became imbedded in the home via the participation of middle- and upper-class women, but it also provided a means out if a woman developed enough skill in pictorialist image-making. In a vivid demonstration of ruling-class appropriation of the amateur photographic community, the patroness of the Austrian Society of Amateur Photographers was the Archduchess Maria Theresa.[116]

Popular-magazine writers assumed that amateur-movie apparatuses would educate one to appreciate beauty by learning the tenets of pictorialism within the family, recalling this schema of still photography, but during the later period of 1913 to 1923. This amateur-film aesthetic defined pictorialism almost exclusively on the combination of natural composition techniques with the ability to evoke emotional and interpretive responses in viewers. If nature provided better lines for amateur photographers, it transmuted into a transcendent, eternal vision in amateur cinematography. For example, magazines advised amateurs to film nature and country scenes; those images both uplifted the spirit and refreshed the eyes. A 1921 article "Filming Adventures in Beauty" in *Arts and Decoration* considered filming cities both visually distracting and too much a part of one's day-to-day existence to qualify as "art."[117] The article hailed an amateur film called *Lyric of the Marshes* for its still photographic pictorialism, its natural settings, its absence of people, and its ability to invoke "cosmic truths."[118] In yet another permutation of pseudo upward mobility, the advocacy of pictorialism here shifted the amateur-film subjects away from daily work life and industrialization into a static, beautiful adoration of nature and the home.

Defined and articulated by magazine writers for filmmakers, pictorialism separated rationalized, industrial capitalism from the more spontaneous and natural middle-class family life and its hobbies. The dominant discourse on amateur filmmaking pictorialism discouraged amateurs away from investigations of labor, capitalism, or industry. Instead, it steered them toward more neutral, personalized, and subjective territory.

While many amateur-film advice columnists acknowledged that motion picture making straddled commerce and art, they dislodged amateur cinematography from commerce by advocating that its artistic practice evoke moods and emotional states in viewers. With this version of pictorialism, the amateur film attained status as art; with emotion, it would emerge as a traditional "great art." For instance, "Painting Moods with a Motion Picture Camera" in a 1923 issue of *Arts and Decoration* cautioned that if one had to film people, they should expose "inner feeling," "real emotion," and "beauty," ferreted out by the skillful use of the camera.[119] These attributes recalled the more general definition of amateurism as a depository for values discarded by corporate industry. The simplification of amateur-film technology extended into and aided this expression of art and beauty. A 1919 piece called "Cinematography, a New Art for Amateurs" claimed the less the operations of the camera interfered with the subject, the easier it was to obtain psychological insights.[120] This advocacy of the psychological and emotional levels of the amateur aesthetic corresponded to the late nineteenth-century discourse that amateurism revitalized industrialization with human values and sensibilities, energy, and spontaneity. By the early 1920s, the amateur-film aesthetic inserted the residual values of high art into private time and hobbies.

This process of beauty and art was also inverted from the production of pictorially pleasing imagery to the social production of the body as a natural, unified, and composed unit. Home movies objectified movement of family members for study, investigation, and improvement—a time-motion study on the body, according to one optimistic writer in 1919:

> Certainly the sight of ourselves moving through a reel, after the uncanny first impression is past, will make the most hardened of us admit that we— well—that we can improve our gracefulness. Animals register more naturally and gracefully because they move naturally and rhythmically.[121]

This production of physical movement projected that the body, like the photograph or home movie, should attain grace through the adoption of natural animal movements and should simultaneously affect more repetitive behaviors through rhythm. Before World War I the principles of scientific management, which broke tasks down into their most simple components to insure efficiency and increase productivity, circulated in other spheres of American life besides the factory; popular lecturers misconstrued efficiency by preaching that it promoted common sense, competence, energy, initiative, and moral character. Some politicians saw the institution of "social efficiency" as a form of social control of laziness and greed. Efficiency societies were organized to promote loss of selfishness, hard work, and big profits. Scientific management infiltrated the home, with women's magazines describing how housewives could analyze and time their work to determine schedules and operate the household more scientifically. The production of home movies in order to analyze family members was perhaps only another articulation of how scientific management had penetrated daily life.[122]

This technical surveillance of the body through an instrument that sees more perfectly and scientifically than the human eye was the family parallel to the use of amateur-film equipment in the workplace to monitor workers. In order to institute the efficient production principles of time and motion studies, managers filmed workers next to clocks in order to evaluate their movements. According to a description in a 1913 *Current Opinion*, films of skilled workers— that is, those who conformed to the efficient production methods sought by scientific management—were shown to slower or newer employees so that they could observe, analyze, and learn how they should behave in the factory.[123] Movies were thought to transfer skills from machines to bodies, according to efficiency experts, and thus they industrialized physical behavior. Surveillance here was appended to amateur film in the home: amateur films materialized the invisible and ephemeral, and this new, mechanical form of visibility was more analyzable and more controllable than amorphous emotions. With smaller equipment and more accurate observation, factory managers and parents could control the worker and the family.

Pictorialism, as an aesthetic paradigm and photographic discourse emphasizing natural lines and residual painterly standards, exerted pressure on the direction of amateur film in several ways. As an aesthetic discourse, it oriented amateur producers to film their homes and personal friends rather than aspects of industrialized modern life. Second, pictorialism, as it was later redefined by proponents of amateur film, aided the promotion of industrial time-motion studies within the home, functioning as a form of standardization of beauty. Finally, pictorialism may have further segmented the ideological and material contradiction between rationalized wage labor and the supposedly more integrated, freer artistic labor of amateur-film production by positioning the quest for the natural and the beautiful within the private sphere.

Nonetheless, the predominant discourse in amateur-photography and mass-circulation magazines running articles on amateur film either openly advocated pictorialism or called for an aesthetic that deployed pictorialist assumptions. The uniformity of this slant is both interesting and significant, particularly in that pictorialism as a movement for art photography generated controversy, disagreement over its principles, and redefinitions within this period. Consequently, it would appear that the infighting and changes that characterized both pictorialism and art photography did not include uninitiated amateurs, who were introduced to the aesthetic as a fait accompli. The values of pictorialism, which emphasized the natural, harmony, a unified idea, and the search for universal, general values, dispersed into the realm of the family and its relationship to amateur production, and advice columnists situated the family as fertile ground for these enduring values.

Filming the Family: Social Uses of Amateur Film

In this early period, the family, as a continually expanding market for consumption of commodities, became closely identified with amateur filmmaking in general, photography, and engineering magazines. Because the family was considered a separate and distinct social structure from business, amateur-film marketing distributed the technological ideology of industrial capitalism to the home. Through its inscription of dominant values that supported the family, this discourse on the role of filmmaking positioned the family as timeless, isolated, and private—ripe for the labors of a well-honed pictorialist.

Although the clientele for amateur motion picture equipment was most likely more financially well off and more technically oriented than the average American at the turn of the century, their mechanical knowledge of both camera and film was mediated with the discourse in magazines that urged the use of the camera almost exclusively as a means to chronicle the family. This insertion of filmmaking into the family on the ideological level may have detained inexperienced amateurs from entering professional channels or moving toward more public, political usage. According to Julia Hirsch in her *Family Photographs: Content, Meaning and Effect,* before the invention of amateur photography in 1888, family portraiture was considered a professional field.[124] One took photographs of one's family, according to this new, more democratic view, to reproduce the family as efficiently as industry produced commodities. These magazine writers encouraged amateur-camera users to remain within the safe boundaries of the home to find beauty. This notion of amateur cinematography affirmed the family as a social construction outside economic, political, and social relations: portraits decorated walls as icons of family presence, and films were projected as individualized narratives of particular family histories. The relationship between the ideologies of family life and amateur film is significant. Susan Sontag in her *On Photography* has argued, for example, that this emphasis on the family during the industrial and economic reordering and readjustments of this period presented a denial of the contemporary situation by relying on preindustrial, residual notions of the family:

> Through photographs, each family constructs a portrait chronicle of itself—a portable kit of images that bears witness to its connectedness. It hardly matters what activities are photographed, so long as photographs

get taken and are cherished. Photography becomes a right of family life just when, in the industrializing countries of Europe and America, the very institution of the family starts undergoing radical surgery. As that claustrophobic unit, the nuclear family aggregate, photography came along to memorialize, to restate symbolically, the imperiled continuity and vanishing tenderness of family life.[125]

While the camera may have more sharply focused the family in a period of its declining economic utility, the production of amateur movies delivered, according to essayists, a mechanical sense of relatedness, intimacy, and pleasure. Derived from the objectification of the family, this pleasure demonstrated discursively how the idea of observability advanced in empiricism organized family private time. This democratization and expansion of scientific epistemology was expressed in a 1917 *Literary Digest* article appropriately entitled "Movies for Everybody." The article proclaimed that private movies were no longer monopolized by the wealthy but were now within the reach of the middle classes who could afford to analyze and dissect their own lives on film.[126]

Amateur motion picture technology interfaced with social relations as an instrument that was imagined to improve the interactions of the family, as observed in a 1915 *Literary Digest* piece:

When the conversation lapses and expires, and lies like a lump in the throat, first aid today shall consist of immediately turning out the parlor light, and wheeling in the family cinematograph, and entertaining the wilted swain with yards and yards of film from the past.[127]

This ideology—appearing after World War I during film-industry expansion—positioned home movies between two different historical articulations. On the one hand, amateur film represented technological progress as a popular tool and remedy for interpersonal relations; on the other hand, home movies retrieved the past so that they could serve and entertain the present. Home movies mined the past as material that could be measured and quantified in footage or reels like workers in time-motion studies.

These values of technocratic capitalism infused the popular discourse on amateur-movie production and positioned amateur film as an adjunct and support to industry. As early as 1899, a writer in the *Photogram* looked forward to the time when the movie camera, like other entertainment or production technologies, would shed its designation as a speciality and luxury item and attain a natural place within the family as a necessary item for emotional survival. Some entrepreneurs fantasized the installation of cameras into homes as working components in the apparatus of everyday life, assuming that technology motivated behavioral change and adaptation. The article in the *Photogram*, for example, set out a manifesto of projections for amateur film:

> In the home, the camera must become as universal as the sewing machine; in the office, warehouse, factory, bank and library, it must become as indispensable as the letter copying press and the telephone . . . it is perfectly true that the many people of whom we have spoken DO NOT KNOW THEY NEED a camera, but this does not in any way effect the main proposition. While it is true that demand creates supply, it is also true—and this is the basis of good trading—that supply creates demand. The women of the world did not know they needed the sewing machine, and business men had to be gradually taught the advantage of the typewriter and the telephone. . . . And so it must be with the CAMERA IN EVERYDAY USE.[128]

Daily use, of course, implied mass markets, an almost preposterous speculation in 1899, nearly twenty-four years before the demand for amateur cameras increased into a sizable market. With other mechanical recording instruments like the typewriter and the telephone, this writer framed the amateur-film camera as a precision device to monitor relations within the home, the office, the factory, or the bank.

A good example of how the discourse on amateur-film technology located it as the new intermediary between both the past and the present and between a nonverifiable subjectivity of personal and family life and observable behaviors that were the subject of scientific management resided in the promotion of amateur-film cameras as recorders of family history. In Mervin Delaway's analysis in an article titled "Make and Project Your Own Home Movies" published in 1917 in *Illustrated World*, technology subsumed both recollections and interactions within the home:

> Think of the pleasure, in after years, when your son or daughter is grown up and leaves home of having a complete film record from cradle days up. Think what a generous filming of scenes of your honeymoon would mean to you now. The greatest single pleasure that is possible to store up for the days of old age is a wealth of reminiscences of happy hours spent in youth with comrades or people you care for in a sincere and lasting way. The old people of today have only their dimming memories to depend on; those of tomorrow will have libraries of this film. This camera ought to add greatly to the joy of every family.[129]

Films, then, in Delaway's view, were thought to bestow permanence on the constant progression of age and cultural change. The passage above underscores the significance of the happiness of memories. These more modern visual memories transposed family history into a commodity that invoked only good times, selectively erasing contradiction, struggle, or disintegration. Indeed, writers in both popular technical journals and mass-market magazines directed amateurs toward creating a narrative spectacle of idealized family life.

Columnists advised filming social events marked by public celebration, such as children's birthdays, garden parties, and weddings. In 1911 one writer in *Popular Mechanics* suggested that parents give their sons and daughters a set of films that recorded the sequences of their childhood for wedding presents.[130] This linear historical narrative of family life in amateur films was eventually linked to the achievement of bourgeois success as a manifestation of natural evolution. One article in 1915 claimed that by graphically documenting their humble beginnings, home movies were excellent teaching devices for parents to show their children how they became more prosperous.[131]

This discourse on amateur film's capacity to chronicle the home dispersed into public exhibition in the form of war films that paralleled home movies but on a national scale. While government propaganda, these films were analogies of the personal and social structures of amateur-film use in the home, adapting private emotions and moods to mobilize the nation around the war effort. For the purposes of this discussion of amateur-film discourse and its relationships to families, the most interesting aspect of World War I newsreels was that they were categorized by some magazine writers as simply a larger scale, more dramatic, and more urgent sort of home movie. In actuality, until the United States entered the War in 1917, most Americans saw faked coverage of the war. After 1917 the Army Signal Corps filmed the war, but this footage was censored by a government committee before release to newsreel companies. Film historian Raymond Fielding has argued that because most photographers lacked combat experience, access to the front lines, and suitable equipment, the war was inadequately documented.[132] However, magazine writers equated this war footage with family-film footage in a way that reflected the arguments for the use of home movies in families.

During World War I the discourse on home-movie form and use emerged in the discussion of military films used for both surveillance of battlefields and for the recognition of loved ones in theaters back home. Technical and popular writers positioned propaganda films as national home movies. Surveillance and memory fused and did double duty; automatic cameras recorded aerial surveillance of enemy territories that were analyzed by the high command for strategy and then shipped to the states for public consumption in war weeklies.[133]

Films of the war effort circulated to newsreels from the government cataloged the progression of the war as home movies chronicled the linear narrative of the family. According to an essay in a 1917 issue of *Current Opinion*, motion pictures were critical not only in "keeping patriotism aroused but in keeping for posterity a pictorial record of every phase of the world shaking struggle."[134] On a grander scale, D. W. Griffith, the commercial-film producer, made a film of American industrial strength in order to boost the morale of the Russians and to demonstrate America's commitment to victory.[135] This identification process precipitated by war movies extended into the public showing of news weeklies, whose popularity may have depended less on their informational value than on their public display of images of soldiers for the audience, if we take an article in the May 1918 issue of *Current Opinion* as an indicator of how audiences viewed these films:

> Right here it may be stated, those simple minded folk who imagine that war will diminish attendance at the movies are vastly mistaken. Already millions of eyes throughout the country are anxiously viewing every bit of war film, in the hope of seeing the beloved lineaments of some near and dear relative who is fighting over there.[136]

During World War I, newsreels transmuted into national home movies resonating with patriotic and family ties.

In this later period from 1911 to 1923, the insertion of amateur film into nuclear families exposed two functions. On the one hand, it colonized the family with the procedures of industry through promoting the empirical properties of amateur film. On the other hand, it served to idealize and immortalize the family. However, by the latter part of this period, between 1919 and 1922, the idea that amateur efforts could provide a springboard to Hollywood fame and fortune surfaced, exhibiting a slight shift in the discourse on amateur film from a technical speciality to a fertile ground for the propagation of the illusion of instant success in and natural talent for "pictures."

Breaking into Movies:
The Political Consequences of Amateur-Film Discourse

By the early 1920s the discourse on amateur film had changed. Rather than only technical information, behind-the-scenes information on filmmaking, and magazines, journals, and books devoted to the discourse of professional techniques and standards began to appear. The dominant film industry's ideological subsumption of the discourse on amateur film operated as a form of political control, because it instituted a power relation between professional-film activity as the standard and epitome of production and amateur film as a training ground to rehearse these same procedures and norms. Thus, an ideology and discourse on the ascent from amateur- to professional-film work developed, accentuating their hierarchical relationship by integrating them structurally and by containing any material contradictions between them that might create an imbalance.

The rise of the amateur theatrical movement in the United States during the years 1860 to 1920 provides an ideological and cultural context for the institution of amateur film as a cultural training ground for entry into professional-film activities. The uses of amateurism as a social mechanism to both transfer dominant ideologies in the guise of participation and to cultivate a more highly groomed appreciation of professional standards in the theater are two trends evident in amateur theatricals that also surface in public discourse regarding the possibilities for amateurs to make it in Hollywood.

Beginning in the early, post-Civil War period as charity benefits produced by the ruling classes, amateur theatricals evidenced the origination of amateur productions of fiction and laid the base for amateur photoplay societies that were to develop later in the 1910s and 1920s. Amateur theatricals wedged amateurism within the realm of women and the nuclear family. By the mid-1890s two trends emerged in professional theater that set the stage for the evolution of amateur theatricals: amateur advice columns and books that contained a perpetration of residual concepts of individual control and artistry and a caste system determined by content that erected boundaries between professionals and amateurs.

Between 1895 and 1896 theater grew into a big business, following the economic trends set in industries like steel and oil. With small groups of business-people obtaining control over entire industries with the formation of the trusts, the theater market consolidated in what was known as the Syndicate, a group of booking agents and theater owners who exerted nearly total control over the entire industry. The Syndicate controlled tour routes between major cities, forced producers to sign exclusive contracts, booked only plays that would garner large audiences, and hired stars with personal followings.[137] Against this, amateur theatricals worked as a deflection of the myths of opportunity on the cultural and aesthetic levels.

In addition to these powerful economic constraints, formidable aesthetic barriers were in place. The latter part of the nineteenth century had witnessed the gradual acceptance among American audiences of realist plays that stressed attention to authentic detail and real-life situations. While it is not within the argument of this study to elaborate on the various forms of realist theater, it is significant that the paradigms of meticulous authenticity—in sets, acting, dialogue, and props—distinguished professional from amateur theater.[138] If amateurs were steered toward less-serious plays, it may have been a reflection of magazine writers' own analyses that serious drama demanded an obsessive rendition of prop, costume, and set detail, along with acting skill that amateurs on shoestring budgets and limited time could not replicate.

In contrast to professional theater of this time, a writer for *Cosmopolitan* in 1890 offered his own version of amateur theatrical history that defined amateurism as a form of charity and social service produced by wealthy women.[139] Amateur theatricals hinged not on original creative efforts but on the free circulation and dissemination of professional plays for private use. Professional plays dominated and infiltrated amateur theatricals: to be an amateur was to act, not create.

The amateur theatrical at the turn of the century also served as a place where people, through performance, could practice and standardize the personal attributes of rational control derived from scientific principles demanded of a more bureaucratic mode of production. Acting and amateurism were seen as important movements for cultivating, according to Charles Waddle in *Cosmopolitan*, "that general quality of action which is amply comprised in the indefinable word 'nerve,' so necessary to and so intensely characteristic of the American idea."[140] Amateurism manufactured appreciation of the dominant theater's professional performances—the aesthetic paradigms and standards by which amateurs imitated and evaluated their own work. Professional theater companies in the 1880s and 1890s, for example, test marketed their new productions in Buffalo, New York, arguing that the large number of amateur theatrical societies in that city created audiences that could better understand and discriminate plays.[141] In 1923, for example, Helena Smith Dayton and Louise Bascom Barratt published a manual for society theatrical producers called *The Book of Entertainments and Theatricals*, which advised amateurs to select plays from the Drama League of America because audiences would have had some familiarity with them.[142] In short, amateur acting shaped cultural consumers into more knowledgeable spectators honed to appreciate professional standards.

In nearly every major city in the United States, women's amateur theatrical clubs and societies flourished. As an example of either their pervasiveness or their perceived threat, a 1905 *Cosmopolitan* article complained that women used amateur productions as springboards to the professional stage, thereby breaking up the family.[143] The author attributed women's stage behaviors to a public extension of the natural vanity of woman: "It gives her the opportunity to show herself and to wear pretty frocks, and makes it possible to get her name in the papers."[144] Some male writers asserted that women were trained to perform anyway in the home, so their amateur theatrical activities were a "natural" extension of their private lives. Arguing that women were better actors than men, a 1911 *Century* article proclaimed:

> A society girl with an attractive exterior, a pleasant voice, and that indefinable quality called "temperament," after a very short training appears well and with an ease that is denied the other sex. Says another cynic, in a possible explanation, "most women are acting half their time."[145]

In a 1913 piece in *Ladies' Home Journal*, Corinne Robert Redgrave, a professional actress who advanced by way of amateur ranks, warned women to rehearse and gave tips on how to utilize time-motion efficiency in order to learn a play: "This lack of definite purpose on the part of the players is quickly conveyed across the footlights; and the audience, without analyzing, says, 'amateurish.' "[146] Discipline, control, and repetition embodied the amateur's version of professionalism.

A discourse on the home as consummately inconsequential compared to business inscribed the content of amateur theatrical production as well. Some advice columnists warned against serious plays and melodrama, equating their production with work rather than with leisure. Heroics, passion, and purpose, which demanded concentration, were to be strenuously avoided as well. The problem, claimed a *Century* writer in 1911, was that the audience knew the real person in a day-to-day context, thus undermining the credibility of the acting.[147]

While the leisured upper classes were instructed to do comedy, the working class was infused with serious high culture, folk dances, and dramas. In an article reprinted in a 1907 *Living Age*, an English author described how a dramatic association showed workers how to produce Shakespearean and Greek plays. The "beauty" of these great works would teach the lower class to stay away from public drinking houses and would revive their sense of history and patriotism: "[Drama] may brighten the life of the laborer and make his labor more intelligent and effective."[148] This task of elevating and pacifying the masses through the importation of classical high art and folk culture extended to the education of children as well. In her 1912 book on how to produce folk plays with school children called *The Dramatic Festival*, Anne Craig argued for drama as a way to combat the plights of urban life.[149]

However, this domain of amateur theatricals was also the emergent site of experimentation, innovation, and opposition. Ideals fostering experimentation merged into the label of amateur, as applied by the popular press. Theater historians have shown that the "little"- or "art"-theater movement began in 1912 out of a desire for both innovation and content (for instance, plays with working-class characters and themes) and an attraction for foreign developments in the theater. Based on goals of art rather than profit, these theaters—like the Toy Theater of Boston, the Neighborhood Playhouse in New York, and the Provincetown Players, which later moved to New York—were run by unpaid volunteers.[150] The description of *amateur* that the mainstream press applied to these productions betrayed three assumptions regarding amateur status. First, productions that did not attract large, mass audiences and earn large profits were, in contrast, amateur. Second, plays based on subjects not broached in the more conventional theater were amateur. Third, plays with a leftist, antiestablishment political orientation were amateur. The application of the term *amateur* appears to have been as much a recognition of economic marginality as it was a tag of derision. In contrast, a *Boston Transcript* article praised the organizational structure and production of amateur theatricals: "The great school of power, in art as in politics, lies in people's doing things for themselves."[151]

This brief overview of the dominant themes in early amateur theatrical history demonstrates how the tensions between the idea of professionalism and leisure activities were negotiated on the level of amateurism. It provides a cultural foundation for the emergence of the making-it-in-Hollywood myth in amateur-film discourse.

While amateur-film discourse and technology promoted a residual artistry and instilled calls for a mechanical surveillance of family life, it also educated its users toward a better understanding of commercial filmmaking processes. As a socialization process, the discourse on professional-film tidbits worked to smooth out the contradiction between amateur film, which was cheap and unorganized in comparison, and commercial practice, which had access to larger and more public audiences. This socialization and production of ideal consumers for the movies moved in two directions. On one level, the discourse of technical magazines urged amateurs to participate in conventional, commercial cinematic practices by learning the mechanical operations of illusions. On the level of economic and political relations, movie-advice books sustained an illusion of mobility from amateur-film status to commercial-film production that evoked the myth of the "self-made man" (or woman), which promoted the idea of gaining wealth and status from lowly origins through hard work and luck.

This abundance of advice books and how-to columns during the period from 1917 to 1923 reflects changes in the economic structure of commercial film, as well as a significant ideological shift in the discourse of amateur film. While the economic changes in the motion picture industry after World War I were certainly more complex and intricate than what a general description can possibly account for, the context of the changes in the popular discourse on amateur film can only be assessed if we consider the impact of the nature of the industry as a historical factor. The larger context of the development of motion pictures as a major industry in the United States from 1917 to 1927 contributed to the reframing of amateur film from a technical playground for hobbyists to a practice field for those with visions of a glamorous sort of upward mobility.

After World War I the motion picture industry became a vertically integrated oligopoly in the United States, with a few firms like Paramount, First National, and Loews controlling production, distribution, and exhibition. United States motion picture companies held an 85 percent share of the world's film business and a 98 percent share of the domestic market and ranked in the top six businesses in the United States.[152] The motion picture market was national. These companies initiated bureaucratic practices that paralleled those of other corporations, such as control over production, employees, and budgeting.[153] Their large economic structure, which occurred with the entrenchment of the star system, longer feature films replacing one or two reelers, and ownership of theaters by major studios, created an image of motion pictures as big business.

Film historian Robert Sklar in his *Movie-Made America* describes the cultural phenomenon of the "starstruck girl" who ventured to Hollywood for fame and fortune in the late teens and early twenties, propelled by the vision on the screen of young actresses "making it." He notes that many advice books were published to offer female motion picture workers insight into Hollywood practices.[154] However, it is possible to analyze these advice books and Hollywood-mania columns from the additional perspective of amateurism. These texts, then, may intersect and mediate two separate areas: the rise of the motion picture industry as a major national business with a publicity apparatus in magazines and books that created an aura of glamour, opulence, and omnipotence, and the already existing discourse on amateur film in technical magazines that would increasingly focus on rehearsing amateur skills in exchange for promises of upward mobility or big bucks in the dominant commercial-film industry. They reflect a tendency prevalent in mass-market magazines of the postwar period that historian Elizabeth Stevenson has termed the "success mania" to earn large amounts of money as a form of adventure, spurred by wartime prosperity despite postwar rises in inflation and unemployment.[155] While certainly not a complete bibliography of all these articles and books on how to enter the film industry, the texts chosen for analysis here do illustrate some of the articulated themes. They deploy motifs common to amateur film during the larger period of 1897–1923.

As an ideological boot camp, these how-to books created an illusion of the accessibility and democracy of professional filmmaking through their copious advice on acting, directing, photography, and writing. They simultaneously drilled consumers in the paradigms of the dominant style and method, thus subjugating more private predilections to the goals of industry. This trend toward behind-the-scenes information began early in the decade in technical-journal information regarding the film industry targeted to amateur cinematographers.

A random survey of article titles in *Technical World* between 1910 and 1923 reveals how some film articles cued in the amateur to professional secrets: "How to Become a Star," "What Really Happens on the Movie Set," "Cameraman Almost Loses Life," and "How Deaths Are Faked in Movies," to name only a small sample. Assuming that audiences understood that most of what they saw in films was faked, most of these articles reinforced and promoted commercial filmmakers as geniuses and experts. Unlike the lowly amateur, they did not shoot scenery or action naturally, as advocated by pictorialism, but artificially, with the assistance of technology. If the amateur engaged with nature for its inherent pictorial possibilities, the professional required artifice to advertise specific control and manipulation of nature. Explaining how one camera faked rain, wind, and storms, a columnist argued that "anybody with the price and time can wander around the world 'shooting' scenery; but in his opinion, it takes genius to be a camouflage artist and create the same atmosphere by means of artificial agencies."[156] These technical journals offered production information emphasizing the wonder, power, and specialized technical expertise of the established, dominant cinema as beyond the reaches and capabilities of the amateur.[157] This discursive context of mechanical trivia and production gossip positioned amateurs as highly trained film consumers.

Hollywood mythology eventually conscripted this association of amateur film with nature and spontaneity into an ideology of talent that would assist one in landing a job in motion pictures—a sort of behind-the-scenes story about professional work standards. For example, in a book called *Opportunities in the Motion Picture Industry and How to Qualify for Positions in Its Many Branches*, an anthology of articles published in 1922 on how to become a "professional" in the Hollywood industry that was aimed at amateurs, one writer instructed amateur actresses that they could become movie stars if they possessed beauty, personality, charm, temperament, style, and the ability to wear clothes.[158] Amateurs interested in clothing design, art direction, directing, or cinematography, in this book's opinion, were told that their "natural" talent and "energy" would assist them on the road to success, but that to gain status as a paid professional, one would have to be disciplined and work long hours. The book divulged the duties of all these various film production positions so that the amateur could ascertain how to fragment "natural talent," effectively encompassing the concept of the amateur's freedom and spontaneity within this ideology of upward mobility and success. This book, and many others like it, reconstituted the idea of amateur film as a kind of lower species on a natural evolutionary order toward professionalism.

The conceptualization of amateur filmmaking as dependent upon the dominant film industry for standards was exemplified in the proliferation of photoplay-writing books from 1918 to 1922. The subject matter of these books formulated and quantified movie plots so they could be more easily mastered and reproduced by amateurs. In essence, these handbooks were written in such a manner as to reproduce the ideological assumptions behind content choices, standardized norms, and procedures that typified the professional industry so that the amateur could incorporate them. A typical example of this quantification of narrative film plots is Aber Wycliffe Hill's *Ten Million Photoplay Plots.* Hill disguised this science of narrative with exhortations encouraging amateurs to experiment but nonetheless itemized the thirty-seven basic dramatic situations available to professional scenario writers. A successful screenplay writer, according to Hill, mixed and recombined these thirty-seven situations with one's list of the thirty-seven basic emotions. This scientific process compartmentalized imagination and originality as reproducible parts. It also revealed the pervasiveness of scientific management as it eliminated personal quirks, spontaneity, or particularized social contexts from filmmaking.

Hill captured the residual essence of pictorialism's fascination for landscape and women when he directed amateurs toward the country and away from the city in order to display artistry and dispel political or social references that might destroy the pleasure of spectators:

> [Good movie settings are] rustic country or woodland scenes, beach and bathing scenes, girls and men in western costumes, behind the scenes in a theater, herds of sheep, cattle or horses, pretty girls in dancing costumes, a pretty girl in a Red Cross costume, snow scenes, steamboat and river scenes, mountaineers in their native element. Compare a scene of this kind with that showing inmates of a hospital for the deformed and you will get the significance.
>
> It is of course necessary, sometimes, to show the seamy side of life in order to secure a contrast with the happier side. The writer should take care, however, that history does not fall for so much of it that the picture will be displeasing as a whole.[159]

This passage indicates the political pressures of pictorialism as late as 1921 in amateur publications. What posed as amateur imagination was in reality the colonization of amateur hopes through the principles of the dominant commercial-film industry, traditional art forms, and fantasies of upward mobility.

This political structure between the concepts of professional film and amateur film maintained and promoted professional film's domination through standardized procedures of narrative construction. At least on the ideological level, amateur efforts, then, were positioned by these writers in a supplementary and hierarchical relationship to professional film. As an area to exercise the perfection of the consumption of commercial films, as a site to learn that professional style and standards hinged on technical control, the discourse on film amateurs in the latter part of the period supported and began to define amateur film as an adjunct to the dominant film system through its supposed and imposed inferiority to professional film. The spontaneous and natural talent that was considered the exclusive domain of the amateur before 1910 was in the postwar period corralled by the ideology of the dominant, vertically integrated industry as a way to break into movies if one could adequately appropriate the more disciplined, controlled, and replicable standards of the professional. Consequently, this discursive shift toward the hierarchicalization of amateur-film ideology to professional filmmaking framed it not as an inventor's technical excursion as before but as a potential filmwork requiring specific skills, a pattern that would expand in the 1920s.

From 1897 to 1923 the definition of amateur film was composed most saliently on the technological level, with the term *amateur* most frequently applied to substandard and noninterchangeable designs. This technological definition of amateur film as an entrepreneurial activity also evidenced secondary characteristics derived from the persisting residual formations of pictorialism, familialism, and success myths. In effect, these secondary components articulated by popular and photographic writers cushioned the technological innovations within more antiquated, residual, and nostalgic aesthetic, social, and economic discourses. Pictorialism, familialism, and ideologies of upward mobility through practice laid the discursive groundwork for subsequent redefinitions and reconfigurations of amateur film. The relationship and position of these discourses changed dramatically after 1923. After the standardization of the amateur-film gauge and the resulting domination of the market by three firms, this technological component declined in importance. The aesthetic level, which merged the ideology of the striving for Hollywood standards and the norms of this early period with a fervent resuscitation of pictorialism, gained prominence in the definition of amateur film after the twenties.

3

Professional Results with Amateur Ease

1923–1940

Movies at Home

By day I lead a sordid life
Submerged in dirt and din;
By night I turn the current on
And let Romance come in.

Entranced, I loll in distant Spain,
And hunt in Zanzibar:
I join the crowds in gay Paree
And ride with Lochinvar.

—A. P. Hollis[1]

PUBLISHED IN A 1927 *Amateur Movie Makers*, these lines summarize the popular discourse formulating amateur film during the 1920s and 1930s: ideas pertaining to artistry, fantasy, and distant lands circulated in leisure time. They necessitated a more logically ordered and controllable form of family life. But such fanciful artistry represented only one dimension of the larger cultural trends regarding amateur film during this period extending from 1923 to 1950: the inscription of an ideology of professionalism on all discursive levels of amateur film.

Technology: Professional Results with Amateur Ease

With the competition among designs, formats, and small inventors resolved with the standardization of 16mm film as the amateur format, amateur-film technology changed from a technical oddity into machinery that utilized professional technical standards. All three major manufacturers of amateur-film equipment during this period were closely identified with professional-film technology manufacturing—Victor Animatograph, Eastman Kodak, and Bell and Howell. Their market domination of amateur-film equipment enforced powerful economic and ideological control over the discourse and definitions of amateur film. From 1923 to 1940 amateur-film technology production became concentrated in two firms—Bell and Howell and Eastman Kodak. The split between amateur and professional cinematography was increasingly defined through the complexity of camera technology and manufacturing.

By the end of the twenties, professional cinematography journals such as *American Cinematographer* advertised amateur equipment and included special amateur movie-making sections in nearly every issue. A 1929 ad for Victor Animatograph heralded its cine cameras "for normal and slow motion pictures" that required "no other adjustment than a quick turn of the button."[2] The Bell and Howell Filmo 70-D legitimated itself in a 1930 *American Cinematographer* ad through a genealogical attachment to Bell and Howell's professional feature-film cameras:

> Bell and Howell standard and Eyemo cameras have established a promise in professional moviedom which Filmo splendidly fulfills. Filmo derives its royalty from precision, dependability, and performance—as fine as that which distinguished its professional parent.[3]

On the same page, these professional attributes were even ascribed to a tripod: "For Eyemo and Filmo cameras, the new Bell and Howell tripod presents amateur portability with professional versatility and operations."[4] This discourse between professional filmmaking and amateur-film consumption reinforced a hierarchical, dependent system of technological norms, a significant shift from the previous period of technological competition. Filmo's advertising slogan from the 1920s codifies these trends: "Professional Results with Amateur Ease!"

This ideological and discursive domination had a powerful economic determinant: all three amateur-film manufacturers in this oligopoly were initially involved with some aspect of professional-film technology. This economic pattern signified corporate, tactical marketing strategies to capture the market for mass-produced cameras. Amateur film was not distinct from or in opposition to professional film; rather, it was its accomplice in the dissemination of professional technical ideologies to consumers. By the late twenties, three firms dominated the amateur-camera market: Eastman Kodak, who owned all of the patents on the production of standard 16mm film stock; Bell and Howell, who held most of the patents on mechanical-camera apparatuses; and Victor Animatograph of Iowa, one of the few firms to survive from the entrepreneurial period prior to 1923.[5] Clearly the strongest competitor, Bell and Howell controlled a majority of the mechanical-design patents on both 35mm and 16mm cameras in the United States. Pathé, Sept, DeVry, and other smaller European firms continued to produce amateur equipment, but they did not achieve the market penetration and dominance of Bell and Howell, because their designs used nonstandard film gauges like 9.5mm that were not readily available in the United States.

These differing technological standards distinguished amateur film from professional film through commercial exhibition. Professional 35mm stock facilitated public exhibition; amateur 16mm stock was limited to private exhibition. Some amateur-cinematography columnists wrote polemical columns on substandard versus professional film gauges. By 1926, three sizes of amateur film prevailed: 17.5mm, 16mm, and 9mm, the gauge employed by the French Pathé camera. Most writers pushed for 16mm, arguing it paralleled professional theatrical film for shooting, editing, titling, and projecting. In 1926 Herbert McKay, who wrote a column on amateur film for *Photo-Era*, explained, "In short, the 16mm film is a miniature reproduction of the 35mm theatrical film in everyway except that there is but one pair of perforations to the frame instead of four."[6] Even though its gauge limited authentic professional possibilities, 16mm's similarity to professional film transformed into a marketing device for the promotion of American cameras. In a 1926 column in *Photo-Era Magazine*, McKay elaborated these exhibition distinctions:

> The amateur, strictly speaking, the one who makes films for private exhibition, seems to be best served by the substandard. Of course, on a world tour, you will want a standard camera so you can "hire a hall" upon your return and exhibit the films.[7]

These promotions of the 16mm format in amateur-photography magazines were not entirely objective endorsements however. Amateur-photography magazines enjoyed incestuous relationships with American camera and film manufacturers. They depended on them for large advertising revenues. Many research scientists and other corporate personnel from Eastman Kodak, Bell and Howell, and Victor Animatograph wrote columns or articles for them (McKay is only one example). And amateur magazines sometimes reprinted corporate publicity material word for word in their pages.[8]

Primarily a home-projector manufacturer, Victor Animatograph developed reduction printing processes and machines to distribute professional films to homes. Kodak, on the other hand, monopolized professional 35mm stock production and transferred their patent control to amateur 16mm film manufacturing. As one of the only American manufacturers of professional-movie cameras, Bell and Howell also exerted nearly total economic control over amateur cameras. The integration of amateur film with professional film helped these firms capitalize on their existing market prestige.

The market position of Victor Animatograph illustrates the adaptation of entrepreneurial firms from the early period toward integration within economic models based on standardization and concentration by the 1920s. Alexander F. Victor founded Victor Animatograph in 1910, the same year he developed an amateur motion picture camera and projector. His own account of these machines in a 1944 Victor Animatograph Annual Report cites the wide press coverage he received rather than his patents.[9] By 1920 Victor had developed a continuous printer that reduced professional 35mm film to 28mm for home distribution.[10]

At the 1918 meeting of the Society of Motion Picture Engineers in Rochester, New York, Victor proposed a nontheatrical standard for amateur film that would be nonflammable and not easily duplicated by splitting 35mm.[11] After Eastman Kodak's invention of the 16mm reversal process in 1923, Victor anticipated infinite possibilities for the home, educational, and industrial markets:

> I reasoned that if enough people bought cameras and projectors for the purpose of making their own pictures, it would follow that a field would be opened for commercial films made for the projectors or copied from existing theatrical material. In fact, I saw that here was the perfect solution to my dream of safe movies for the home, the school, and industry.[12]

Victor's first 16mm camera closely resembled the design and proportions of the Bell and Howell Filmo. Threaded with a simplified loop, the labyrinthine threading patterns of professional cameras were eliminated. However, the spring-driven Bell and Howell Filmo offered greater advantages for amateurs, because it did not require a tripod. These similarities suggest the difficulty in pinpointing which firm actually originated the 16mm design. Although Bell and Howell held the patent, Victor, an entrepreneurial inventor with experience in the nontheatrical market, sold an almost identically designed camera body the same year.[13]

Unlike Victor Animatograph, Kodak did not widely engage in distribution, industrial uses, or camera manufacturing. Although Kodak produced the Cine-Kodak, refining it through the twenties and thirties, camera manufacturing was secondary to amateur-film stock manufacturing. Eastman Kodak's nonchemical patents from 1923 to 1950 affirm that the company's improvements concentrated on two distinct areas: manufacturing improvements and amateur still and cinematography accessories.[14] Numerous patents for the manufacture of raw stock and printing devices, such as cams, drives, winders, measuring devices, fuses, spindles, silver-recovery processes, and edge printers, further strengthened Kodak's monopoly position as virtually the only manufacturer of professional and amateur stock. If Victor cornered the nontheatrical-projector market, Eastman Kodak, with some limited ventures into amateur-camera mechanical innovations, primarily remained a raw-stock manufacturer.

Despite Alexander Victor's claim to have initiated standardization of nontheatrical film, evidence suggests that Bell and Howell, the most prominent holder of motion picture patents and standardized professional equipment, and Eastman Kodak, who controlled virtually all film-manufacturing patents, colluded in 1922 to agree on 16mm film as the amateur standard.[15] Their agreement gave Bell and Howell a distinct edge in the amateur-camera market; through a combination of patents and manufacturing expertise, Bell and Howell controlled a large share of the amateur motion picture camera market. Its corporate story during this period reveals the contours of amateur-technology development.

Simplification, durability, and precision engineering grounded Bell and Howell's technological development, spurring adaptations and transitions between amateur and professional lines. This fastidious manufacture of amateur equipment, inherited from their prominent position in the professional-camera market, legitimated Bell and Howell's cameras as the top-of-the-line amateur camera marketed to the upper middle class. By promoting the rigorous inspection process, Bell and Howell advertising assured amateurs that their equipment received as much attention as a professional camera. The company's publicity strategy reverted to a residual historical discourse of the careful and meticulous craftsperson to efface this mass production of amateur cameras. An article entitled "Bell and Howell Manufacturing Precision," published in *Photo-Era* in 1931, extolled this position:

> Certain parts of Filmo equipment, we are informed, are held to tolerance of one ten-thousandth of an inch, and lynxed-eyed inspectors see that no lapses in tolerances are permitted in these or other instances, every manufacturing operation being given the acid test right up to and including the final touch that results in the finished product.[16]

As a powerful marketing strategy, a professional craft-manufacturing aura lured camera store owners to feature Bell and Howell equipment. *Selling Filmo,* the internal Bell and Howell sales magazine, suggested salespeople encourage their camera and department store buyers to tour the Bell and Howell manufacturing plant to observe firsthand the precision and care taken by amateur-camera factory workers.[17] During the twenties, the company emphasized "precision" with a lifetime guarantee on all amateur motion picture equipment.

This infusion of professionalism had two important effects. First, in the context of film-industry discussions of amateur-film gauges and substandard formats, this professionalization of Bell and Howell's amateur-film technology obfuscated its substandard design with the incorporation of an ideology of high-quality technical and manufacturing standards.[18] It defined amateurism technologically. Second, this professionalization of amateur-movie cameras, although actually corporate advertising for Bell and Howell's plant, blurred the very real distinctions between Hollywood filmmaking, which shot 35mm stock, and amateur filmmaking, which now exclusively used 16mm stock. For example, in a 1926 *Photo-Era* piece, Herbert McKay praised the Filmo as the closest approximation of professional gear in miniature dimensions.[19] This shift toward a technological rather than a behaviorial definition of professionalism was further evidenced by accessories: photography writers viewed the Filmo as the most "professional" amateur camera, because accessories, supplies, lenses, and lights utilized by standard cameras and professional cinematographers were available.

While this fluidity between amateur and professional design was nothing more than a fantasy for the amateur, it was, on the other hand, a source of innovation and improvement for the development of professional equipment. The Bell and Howell Filmo 70-D's simplified threading was adapted two years later in the Eyemo, a 35mm enlargement. Newsreelers widely used this camera. It was relatively easy to hand-hold without a tripod. Hollywood cinematographers liked the Eyemo for shooting difficult angles. The Eyemo elevated spontaneous shooting from amateur ranks to professional news ranks. It could be easily accommodated to the efficiency demands of the competitive news market:

> The paramount requirement at such a moment [for newsreelers] is SPEED, SPEED and MORE SPEED. To this requirement the seven pound automatic Eyemo professional camera came as a blessing. It eliminated the tripod, burdensome carrying cases and luggage which were associated with the heavier type of standard motion picture cameras.[20]

Flexibility and compactness increased efficiency—a component of professionalism—in the industrial process of news production.[21] The Eyemo utilized 35mm standard film, better lenses, a more durable metal, and larger magazines.[22]

Bell and Howell also differentiated its amateur motion picture cameras according to gender. During the 1920s, amateur-camera ads promoted women as filmmakers. These ads pictured women filmmakers chronicling their children in the home or in nature; they equated amateurism with the nuclear family. The image of a woman holding the camera signified the camera's lightness and compact style. The ads emphasized the ease of operation and automation of Filmos. The woman's image ameliorated the aura of camera equipment as complicated, heavy professional machinery.[23]

The social contradiction of amateur technology dispersed into two levels: technology (positioned as descending from professional design) and usage (situated increasingly within the home). In 1928 Bell and Howell even originated an amateur camera especially for women called the Bell and Howell Filmo 75. The Filmo 75 weighed only three and a half pounds, with dimensions of 1 5/8 by 4 by 8 3/4 inches. It was shaped like an oval case with one small lens. Selling at approximately 30 percent less than the 70-D, the camera itself was designed to fit the fashion needs of women; its flat sides meant it could fit into a pocket or purse. The filigreed camera body was available in three colors—silver birch, ebony black, and walnut brown.[24] Bell and Howell executives reasoned this color differentiation would appeal to the "decorative" instinct of women.

This pattern of professionalizing amateur-film equipment transposed during the Depression and World War II when amateur equipment adapted to professional requirements. Owing to the fact that Bell and Howell was essentially geared to the luxury leisure market, the Crash of 1929 propelled a severe revenue drop. Bell and Howell curtailed its manufacturing operations by 60 percent. The semiprofessional and audio-visual field, primarily targeted at education, expanded from 1929 to 1932. As early as 1926 in *Amateur Movie Makers*, Joseph McNabb, president of the Bell and Howell Company, wrote that amateurs could use their filmmaking skills for industrial, scientific, and educational films.[25] In 1929 an article called "Recreation Annexes the Movies" published in *Amateur Movie Makers* argued that amateur-film equipment could emerge as an indispensable educational tool.[26] By 1931 *Literary Digest* promoted amateur cameras for factory time-motion studies to increase productivity and to train workers, recalling earlier attempts, but now articulated more ardently.[27] Bell and Howell cornered this market with a patent on the first 16mm optical sound projector, the Filmosound.[28]

With declining camera sales, manufacturers tried to recapture the market by lowering the cost of home-movie production. Writing in the *New York Times* Sunday hobby section in 1937, John Markland reported that three factors galvanized demand for amateur equipment: the availability of color film, the introduction of moderately priced 8mm cameras, and "the development of many new accessories that give the 'professional' touch to home made movies."[29] As early as 1928, Kodak had introduced the Kodacolor process for amateurs. Kodacolor enjoyed limited success however; color filters absorbed large amounts of light, consequently necessitating shooting under very bright illumination to achieve an acceptable exposure.[30] By 1937 three amateur color-movie systems existed: Dufaycolor, Kodacolor, and Kodachrome. Dr. Kenneth Mees, head research scientist for Kodak, observed that amateur color film preceded professional color, because amateurs generally did not desire a duplicate print.[31]

Responding to amateur color and double-8 film development, Bell and Howell altered its marketing and manufacturing strategies. Declining sales figures prompted the company's shift to producing less-expensive cameras. Sales dropped from $4,451,610 in 1929 to $2,861,985 in 1930; $1,796,654 in 1931 to $878,261 in 1932. After the introduction of 8mm in 1934, the company's net jumped to $1,276,078 and continued to rise in subsequent years.[32] According to the 1930's vice-chairman Everett F. Wagner, the shift to 8mm equipment presented a dilemma for Bell and Howell, now faced with maintaining its market prestige based on precision engineering while simultaneously lowering production costs. Wagner's own assessment of the problems illustrates these pressures:

> Marketing had to deal with the problems of broad mass market selling and distribution. Engineering had to concentrate on designing attractive, innovative, low cost product, yet maintain the quality and precision inherently required to produce good pictures. Manufacturing had to advance the state of the art to mass produce quality product and achieve precision at ever decreasing costs.[33]

These financial and managerial constraints formed the backdrop to the company's new technological directions.

By 1934 Bell and Howell had introduced the model 134 camera. It used Eastman Kodak double-8mm film, lowering the cost of movie-making. Both companies hoped the relative economy of double-8 would expand the market. Once again, Eastman Kodak and Bell and Howell agreed on 8mm as the standard amateur gauge. Double-8 film ran through the camera on two passes. It could be processed on regular 16mm finishing equipment and therefore did not require further capitalization or equipment.[34] By 1936 Bell and Howell's sales had risen by 60 percent, doubling itself in 1937.[35] During the thirties, Bell and Howell also patented 16mm cartridge-loading cameras called the 121 model and 141 model, which were later adapted for gun-spotting use by the military in World War II.[36]

By 1941, prompted by the growth of the audio-visual market, Bell and Howell had developed a professional 16mm movie camera, essentially a smaller, 16mm version of the Bell and Howell professional 2709 camera. This camera used the more professional intermittent movement, producing extremely accurate registration of the projected image. The quietness of the intermittent movement made this camera usable for sound recording.[37] William Stull, of the American Society of Cinematographers (A.S.C.), wrote in a 1941 description that appeared in *American Cinematographer* that this camera would lower barriers to entry into feature-film production:

It should also have an increasingly spectacular future in studio work, not only in making 16mm tests for 35mm production, but even in actually filming independent feature productions for joint 16 and 35mm release.[38]

However, World War II retooled all domestic production for wartime materials, unfortunately curtailing the possibilities for this expansion of independent production.

The United States government and World War II rescued Bell and Howell from the financial setbacks of the thirties. During the war, Bell and Howell was the prime contractor for over $100 million worth of military optical and camera equipment.[39] To sustain the production of this equipment, the government Defense Plant Corporation financed a $2.24 million, 220,000-square-foot plant in Chicago, which remained the company's main manufacturing site after the war years.[40] As a direct result of profitable wartime contracts, the company went public in 1945. Bell and Howell not only manufactured cameras but also optical equipment such as tank telescopes, bore-sighting tool kits, reflector sights for remote gun control systems on B-29 bombers, and rifle sights.[41]

Bell and Howell's wartime equipment demonstrates a movement from amateur technology to professional, military surveillance tools. Basically, the company "militarized" amateur designs by installing remote-control devices and by manufacturing the equipment in military green metal. For example, the gun camera was adapted from the earlier, unsuccessful model 141, 16mm cartridge camera. Normally mounted in fighter aircraft wings to record the accuracy of machine gun fire on the target, this camera functioned as a time-and-motion-study camera to evaluate gunners.[42] This surveillance and testing use of compact amateur cameras extended into the Intervalometer camera, a further refinement of the 1412 camera that automatically took a picture each second.[43] Both the Eyemo and Filmo were manufactured in a heavier gauge metal and used prethreaded, interchangeable magazines, which accredited their use by the Signal Corps in combat field work.[44] This pervasive domination of amateur-film technology by professional-film standards was even more pronounced on the aesthetic level: Hollywood-style, configured production norms, denigrating any deviations.

Doing Things Well: Hollywood Professionals, Amateurs, and Aesthetic Technique

In 1923, the same year that Eastman Kodak and Bell and Howell standardized amateur-film stock to 16mm, *Living Age* reprinted an article entitled "The Importance of Doing Things Badly."[45] The author reasoned that the impoverishment of private pursuits and hobbies evolved from two sites. On the one hand, the practice of the arts demanded skill; on the other hand, the higher, more exclusive professional standards seemed unattainable. By 1926 this sentiment of "doing things badly"—a concept that defined amateurism as increased participation—reverberated as an argument against the constrictions of skill. An article titled "The Amateurs and the Dilettante" published in *Living Age* elaborated:

> If all men postponed engaging in any creative or recreative activity until they could do it expertly what would become of all the experimental vitality of human life? It takes a certain confidence in the value of experience, as such, to be a good amateur, and the modern world is probably too conscientiously utilitarian for that.[46]

Popular discourse on amateur movie-making during the twenties and thirties expressed two competing definitions. In his 1927 statement to the meeting of the National Board of Review of Motion Pictures, reprinted in *Amateur Movie Makers*, Roy Winton warned that amateurs should not be derided; they could experiment and distinguish the cinema as an art. His argument invokes nineteenth-century definitions of amateurism as a defense against commercialism:

> In the Amateur Cinema League we are trying to get back to the original meaning of the word "amateur." We are concerned about where this Eighth Art is going and we are concerned about it aesthetically as well as socially and ethically. We do not look on it as a means to an end only. We believe that, like every other art, it should be self-justified and that if it can present beauty to humanity it can stand on its own feet.[47]

Winton's proclamation clearly summoned conceptions of amateurism that positioned freedom, creativity, and art as separate concerns from the enervation of more industrialized and bureaucratized work. However, these somewhat utopian definitions were eclipsed by a more pervasive and popular idea regarding amateur film—that it was not Hollywood. *New York Times* writer Phillip Sterling offered a succinct definition of amateur film in his 1937 article "Sowing the 16mm Field": "Because the 16mm world has always aimed to maintain cordial relations with the entertainment industry, the term amateur is applied indiscriminately to anyone who doesn't work in or for Hollywood."[48]

From the 1920s on, aesthetic discourse constructed amateur filmmaking based on skill. It emphasized expertise and the perfect execution of Hollywood narrative paradigms. To continually ape Hollywood style was to perpetually create Hollywood as the cultural norm, consequently positioning imperfection or digression as amateur and illegitimate. But in a significant cultural and social reversal, this period also evidenced two strains of experimentation: professional cinematographers tested and created new visual effects with amateur cameras, and a small coterie of political and avant-garde filmmakers viewed this simple and inexpensive technology as an accessible way to produce personally meaningful images.

The home movies in the George Johnson Collection dating from 1928 to 1941 show children riding horses, sunbathing, swimming, dressing in cowboy costumes, playing in the snow, crawling on the stairs, and looking at the cameras.[49] The aesthetic strategy, if one could call it that, of the Johnson films demonstrates a total disregard for Hollywood style, harmonious compositions and smooth narrative editing. The films are for the most part shot in shaky medium shots. Each shot documents a different family event, and any attempt to break an event down into separate narrative shots is completely absent. Indeed, contrary to advice columns, the Johnson films are not even edited: they simply present an inventory of children's leisure activities executed in single-medium shots with no interest in composition. These reels insinuate that amateur filmmaking occurred exclusively within the nuclear family, and these images of family harmony and leisure were supported by the photographic press. A 1929 article, simply titled "Home Movies," in *Parents Magazine* commented that the arrival of children fired home-movie production: "The love of parents for their children is the most important factor in the present rapidly accelerating popularity of home movies."[50] The increase in home-movie production as a hobby coordinated with a much larger social context: the rise of parenting as a science during the twenties and its popularization in special magazines devoted to perfecting "parenting skills" (e.g., *Parents Magazine*), the increase in social science studies of families, and the development of behavioral psychology as an academic field.[51]

This persistent equation of amateur movies with the home registered two important ideological consequences for the new definition of amateur aesthetics. First, popular discourse instructed filmmakers to exalt the everyday details of family living to a level of spectacle, wonder, and importance. In an unconscious homage to turn-of-the-century pictorialism, an article in a 1939 *Woman's Home Companion* exhorted women filmmakers to "remember that simplest things are the best . . . the things that happen in your own household every day make the best moving pictures."[52] The writer further suggested such titles as *A Day in Our Home*, *The Sunday Motor Trip*, and *The Saturday Afternoon Picnic*. The writer uncritically assumed narrative could control, maintain, and unify the activities of the home. For example, Herbert McKay cautioned in a 1926 *Photo-Era* column that "action should not be meaningless motion. It should have a story to tell. . . . The usual patchwork of haphazard scenes is confusing and irritating."[53]

Second, aesthetic discourse emphasized action as an integral component of family memory, reinforcing that philosophical, analytical thinking or spontaneity were not as critical as sequences, progression, and continuity development. An article called "Pictorial Diary for a Lifetime: Home Movies for Christmas" that appeared in the December 1928 issue of *American Home* exemplifies this attitude:

> Perhaps the greatest value of the home movie lies in its ability to record in close-up, semi-closeup, or long shot, the various members of his family and household, not in stiffly posed "still" pictures, but in action, just as they really are.[54]

This discourse on action articulated reality as observable. Although a bastardized version of empiricism and scientific management, it etched industrial concepts onto private life.

In this context, Hollywood technique functioned as a powerful management system to control and order reckless amateur home-movie production. An interesting example of this discourse regulating cinematic chaos is a 1929 "Amateur Movie Making" column in the professional-film magazine *American Cinematographer*. William Stull, the author, advised:

> Look at your own latest cinematographic effort. Then in the theatre compare it with similar shots in the professional picture. It is not difficult. You shoot on the beach. You do not like it. Pick a picture that has beach shots in it. Look them over and see what the professional did to make his shots effective.[55]

This exaltation of technique camouflaged the material contradictions between the limited resources of the amateur and the corporate backing of a Hollywood spectacle.

As further evidence of this discursive colonization, Hollywood style was lionized as the pinnacle of cinematic perfection for amateurs. Professional cinematographers not only dispensed advice to amateurs in a special column in *American Cinematographer*, the trade journal for professional cinematographers, but also held seats in the majority of amateur movie-making societies.[56] Professionals touted tripods to stabilize "technique," limiting the hand-held freedom of 16mm portability. Image stability and comprehensibility, as foundations of the epistemology of Hollywood professional style, were equated with representational transcendence.

Indeed, one writer in a 1937 *Popular Science* article titled "Simple Ways to Improve Home Movies" advised using Hollywood style to placate restless and unruly home-movie audiences:

> Your friends, when they view your home movies, do not expect to see pictures that rival the technical perfection of the productions shown at the local movie palace. However, this is no excuse for showing movies so glaringly faulty that they annoy your audience.[57]

This aesthetic discourse positioned the professionalism of Hollywood style as the consummation of technical skill and control rather than as a constituent of the industrial process of studio filmmaking.

Problems in amateur films, therefore, revealed a loss of control, order, and skill. Advice to amateurs in popular science magazines and photographic magazines focused on what professionals defined as the three most common "mistakes" of amateur movies, according to a 1939 *Popular Science* piece captioned "Home Movies: How to Shoot Them like a Professional": swinging the camera too quickly during panorama shots; "firehosing" the camera, which meant moving it around too much and without purpose; and lack of planning.[58] Panoraming—the movement of the camera from one side to another—was considered disturbing to audiences if executed too quickly. If the filmmaker lacked a tripod, the same writer advocated conforming one's body to mechanical norms to eliminate unnecessary movement: "In essence, the idea is to convert yourself as far as possible into a rigid camera-holding fixture from the waist up and move the camera as little as possible, and then only by swinging the whole body at the waist."[59]

Extending this homology between order and Hollywood, many advice columns in the late 1920s and throughout the 1930s pressed for preproduction planning to eliminate shaky, haphazard camera work. *American Cinematographer* in 1929 encouraged technique and technical mastery as the first phase on the road to achieving cinematic "perfection":

> "Snapshooters." . . . They are the ones who have not yet passed the "you press the button we do the rest stage"—the ones who have not become *conscious of the vast unexplored world of new experience. . . . As the individual grows artistically, technique grows to mean more and more to him. It is no longer a set of dull rules and observations to hinder him, but a living, vibrant aid in perfect, artistic expression.* (Emphasis added)[60]

Aesthetic embellishments simply aroused emotions. Perfect artistic expression articulated complete socialization into a highly codified artistic style that displaced the social and organizational attributes of professionalism into a canon of formal rules for artistic expression.

Pictorial composition marked the professional class of cinematographers; it organized visual elements and demonstrated technical skills in achieving pictorial harmony, according to a 1927 *Amateur Movie Makers* article.[61] While cautioning amateurs against "shooting recklessly . . . with no thought," Hal Hall in a 1930 *American Cinematographer* article defined this version of cinematic perfection: "Composition or pictorial beauty . . . a picture has a two fold aim: it aims to represent an object or objects and also to be a decorative design."[62] To please the spectator's eye, a shot should not have a cramped visual style; should have proper focus and exposure; and should show a soft, undulating line, he continued, echoing nineteenth-century pictorialist photographic theory.[63] For example, the amateur movie-making column in the June 1929 issue of *American Cinematographer* explained: "He must be sure that there are no jarring, discordant notes in any part of the picture, that the action is intelligent and attractive, and that the whole forms a pleasing composition."[64]

However, these ideas on beauty and order disguised representation. Naturalness was prized as a purer form of uninterrupted observation. This "naturalism" shifted in one instance in a 1934 *Popular Science* feature into a surreptitious surveillance of one's own family members in order to obtain the most "natural" shot: "It goes without saying that the best shots you are likely to get of either children or grown-ups are those taken when your subjects are completely unaware that a camera is trained on them."[65] Naturalness represented a pure, uninterrupted, value-free form of observation that could better evoke an emotional response. Naturalness merged with assumptions pertaining to amateur acting as well in a 1929 *Amateur Movie Makers* feature called, polemically, "Acting vs. Naturalness" that instructed actors not to expose their efforts at adopting a role.[66]

Within Hollywood aesthetic discourse, however, naturalism did not denote undisciplined aesthetics. Stylistic devices cultivated naturalness, appending emotional codes to home movies, according to *American Cinematographer* in 1929: "Doesn't he look natural is the greatest compliment, but if we are to provide entertainment, we need a kick."[67] Writing in the December 1929 *American Cinematographer*, William Stull explained: "Therefore, the amateur's first commandment should be: thou shalt not show thy family or friends any of thy screen work which is not as perfect as thou canst make it."[68] As late as 1937 *American Cinematographer* reasoned that controlled artistic expression unlocked spectators' cinematic satisfaction. Spontaneous actuality could not top "feeling": "The camera should be an instrument of illusion."[69] In his column on amateur movie-making in a 1930 *American Cinematographer*, professional cameraman William Stull again argued images should evoke emotional responses:

> Now art is primarily the attempt of one individual to convey some definite thought or emotion to others. Therefore the first thing is to decide just what emotion you want to convey in your films. Then you can easily adapt your mechanical processes to the task of expressing emotion.[70]

Professional cinematographers addressing amateurs believed the resulting film would lack "perfection" without this affective component. Too many distorted camera angles were thought to provoke too disturbing a response in spectators.[71] The film would be reduced to "unprofessional" status. These advice writers discredited any form of cinema that recorded reality but did not evoke emotions; without technique and narrative purpose, films were seen as lifeless, stark, and discordant.[72] Composition and camera placement transported professionalism into amateur filmmaking.[73]

The infusion of narrative story lines into random shots further illustrated how Hollywood style continually exerted pressure on amateur filmmaking to imitate dominant standard practice. Paul W. Kearney, writing in *Parents Magazine* in 1937, for example, did not consider random shots visually interesting because they were unorganized and lacked a definite purpose.[74] Professional-advice columns indoctrinated amateurs with preplanning as a form of control of spontaneity and saw narrative sequences as more purposeful than, as Karl Barleban put it in a 1929 *Amateur Movie Makers*, a "jumbled mass of incidents."[75] To learn sequencing, Barleban told amateurs to study the construction of photoplays in movie theaters.[76] Stull, in a 1929 *American Cinematographer*, considered shooting "off the cuff" in a documentary manner a transgression against this hallowed aesthetic paradigm: "The primal purpose of all pictures—even the most banal snapshots—is to tell a story."[77]

Story lines helped amateurs to further organize and control their efforts. For example, Sterling Gleason linked organization to economy in the 1933 *Popular Science* article "Amateur Movie Makers Use Professional Tricks": "The more experienced [amateur filmmakers] with an eye to economy, organize their production methods."[78] William Stull in a 1930 *American Cinematographer* observed that "most amateurs use their cameras as if they were machine guns—jerk them around hither and yon as though they were spraying a rival gang with bullets."[79]

Another articulation of these ideas on perfection and narrative as metaphors for professionalism in amateur cinematography was staging. Stull justified this control in his June 1930 column in *American Cinematographer*:

This leads to the conclusion that successful amateur movies must be deliberately staged. This is true of even the most apparently spontaneous films, for cinematic action, like extemporaneous speeches, is always best when carefully prepared for in advance.[80]

Nearly every article regarding amateur film in professional-film technical journals during the thirties stressed staging and preparation—the codification and naturalization of Hollywood narrative style—even though other professional media during this same period like the Film and Photo League, Joris Ivens, and Pare Lorentz experimented with documentary style.[81] Even holidays were not immune: the family could be rehearsed and staged, according to the Amateur Cinema League.[82]

The organization of amateur filmmaking production clubs even replicated Hollywood structures. To achieve "drama," professionals recommended more extensive amateur crews, with a division of labor imitating Hollywood productions. Lamenting that an amateur filmmaker must function as cinematographer, director, producer, and film editor, these writers in *American Cinematographer*, *Popular Science*, and *Photo-Era* advised separating these functions among family members. Contending dramatic film executed by Hollywood professionals surpassed the amateur's skimpy one-person crew, amateur-movie column writers in *American Cinematographer* still saw drama as the end result of a well-planned, well-ordered, prescriptive shooting script, which was within the reach of the amateur filmmaker.[83] To counteract this labor shortage, Herbert McKay in a 1928 *Photo-Era* piece suggested forming an amateur filmmaking club and screen-testing members to record what acting roles they could fill.[84] This homology to Hollywood redirected amateur organizations to reproduce hierarchalized industrial productions.

Furthermore, the presence of amateur movie-making clubs in the 1930s indicated the extent of this concentration and institutionalization of amateur film as an adjunct and promoter of Hollywood. In 1934 the *New York Times* estimated that over two hundred clubs and research bureaus across the United States were organized to help amateur moviemakers.[85] The Amateur Cinema League, the oldest of these organizations founded in New York City in 1926 and the publisher of the magazine *Amateur Movie Makers*, had two hundred fifty amateur-cinema clubs on its rolls by 1937.[86] The *New York Times* speculated that there were over one hundred thousand home moviemakers in 1937 and five hundred services for rental of films for home viewing.[87] With this nationalization of amateur movie-making discourse, normative, technical amateur-advice books were published. These books codified and popularized these normative assumptions.

For example, in 1932 *The ACL Movie Book: A Guide to Making Better Movies* was published by the Amateur Cinema League; it was subsequently published in three more editions.[88] The 1940 edition of *The ACL Movie Book* described the range of activities in which the Amateur Cinema League was engaged: technical consultation on equipment, continuity and film-planning advice, film reviews of members' work, publishing *Amateur Movie Makers*, and running film contests.[89] This text reiterated the requirements of good composition, a unified narrative theme, and rehearsals.[90] It also conflated all other forms of non-Hollywood filmmaking with the amateur; the book included a section on special-purpose films for business, religion, education, and scientific work.[91]

In addition to its publications, the League also organized yearly "Ten Best" film contests for amateur films starting in 1930.[92] Many other amateur-film contests and competitive screenings evolved during the 1930s: a British contest sponsored by the Institute of Amateur Cinematographers that offered awards to professional films; screenings sponsored by society people in their private homes; the Quebec Film Contest; an International Amateur Film Contest sponsored by the Division of Film Study at Columbia University.[93] These contests and screenings pointed to two emergent trends in the popular discourse on amateur film: a nationalization of aesthetic norms, now rewarded in competition, and the concentration of amateur-film technology and discourse within major institutions like corporations or magazines. Indeed, the publication of information relevant to these screenings and contests in the society and travel pages of the *New York Times* suggests an urban, upper-class constituency.

Further evidence of this institutionalization of amateur-film aesthetic discourse and its collusion with "perfect" Hollywood studio style was the appearance of amateur-advice magazines published by Eastman Kodak and Bell and Howell. Published in the late twenties—just a few years after the introduction of standardized 16mm film—these magazines disguised their corporate product-marketing agenda with articles on famous amateurs, production notes from amateur and professional films, stories illustrating the durability of cameras under the most inhospitable conditions, technical question-and-answer columns, and essays on proper composition and narrative style. Eastman Kodak published *Kodakery*, a magazine for amateur photographers that sold for a nickel and began publication in 1913. *Kodakery* ran at least one article in each issue on amateur movie-making. By 1923 its ads for the Cine-Kodak stressed family and beauty.[94] Bell and Howell published *Filmo Topics* monthly from 1925 to 1941.[95] The articles were publicity ploys and aggressive marketing plans to draw consumers into the mystique of movie-making in order to lure them into buying additional accessories and gear.

To Exotic Lands

The use of 16mm cameras for documentaries—especially travelogues of foreign countries—by actors, cinematographers, editors, and directors flourished,
most likely to advertise amateur filmmaking with product endorsements from
the Hollywood community. Many articles in the *American Cinematographer* in
1930 described shooting with Filmos in the Far East, Africa, or Europe to underscore their durability, ease of operation, and glamour. Typically, the articles featured stories about the portability and ease of operation of 16mm under the
harshest and most extreme weather conditions. Ironically, professional cinematographers, relaxing off the set with their amateur movie-making gear, complained about winding the footage crank and the slow processing of stock.[96] As
ambassadors of Hollywood and its dominant aesthetic ideology, these directors
and actors legitimated amateur film as a technology and a practice by invoking
their own "professionalism."

The compatibility of foreign travel with amateur filmmaking activity also
diffused into amateur filmmaking magazines. Vacations required order, organization, and planning—just like work or a Hollywood film—to produce the most
optimal visual record. Herbert McKay warned in a 1932 *American Photography*
article "The Cine Amateur" that

> the vacationist who does nothing but loaf and sleep and dance and play
> bridge has only a week or two of vacation, but the one who records all of
> these phases of the two weeks with his cine-camera takes home a generous
> slice of vacation to spread over the dull crust of routine throughout the
> year.[97]

The most efficient and accurate method to document one's vacation demanded
a scenario before departure. This would insure that narrative continuity would
organize one's memory of the vacation, according to a 1931 article by McKay in
Photo-Era.[98]

Control, perfection, and narrative organization of travel also surfaced in
personal testimony of vacation filmmaking in *Amateur Movie Makers*. These
first-person filmmaking melodramas described the treacherous escapades and
encounters of trips to Mexico, Africa, or Europe.[99] These articles reinforced an
illusion of residual rugged individualism in filmmaking; they applauded the
camera operator who skillfully outmaneuvered spontaneous events that threatened the flawless execution of composition and narrative.

Travel filmmaking also assumed cultural power over foreigners. Articles
discussed how American tourists could manipulate indigenous peoples and

their "unknown" customs. For instance, a 1931 article in *Photo-Era* entitled "Movie Making by Up-to-Date Travelers" insisted that the amateur camera was a passport:

> The camera is an "open Sesame" or an international introduction; it encourages one to wander off the main track into strange byways, up those little side streets where pictures may lurk around the corner.[100]

In 1927 *Amateur Movie Makers* vigorously urged travelers to avoid stereotyping foreign countries by filming "natives" under the vague supposition that they were more "picturesque" than architecture.[101] As an example of the upper-class character of amateur travel films during this period, in 1927 the Amateur Cinema League of New York organized a "moviemaker's cruise" to the Mediterranean. The ship was equipped with developing and projecting apparatuses and amateur-movie experts who critiqued passengers' daily rushes.[102]

Concrete examples of travel films from the late 1920s and 1930s are extant, housed in the Human Studies Film Archive of the Smithsonian Institution. A wide array of people spawned these films: wealthy hunters on safaris in Africa, explorers searching for minerals and precious metals, wealthy people touring Egypt, archaeologists on digs in China, military men stationed in the Philippines, teachers in India, missionaries in Iraq and India, and adventurers in Tahiti.[103] Their amateur status was derived from the fact that they produced these films for themselves to document very idiosyncratic moments. They were not trained in the professional pictorial style of composition or editing to seduce the spectator. Their technical and aesthetic competency varied enormously.

Whereas advice columnists exhorted amateurs to maintain Hollywood continuity at all costs and issued numerous directives demanding aesthetic control, the actual films betray the almost innocent idealism and naive ideological positioning of these directives. These films illustrate how out of touch with the contingencies of actual amateur-film production these experts were. For the most part, these foreign-travel films exhibit anything but mastery over narrative, composition, story lines, or emotion. Intriguingly, few films are even edited. Their makers were obviously content to settle on their rushes as the final product, equating production with the finished product for exhibition, if they were even shown at all after they were made. Amateurs clearly harbored a different agenda from that of Hollywood advice columnists.

Four different groups of amateur filmmakers in the 1930s can be analyzed from this collection, demonstrating the range of the use of amateur cameras: travelers, explorers, scientists, and missionaries. These four separate groups exhibit a progressively more intimate and complex relationship with the countries and people they film. Tourists preserve distance from their subjects, while explorers' footage lingers in one location. Scientific films feature many pans and aerial shots of geography and natives. Finally, missionary footage contains many portraits of the daily life of indigenous people, imagery absent from the other three classifications. This progression from distanced catalogs of culture and terrain to more intimate images of private life suggests that the social relations of the makers with the culture imparted the style and content of shooting with more force than did aesthetic discourse. The longer the filmmaker stayed in a location, the less distanced and formal the cinematography became.

Mortimer Fuller's "African Hunting Trip," 1,345 feet shot in 1930, provides a paradigmatic example of tourist footage. Most travel footage shot by amateurs in the Third World imparts an endless swirl of rapid shots, photographed in some ways as though the motion picture camera were a still camera. They lack any sense of composition, editing, or narrative; shots are related only by the narrative thread of where the traveler was at any given moment. Considering that many of these films were shot during the Depression, the fact that they were made at all indicates the upper-class status of the makers, who appeared to be insulated from the economic woes of the era.

Fuller clearly evidenced class privilege to even afford a safari in Africa during the Depression. His numerous unedited images in "African Hunting Trip" feature two kinds of content: pans of the African steppes and mountains cluttered with gazelles, antelopes, rhinos, and giraffes, and static images of white hunters posing with their prey looking directly into the camera. African guides are curiously absent except as accessories: holding up carnage, pushing jeeps through rivers, skinning animals. The black guides are displaced to the periphery. Most of the photography remains in medium or long shots. While Fuller calls the film "African Hunting Trip," there are no images of actual hunting scenes. Perhaps the technical difficulty of shooting quickly in the heat of the action inhibited Fuller; perhaps he was more interested in hunting than in home movie-making. At any rate, the images of terrain, animals, and hunting trophies mark the experience, registering its occurrence and place. But these images engage in a curious anticipation and nostalgia for the event—they are either before or after the hunting incident.

Two scenes, if a series of jump cuts related by content can be called scenes in any conventional narrative sense, convey the intricate power relations of the imperialist gaze of home movies. The curators at the Smithsonian recorded Mortimer Fuller's annotations of his footage, supplying a rare record of an amateur filmmaker's intentions.

The first scene conveys the conflation of the scientific medical gaze, voyeurism, and imperialist power to regiment black women's bodies. A group of African women are lined up, some with children on their backs, others with baskets of grain under their arms. They are bare breasted. They look directly into the camera lens. A series of close-up pans scan their breasts. Mortimer Fuller interprets in voice-over:

> This is a group of natives. Dr. Wainwright used to go to a town and get the natives lined up—the females—because he was looking for breast cancer, and trying to find out if it was more prevalent or less prevalent in them than it was in the Americans.

Mortimer's annotation suggests that white hunters equated black people with animals, treating them all as objects to be hunted, researched, analyzed, organized, and controlled. A rather bald, unmediated presentation: in this scene, white science attempts to rationalize voyeurism not accessible in United States culture. The probing pans of the cinematography expose the authority of the maker. The nervous shooting and rapid pans also map sexual anxiety.

A second scene illustrates the exchange relations between white tourists and indigenous people. Clearly not a narrative with emotional evocations and clearly not a documentary dependent on noninterference, many scenes of contact between whites and blacks trace colonialism's visual contours. Mortimer Fuller photographed an African man riding a motorcycle in what looks like the sandy expanse of a village square. Fuller recorded the man in a series of long medium shots. On occasion, the man rapidly glances at the camera as he steers the motorcycle. This image seems almost surreal. Before this shot, the only modern, engine-powered vehicles we view are safari jeeps, always driven by whites. Fuller explains: "This is the Sultan of the village. He had a motorcycle. He was so pleased we wanted him to ride it. We gave him a couple of shillings. He went round and round a circle." Fuller's narration shows how exchange relations materially altered cultural contact. The sultan riding the motorcycle in a circle is trapped and corralled by the white home moviemaker in a burlesque of contradictions: a Third World "primitive" driving modern technology as spectacle for the amateur camera. The amateur camera dominates a sultan, while the sultan emerges as pure performance, stripped of his power.

A more explicit domination and exploitation of Third World people is evidenced in "Jivarro Indians of Ecuador," 590 feet of 16mm film shot by gold-mining explorers Vincent Blava and William Ryan in 1936. Again, the cinematography ignores actual gold mining, concentrating instead on images of white explorers' leisure-time activities with the Jivarro. The unedited film includes many static medium shots of Jivarro walking around their village, shooting glances at the camera.

Evoking "African Hunting Trip," this footage contains many shots of indigenous people lined up in a row and examined by the panning camera, as though their cultural difference could be branded by the camera's eye. One series of jump cuts is indicative of this perspective. Nine medium and close-up shots follow Jivarro lined up in front of thatched huts. They look directly at the lens as the camera moves in for a series of close-ups of different individuals. However, unlike the African footage, this scene concludes with a series of medium close-ups of daily life: building a canoe, eating in the hut, eating outside. White explorers eat in the hut with the Jivarro, documenting their contact.

Blava and Ryan execute two different kinds of shots that emphasize both cultural difference and economic power over wage labor. The first group of shots compares white explorers to the Jivarro. In one image, a white explorer dressed in safari gear sits on a log with three Indian adults and two children. The explorer is obviously larger than they and clothed in Western dress. In another image, an Indian stands with his ax in wood, while the white explorer next to him stares into the camera. Later in the rolls, a white explorer and a Jivarro man each smoke a cigarette framed in a medium shot that compares their individual movements. The white explorer is poised and blows smoke into the camera lens, whereas the Jivarro male holds the cigarette awkwardly, anxiously watching the white man. These random shots illustrate how the amateur camera avoids narrative structure and focuses instead on contact between the First and Third Worlds as a leisure-time exercise in the colonization of daily life. The camera insists on cultural difference in nearly every shot.

The second group of images can loosely be categorized as images of Jivarro working for the explorers. Resonating a similar set of absences as the African footage, the Jivarro footage does not include any scenes of the actual work of mining, suggesting that amateur filmmaking was reserved for leisure time after work, even in alien locales. Blava and Ryan engage in a form of casual ethnography that repeatedly documents their contacts with the Jivarro. The Jivarro are photographed as picturesque primitives, where daily activities emerge as exotica because they are not contaminated by industrialization. These shots suggest the adaptation of the myth of the noble savage in amateur footage.

Two scenes evidence this attitude of superiority. In one lengthy sequence, the explorers take what looks like a river trip with the Jivarro. Throughout these various medium shots of the river, the Indians, the explorers, and the boats, the camera records the servitude of the Indians to the white explorers. The Indians labor while the whites enjoy leisure on the river. The Indians paddle the boats in which the whites ride. They push white men across rapids on a platform. A series of tracking shots from the inside of the boat ensue, ostensibly photographed by one of the whites while the Jivarro paddle. These tracking shots film the flora and fauna of the jungle as it edges toward the river's banks. The final one hundred feet of the film contains images of Jivarro building log structures under the supervision of Blava and Ryan. Filled with medium shots and pans of groups of Jivarro shimmying up high poles or hauling long logs in large groups, the whites simply watch them labor, either in the scene as they sit on logs directing the building or with the movie camera as they record the scene.

Although these rolls contain some of the rare images of whites eating with the Third World people they film, these unedited images of the Jivarro suggest that for white explorers, the adventure to unknown lands and cultures is invested with the domination, control, and defining differences that confirm their cultural superiority.

The third group of amateur films extant from this period includes films produced by scientists conducting research in foreign lands. An emblematic film in this category is "Sinanthropus Site at Chou Kou Tien, China," produced in 1935. Four hundred feet of black and white film, this footage was shot by geologist George B. Barbous at the site and excavation work of Chou Kou Tien in China. Echoing the other films shot under dramatically different circumstances, this footage features tracking shots from boats, numerous long shots of mountains and rivers, images of Chinese laborers carrying white scientists on chairs across the mountains, and shots of Chinese digging at the excavation site while white scientists peer over their shoulders. Medium shots of Chinese men staring into the camera arranged in a line interspersed with white men obviously try to visually compare height and facial dissimilarities.

Science and discovery reframe these otherwise random aerial shots of excavation sites. Intertitles label each excavation site: "Eastern Entry to Village over Fords," "Chou Kou Tien Has Long Been Known for Its Coal Mines," "Sinanthropus Locality from the North," "Locality One," "View from the Summit of Sinanthropus Site," "Driving Blast Holes in Limestone Walls," to name only a few for illustration. The majority of the images simply denote the various sites. The titles describe what follows, verifying and filling in its scientific status. The footage is photographed entirely in medium and long shots. It documents the various components of the dig in a rather Taylor-like manner, breaking the dig down into discrete units of analysis. The distance from the sites locates this film in the realm of science: the shots are designed to give an overview mapping of the archaeological dig. The Chinese workers occupy the periphery of each shot; they are trivialized in relation to the more important archaeological excavation.

At the end of the film, a title comes up that states "Off Duty—Archery—Pei and Bein." After the rather remote style of long shots of work and terrain in the previous sequences, these six, closer medium shots of Chinese men shooting arrows into targets and camels sipping water seem misplaced. They depict leisured activities of easy camaraderie after the excavation. They insinuate the archaeologists' and geologists' intersubjectivity with the Chinese, a rupture into the ordered, detached scientific gaze of the excavation footage. In contrast to the films of leisure-time pursuits in the Third World, Chou Kou Tien documents the work of the expedition.

The last group of films by missionaries and teachers in the Third World exhibit a far different and more sympathetic view of their host countries. Because their makers lived for extended periods of time with these Indian, Polynesian, or Iraqi cultures, the camera aims more directly at everyday occurrences, such as building houses, cooking food, ceremonial dances, women washing. Proximity, time, and purpose propel the filmmakers into the cultural domains beyond the frenzied, alienated glance of the tourist.

"Robert Haupt's Travel Footage of India" is an excellent example of how residency in a place changed the position of the home moviemaker, enticing the camera deeper into the private sphere of a culture. This 965 feet of black and white film was photographed from 1933 to 1937 by Robert Haupt, an American teacher in India. Haupt's annotation explains that most of the footage in these reels was shot on excursions he embarked on while in India when he was not teaching.

However, despite its touristic context, the content of this footage is more unique than the generalized glance of the casual tourist. One sequence in the film shows people wading across the Ganges, with cutaways to a water wheel, sacred monkeys, and a double-amputee holy man sleeping on a bed of thorns. These details indicate both a familiarity with the culture and a very specialized, pointed vision. They contrast sharply with the generalized, remote pans of other amateur-film footage.

A fairly long sequence records a Mela, a holy festival for Hindus. Haupt filmed the huge crowd from the nucleus of the action. Unlike tourists who filmed rather immobilized, sanitized representations of Third World people as a form of performance for the First World, Haupt encountered two rituals of self-mutilation. Rope dancers swirl together connected by ropes strung through incisions in their backs, and hook swingers spin from a pole to which they are attached with hooks wedged into their shoulder blades. In the voice-over annotation, Haupt reveals the enormous effort he undertook to attend the Mela: he traveled as far as he could go in a car, then hiked in, all the while acutely aware of the clandestine nature of his attendance at the Mela. His is not the lazy, enervated gaze of the tourist on safari, but the probing camera of an insider in a culture.

While medium shots of docks, cities, animals, people, and market scenes dominate the major portion of this Indian footage, these scenes of the Ganges and the Mela surpass the distanced view of the tourist. While they are not edited in any logical style nor photographed with the proper pictorialist formal dimensions, they nonetheless are examples of shots taken during the middle of an event where the Hindus were performing a ritual.

The footage concludes with numerous medium and high-angle shots of the students at Haupt's school in the courtyards, eating and participating in a track-and-field festival with events like long jumps, running races, and pie-eating contests. While the images of American children dressed in white uniforms sketches the colonial outpost, the footage is also significant in that it shows Haupt's workplace and his connections with his students. They obviously know him inasmuch as they look into the camera and laugh.

Some general visual characteristics of these various genres of amateur-film production in foreign lands can be deciphered. They unfold the enormous gap between written advice from seasoned professionals and actual amateur-film production activity on foreign trips in the Third World. Although the argument that these films present resistance to these aesthetic prerogatives could be made, their shaky camera work, inability to change composition, and absence of narrative may more simply demonstrate that amateur-camera usage was not oriented within the discourse of film production.

Somewhere between an ingenuous ethnography and a Sears catalog of the marvels of the Third World, these films trace encounters between privileged and mobile First World people who control technology (cars and cameras) and the Third World. These travel films inventory foreign people, animals, geography, and cities. Most of the cinematography is frontal from eye level. It remains in a static medium shot, far removed from the subject. In essence, the filmmaking here attempts to immobilize, separating the "other" or the terrain from context and interaction for visual quantification. The amateur camera transforms people and terrain into artifacts. Camera movement only occurs when the operator rides a boat, plane, train, or automobile, themselves indicators of economic resources, mobility, and access to transportation.

Many scenes in these films pose American tourists waving directly to the camera in front of important archaeological sites or interesting terrain. They deploy the same gestures of home movies photographed in the States in the confines of the nuclear family—only the backgrounds are different. White culture is transported to the Third World, unchanged by any interaction or contact. These films do not apply the narrative language of cinema. It would be stretching to consider them documentaries in any sense of the term, although they do function as perverted marginalia of colonial encounters. Frequently, tourists pose with indigenous peoples motioning in various ways to underscore their cultural difference, such as patting Africans on the head or looking Japanese housekeepers up and down.[104]

Nearly all of these films are photographed outside, signaling both the technical limitations of exposing indoors and the ideological implications of filming only in large, accessible public places. This exterior shooting also marks the geographical and ideological distance between the camera operators and their subjects. All terrain, all people, all animals are simultaneously generalized, itemized, and tagged by the amateur camera. These convenient locations frame how tourists remain outsiders to these cultures. Very few of these films even bother to establish the context for their images—people, places, and animals simply materialize and then float in medium shot.

In many ways, these films demonstrate how foreign-travel home movies of all sorts commodified and quantified other cultures for consumption in the United States. The films evidence displacement from one's own culture. These films tabulate the difference between the "looker" and the "looked at." The distance etched between the camera operator and the people and their terrain insinuates foreign culture as spectacle and tourism as passive consumption. The camera work here suggests a quick, rushed glance, a surface scanning. The mobile tourist regulated encounters with cultural difference through the camera. When circumstances like exploration, science, or missionary work altered the material context of the maker and determined a longer stay in the foreign culture, the camera moved into the private sphere with more frequency and more intimacy.

Experimentation

Although Hollywood professionals proselytized narrative style to amateurs in cinematography magazines, popular science magazines, and corporate publications, their own deployment of "amateur" 16mm cameras betrayed distinctly nonnarrative inclinations. Professional cinematographers adopted 16mm film for experimentation and documentary, because it was significantly cheaper than 35mm stock. Despite the fact that Hollywood actors such as Lon Chaney, Claudette Colbert, and Kenneth McKenna expounded on how they learned "good" amateur technique by filming the pros at work on movie sets in the pages of *American Cinematographer*, many professional actors employed 16mm Filmos to test and correct their own acting style for Hollywood films. William Stull wrote about how this process aided a young opera singer turned film actress in the the July 1930 issue of *American Cinematographer*:

> When I suggested this to Miss Moore the other day, she quite agreed with me. Her work with her own Filmo, she told me, had been a great help in

teaching her how to time her own movements when she faced the big studio Bell and Howell.[105]

On Hollywood backlots, 16mm cameras were reframed as professional tools to measure cinematic acting ability and to train beginning actors in screen technique.

Whereas Hollywood narrative conscripted leisure-time amateur filmmaking into an imperfect clone of dominant aesthetic practice, Hollywood professionals engaged amateur equipment for experimentation and innovation in studio aesthetic style. Dan B. Clark, A.S.C., who shot the Tom Mix series and the Mazda light tests, trained his apprentices with both Leica still cameras and 16mm Cine-Kodaks. He instructed them to produce short documentaries about the feature films they crewed on to practice studio framing techniques. Wesley Ruggles, director of *Cimarron*, used his Filmo to visually sketch out his ideas for his cinematographers.[106] Ruggles also archived locations, actor's interesting mannerisms, and informal tests for historical accuracy of sets with his 16mm equipment, creating a catalog for home study, according to a piece in a 1930 *American Cinematographer* article.[107]

In an October 1930 Bell and Howell ad in *American Cinematographer*, John Arnold, an MGM cinematographer, proclaimed that he experimented with angles and cinemachinery with Filmos.[108] Many cinematographers attached Filmos to their studio cameras to record the scene for their own portfolios and to view their work prior to its screening for producers.[109] John Arnold experimented with optical printing effects, Kodacolor, and bipacking with 16mm cameras.[110] The lower cost of 16mm film was the primary impetus toward this usage.

Oddly enough, Cecil B. De Mille may have been the first Hollywood studio director to connect realism, intimacy, and documentary technique with smaller, and especially more portable, 16mm equipment and lightweight 35mm Eyemos. This hand-held technique contradicted the Hollywood-aesthetic mythologies of "perfect" composition perpetuated in amateur magazines. De Mille claimed he photographed moving shots in *The Ten Commandments* crowd scenes, the riot sequences in *The Godless Girl*, and the zeppelin sequences in *Madame Satan* with Filmos and Eyemos. He attested that this hand-held method heightened emotional appeal and increased audience participation. According to a 1930 *American Cinematographer* article, De Mille allowed only the most experienced and expert narrative cinematographers to experiment with this spontaneous "documentary" camera style. The compactness of the Eyemos and Filmos, in De Mille's estimation, permitted cinematographers to obtain angles and positions too tight for larger studio cameras.[111]

However, other factors besides aesthetic experimentation might have induced Hollywood cinematographers to utilize 16mm cameras. Luxury-market camera sales dropped significantly after the economic disaster of the Great Depression in 1929. With many 16mm ads in 1930 featuring testimonials by professional cinematographers, Bell and Howell and Eastman Kodak may have attempted to offset financial losses incurred in the rapidly declining leisure market by redirecting their marketing to Hollywood professionals, whose industry was also affected by the Depression.[112]

Hollywood studios were not the only site of the use of 16mm technology for stylistic innovation. Another form of cinematic experimentation challenging the dominance of Hollywood professional visual standards in amateur-film discourse appeared in the late 1920s and early 1930s. While difficult to document its impact on actual amateurs, experimental filmmaking was fueled by its direct opposition to the more popular discourses on Hollywood style, compositional harmony, and pictorialism. A small group of photographic journalists interrogated films to see whether their approaches to style, content, and construction could be easily attained by the amateur. This emergent and sometimes resistant discourse surfaced in some disparate areas: film criticism, advocacy of expressionistic film techniques, and Marxist film critic Harry Alan Potamkin's theories on amateurism.

Although at best only a diversion from the more pervasive emphasis on Hollywood style in amateur magazines, this linkage of an experimental disposition with amateur filmmaking was nonetheless significant. It suggests that the presentation of Hollywood-aesthetic ideology was not a totalizing phenomenon. At least on the discursive level, magazine writers did not distinguish between amateurs who shot home movies and amateurs who produced "art" films. If anything, magazine writers considered amateur experimental filmmakers more ambitiously committed to amateurism than those who merely recorded their families.

Other historical factors may have contributed to this discussion of experimental technique in amateur-film circles. The initial period of American avant-garde film from 1928 to 1932 followed intense experimental-film activity from 1924 to 1928 in Europe. This spurt of experimental film maintained strong ties to professional film. Robert Florey, director of *The Life and Death of 9413—A Hollywood Extra* (1928), for example, worked for the major studios as an assistant director. Paul Fejos directed *The Last Moment*, an experimental film in the German expressionistic camera style of angles and shadowy lighting, in Hollywood. It earned Fejos a job directing minor pictures at Universal. These filmmakers, along with others like Ralph Steiner (director of H_2O [1929]),

Howard Weinberg (director of *Autumn Fire* [1930] and contributor to *Amateur Movie Makers*), James Sibley Watson and Melville Webber (directors of *The Fall of the House of Usher* [1928]), produced these films as "leisure-time activities." However, unlike most amateurs, their work could be distributed because it was shot in 35mm.[113]

During the mid-to late 1920s, such films as Robert Flaherty's *Nanook of the North* (1922) and *Moana* (1926), Sergei Eisenstein's *Battleship Potemkin* (U.S.S.R., 1925), Carl Dreyer's *Passion of Joan of Arc* (France, 1928), Charlie Chaplin's *Gold Rush* (1925), and F. W. Murnau's *Sunrise* (1927), all films praised for their artistry, were exhibited, establishing a place in major exhibition areas for films extending cinematic art.[114]

After the introduction of sound in 1927, Hollywood films (according to conventional historical interpretations) forfeited some of their more innovative camera styles, because sound equipment limited the mobility of the camera. The interest of amateur magazines during the following four to five years in silent experimental work constituted a reaction to Hollywood's technological developments through a reassertion of the art of silent cinema. In fact, for a few months around 1930, the Amateur Cinema League and the American Film Arts Guild imported European-produced noncommercial films for distribution.[115] By 1931 the Workers' International Relief, a leftist organization that assisted strikers, distributed many Soviet films noted for their artistic and political innovations, like Vsevolod Pudovkin's *Storm over Asia*, Sergei Eisenstein's *Days That Shook the World*, Dziga Vertov's *Man with the Movie Camera*, and Victor Turin's *Turksib*.[116] During this period, some filmmakers like German Walter Ruttman, the director of *Berlin: Symphony of a City* (Germany, 1927), and Soviet Dziga Vertov shot documentary films. Their city symphonies influenced American filmmakers like Jay Leyda and Howard Weinberg, because they used everyday occurrences in cities as the content rather than scripts.[117]

Historian David Curtis has also contended that Hollywood studios experimented with optical printing, traveling mattes, rear-screen projection, and camera movement by the early to mid-1930s. These effects created a larger cinematic cultural context for nonnarrative visual experimentation.[118] On the one hand, these developments displayed and validated visual experimentation; whereas, on the other hand, the technology to produce these effects was unavailable to amateurs.

These discussions about experimental or art films in the amateur-film press may not represent a revolutionary rejection of Hollywood visual norms, an unlikely stance in magazines that so energetically embraced Hollywood; rather, they suggest an effort to expand and strengthen cinema as an art. With the historical prerogative of amateurism as the guardian of art not contaminated by capitalism, it is not surprising that magazines like *Amateur Movie Makers* would promote experimental cinema.

During this same period, Bertolt Brecht analyzed these distinctions as political interventions limiting equal access to artistic production. Claiming that the dominant culture devalued and neutralized songs, rituals, stories, and dances performed in private life as a practice of class oppression, Brecht argued for a redefinition of "folk" or "popular" culture in his essay "The Popular and the Realistic" published in the 1930s. In this essay, Brecht locates cultural struggle in the interstices between elite art and folk art: "The history of all the falsifications that have been operated with this conception of Volkstun [folk] is a long and complex story which is part of the history of class war."[119] Rather than positing that the great institutions of art severed folk practices from more overtly political concerns, he contends that these two spheres work dialectically. On the one hand, powerful economic and ideological interests restrain folk art, peripheralizing it as a static, dehistoricized, passive activity. On the other hand, he defines popular as the active participation of people in the development of culture—"taking it over, forcing it, deciding it."[120] The dominant cultural practice frames amateurism as nonprofessional, because it fails to conform to professionalism:

> Anybody who seriously sets out to study the art of the theater and its social function will do well to pay some attention to the many forms of theatrical activity that can be found outside the great institutions, i.e., the rudimentary, distorted, spontaneous efforts of the amateurs. Even if the amateurs were only what the professional takes them to be—members of the audience getting up on stage—they would still be interesting enough.[121]

Amateur-movie magazines analyzed the formal techniques and different modes of production exhibited in such films as *Battleship Potemkin*, *The Last Laugh*, *Ten Days That Shook the World*, and French experimental shorts, emphasizing the low-budget opportunities they offered. These writers did not attack Hollywood; rather, they promoted amateurism. George Hess praised Eisenstein's films in a 1933 review in *Personal Movies*, because "all the directorial devices throughout the picture are simple; simple in that they are free from all evidence of pretentious artistry."[122] Eisenstein's *Thunder over Mexico* garnered particularly high critical honors from Hess: he allowed that amateurs could concoct nearly every stylistic device in it.[123]

Ideologically, these reviews severed amateur film from Hollywood hierarchy to secure a more important goal: artistic freedom. Alfred Richman in a 1929

article entitled "Technique of the Russians" in *Amateur Movie Makers* underlined
the similarities between Eisenstein and amateurs:

> Eisenstein, in *Ten Days that Shook the World* uses virtually only amateur
> "actors," resorts to constructed sets as little as possible, studies pro-
> foundly the theory and experiments constantly with technique of the cin-
> ema and is interested, primarily, in the artistic integrity of his produc-
> tions, *we see how much he has in common with the aims of the amateur
> movement.* (Emphasis added)[124]

These films offered a new, alternative paradigm for amateurs: simplicity and
experimentation rather than complicated technical control by experts. C. W.
Gibbs, writing in *American Movie Makers* in 1929, completely challenged Hollywood's compositional etiquette of not rankling the spectator by urging amateur
filmmakers to "startle" their audiences through modernist effects: unusual camera angles, moving lights, extreme close-ups, multiple images, distorting lenses,
and the use of flashbacks not connected logically to the previous scene.[125] One
article even advanced the radical notion that small movie houses screening experimental shorts and amateur projects should attack the inherent conservatism
of commercial films.[126] This sporadic articulation on artistic freedom and experimentation resisted the discourse of professional film in two ways: first, it
defied the dominant conventions of narrative with formal experimentation. Second, it alerted amateurs to films produced outside of Hollywood confines.

The combination of Russian film technique at this time was believed to be
politically dangerous. The mainstream press diagnosed the perils of this coun-
tercinema. In a biting review of Turin's *Turksib*, the *New Republic* in 1930 dele-
gitimated the film by dubbing it a Russian "home movie" about a railroad.[127]
Bruce Bliven, the author of this *New Republic* article satirically called "Home
Movies in Excelsis," wrote:

> A few such sessions [of out-of-focus film screenings] are enough to make
> anybody wish there might be a law restricting the use of motion picture
> cameras to professionals who work in studios and have the discretion
> enough to let their mistakes die on the cutting room floor.[128]

During the late 1920s, many leftist critics and filmmakers envisioned the political and social possibilities of the Russian cinema for mass mobilization. Possibly
in reaction to this discourse, the conservative *New Republic* conversely praised
a travel film produced by the wealthy Pinchat family. The article complimented
their Caribbean and Pacific cruise films as "professional," noting their natural
beauty and good composition. It flailed *Turksib* for its overabundant concentration on machinery and on excessively short and disturbing scenes. This dis-

course mapped a cultural-class warfare between professionals and amateurs. Professionalism was ascribed to the leisure class's vacation films, whereas amateurism disenfranchised a film with social and political intentions: "Though on the whole, the USSR's home movie is less interesting than of the American 'capitalist' family: a fact from which no moral whatever is to be drawn."[129]

Radical amateur columnists, like Harry Alan Potamkin and other authors of amateur-advice books, viewed positively the cheapness and flexibility of amateur cameras. According to a 1927 *American Movie Makers* editorial, these cameras would "liberate the cinematic art from restrictions of commerce" and induce experimentation by thousands of amateur-movie equipment owners for the reason that profits and losses did not matter.[130] An extremely utopian anonymous writer in *American Movie Makers* in 1926 even located experimental opportunities within the reach of every family.[131] Indeed, some writers thought this inexpensive equipment could create an entirely new form of communication. This December 1926 description of the purposes of the Amateur Cinema League published in its publication *Amateur Movie Makers* illustrates this idealist position:

> Professional pictures must appeal to mass interest and mass interest does not always embrace things that ought to be known. On the other hand, the amateur has no necessity for appealing to mass interest. He is free to reproduce and record any action his fancy or the fancy of a friend might dictate.[132]

Leonard Harker's *Cinematic Design*, published in 1931 by the American Photographic Publishing Company, also promoted amateurism as fertile ground for art. Dedicated to F. W. Murnau and stressing constructivist principles of geometric design, *Cinematic Design* explicated form, rhythm, color, and relativity in motion pictures. The final one hundred pages of the book featured scenarios for amateur cinematographers. They reproduced the strategies of city symphony films produced in Europe in the late twenties: *Symphony Natural, Symphony Synthetic, Symphony Mechanique*, to name only a few. Fairly explicit about the purpose of amateur cinema, in the preface Harker explains:

> Whereas the purpose of the professional film is to furnish cheap entertainment for the masses, the amateur will devote his attention to the development of cinematics as a highly original art form, eventually finding a market for small audiences of more cultural tastes.[133]

Harker's vision of aesthetic liberation linked amateurs with formal visual experimentation but simultaneously concealed a latent elitism that assumed general audiences were ignorant of the complexities of personal-art cinema.

However, in the social context, these joyful exhortations for artistic expressions not defined by commerce constituted a politically reactionary strategy. They invested leisure time with the illusion of control and the fiction of a residual nineteenth-century ethic of the individual craftsperson.

Robert Florey's *Life and Death of 9413—A Hollywood Extra* (1928) provides a good example of an experimental film created in amateur domains that lambasted dominant Hollywood visual ideology and social practice. Sound production required enormous technological resources and deepened the divide between amateur and professional filmmaking by sustaining extremely high barriers to entry. In a 1929 essay for *New Republic* titled "Home Movies,"[134] Gilbert Seldes noted that several professional cinematographers and photographers produced films that junked Hollywood style, such as James Sibley Watson's *Fall of the House of Usher* and Ralph Steiner's H_2O.[135] In the same vein, Herman Weinberg, in a 1929 *Amateur Movie Makers*, touted *The Life and Death of 9413—A Hollywood Extra* as a triumph of amateur experimentation imaginatively exploiting limited resources. Florey's film critiqued Hollywood's abuse of actors by following an actor—9413—through his hopes for success, his rejection, and his subsequent death. Florey, a Hollywood cameraman by trade, employed cutouts, erector-set miniatures, and expressionistic lighting rather than elaborate soundstages.[136] Florey, the professional cinematographer, critiqued his own employer—the Hollywood studios—in this film. The experimental style of the film countered the logical organization of dominant narrative style and turned the liability of diminished resources into an asset.

The only amateur theorist during this period was Harry Alan Potamkin. A member of the leftist Workers' Film and Photo League, he argued that cinema offered new positive tendencies "towards the compound, the reflective, and toward a new logic."[137] Cinema, he wrote, could initiate a new logic: it could break dependence on literalness through montage, a direct assault on Hollywood continuity. As a technique to reorganize film abstractly, rather than eternally, montage decomposed and reconstructed continuity and natural pictorialism.

In his 1930 essay "The Montage Film," which first appeared in *Amateur Movie Makers*, Potamkin advanced montage films such as Ruttman's *Berlin: Symphony of a City*, Alberto Calvalanti's *Only the Hours*, and Dziga Vertov's *Man with the Movie Camera*. Constructed with abstract principles, these films were accessible to the amateur.[138] As films about actual cities, these documentaries presented a powerful strategy: amateurs were cajoled to film and critique everyday aspects of American life or people—such as lunch hours, transportation—outside the private confines of the home and the nuclear family. It is significant that Potamkin cited examples of films about public places; these examples attacked amateur-movie magazines' emphasis on private life and personal travel.

In a 1929 essay entitled "The Magic of Machine Films," also published in *Amateur Movie Makers*, Potamkin reasoned that machines impacted life on nearly every level. The amateur camera, therefore, should force itself upon the machine and confront it to record it, construct it visually, and examine its operation in detail. To accomplish this, Potamkin advocated many formal techniques such as slow, fast, and stop action. He did not consider these aesthetic devices to heighten emotion; instead, he saw them as instigating analysis of abstract principles in spectators.[139] On the surface, Potamkin's directives to amateurs may resemble merely formal manipulations. However, within the social, historical, and discursive context of amateur cinematography in this period that exalted naturalism, emotionalism, and beauty, these techniques constituted small, discursive acts of resistance to the dominant ideology of Hollywood narrative. This experimental liberalism was short-lived however. With the onslaught of World War II, the smallness and portability of amateur-film equipment would move it and some amateur filmmakers beyond the coziness of the nuclear family. Only this time, the military, rather than Hollywood or amateurs, would command its deployment.

4

Cameras and Guns

1941–1949

The business of fighting our enemies in the current global war is not being done entirely with bombs and bayonets. Playing an important part on every battle front and in every bombing mission, motion picture cameramen, many from Hollywood, are marching and flying side by side with fighting men, shooting film instead of bullets.[1]

AMERICA FOUGHT World War II with cameras and guns. While the guns downed Japanese or German planes, 16mm cameras raised morale in propaganda films for the home front. These 16mm combat films instilled a new stylistic realism to Hollywood narrative films. World War II advertised and legitimated 16mm amateur equipment more than Kodak or Bell and Howell could ever have imagined. Besides igniting technological progress and innovation in this smaller, less-expensive gauge, World War II brought amateurs and Hollywood professionals together on the battlefields. Indicative of this collaboration was an *American Cinematographer* piece headlined "While Camera Planes Win Wars."[2]

World War II precipitated major changes in amateur film through its massive incorporation of 16mm amateur-film equipment for military purposes. The crisis of World War II, with its militarization of all amateur-film technology, suspended the overarching trend of defining amateur film as home movies for about a five-year period. This intervention into amateur-film discourse's linkage with the bourgeois nuclear family was for the most part due to the fact that the consumer market for amateur film did not exist during World War II because of the rationing of 16mm stock. Therefore, amateur-film technology and raw stock were framed with the discourse of patriotism, nationalism, and support for the war effort. Although substandard-film technology and the aesthetic infusion of Hollywood narrative style had functioned as powerful constituents of the cultural definition of amateur film during the 1920s and 1930s, by 1942 the war dramatically repositioned amateur film as a more standard technology and modified aesthetic norms toward a more documentary style. The idea of simulating experience emerged: "A motion picture is a substitute for experience."[3] Through the military's use of 16mm film, this amateur gauge gradually shifted its social and cultural position from a hobbyist's domain to a semiprofessional industry. It would emerge from the war as a more legitimate, standardized, and utilitarian technology.

The relationship between Hollywood professionals and the United States military during World War II has been well documented. In 1945 the editors of *Look* magazine published an account heralding Hollywood's patriotism in cooperating with the motion picture needs of the military titled *From Movie Lot to Beachhead*.[4] This book described how Hollywood actors entertained the troops, how directors made training films, how actors enlisted, and how Hollywood professionals contributed to the training of camera operators in the Army Signal Corps. One-sixth of all workers in the production, distribution, and exhibition of motion pictures were in the armed services. This figure represented 40,000 out of a total number of 240,000 industry workers. It included 132 members of the Screen Directors' Guild, 230 members of the Screen Writers' Guild, 40 camera operators, 75 electricians and sound technicians, 453 film technicians, and 80 machinists.[5]

Although the relationship between the Hollywood film industry and the military envelopes a broad range of historical issues, their connection is significant for this discussion of the war's deployment of amateur film. Their liaison explains three important transformations.[6] First, by World War II the discussion of 16mm equipment and its use changed: it shifted from an aesthetic discourse in mass-market and specialty amateur-cinematography magazines to a concern with its utilization in war conditions in professional-cinematography magazines. *American Cinematographer* considered how to fully exploit 16mm's flexibility and lightness for documentary, in sharp contrast to earlier exhortations for narrative. Second, this relationship demonstrated how Hollywood had garnered cultural power as the standard setter for motion pictures—to the point of training combat camera operators. Third, the intermingling between Hollywood and the military during World War II spurred hand-held combat camera techniques to infiltrate Hollywood visual codes in the postwar period. This collaboration between Hollywood professionals and combat photographers engineered a new visual standard based on audience participation.

For example, in a 1944 *American Cinematographer* James Wong Howe, the famous Hollywood cinematographer, asserted that the proliferation of documentary films during World War II trained audiences to digest a rawer, less-polished cinematic realism. He observed that "the audience cannot help comparing them [newsreels from the front and narrative films] and can draw only one conclusion: that the Hollywood concept is artificial and therefore unbelievable."[7] He cautioned that this documentary "perfection" uttered its own syntax: "Perfect, that is, in realistic terms, certainly not perfect in Hollywood terms."[8] Empiricism and realism framed the eye and direct observation as an extreme exaggeration of scientific applications of cameras. This merger appointed the camera an infallible measuring instrument, the quintessential tool of an accurate science. This visual style anticipated the development of cinema verité in the fifties. "Equipment now in use by the Army and Navy, developed from the necessities of war expediency, cannot help contributing to the motion picture industry a new and much needed mechanical flexibility and simplicity," Howe predicted.[9] Yet he warned that story construction would always remain the cinematographer's primary objective. This ideological contradiction between the empirical capacities of the camera and its more subjectively etched aesthetic and narrative ambitions expanded graphically during World War II. It is a matter of record that 16mm cameras were used for reconnaissance and engineering tests, as well as for "artistic" documentation of American war efforts.

To fully understand this dramatic reversal toward a more participatory and less-controlled standard of realism, the historical context of documentary conventions can better situate the Army Signal Corps' recuperation of amateur-film technology. Preplanned, controlled norms—engraved with the pictorialist aesthetic—spread over a wide discursive expanse of documentary filmmaking, propaganda films, newsreels, broadcasting, commercial still photography, and government directives.

Innovations in Amateur Filmmaking

Documentary Conventions

Feature-film directors like William Wyler, John Huston, and Frank Capra shot combat footage and directed training films during the war. Perhaps the most celebrated of all was Hollywood director Frank Capra's *Why We Fight* series—compilation documentaries produced with footage culled from captured enemy combat footage.[10] Capra also appropriated footage from such diverse documentary filmmakers as Humphrey Jennings, Joris Ivens, Leni Riefenstahl, and Harry Watt. Joris Ivens, an independent filmmaker who later joined the Capra unit, had extensively photographed the Spanish Civil War. He was one of the few independent documentary filmmakers to have photographed wars on the front lines. Most documentary filmmakers in the 1920s and 1930s launched into more romantic, stylized topics that conformed to the tenets of pictorialism, typified in films like Pare Lorentz's *The River*. The documentary explosion of the 1930s—in journalism, film, photography, and eyewitness accounts—elaborated social commitment with a highly stylized and personalized approach. "Feeling" and "experience" overrode accuracy or intimate camera work. With their emphasis on classical composition and sorrowful faces, Margaret Bourke-White's photographs of migrant workers stand as consummate examples of this emotional aesthetic.[11] Erik Barnouw in his *Documentary: A History of the Non-Fiction Film* has noted that the *Why We Fight* series relied on fictionalized recreations to "fill in" when actuality footage was not available.[12] Thus, documentary film did not extinguish narrative control and emotional states.

As discussed in the pages of *American Cinematographer*, documentary camera technique also emulated Hollywood style. Fascination with documentary form escalated with World War II; even John Grierson and Joris Ivens penned essays for *American Cinematographer* on proper documentary form. In a 1937 article titled "Documentary Film Patterned from Prizewinners" in *American Cinematographer*, Barry Staley encouraged amateur documentary production. However, he admonished that documentary form required more thought and planning than a haphazard "celluloid scrapbook of events."[13] By 1942 *American Cinematographer* writers encouraged amateurs who owned 16mm equipment to produce Civil Defense films.[14] The overused axiom "Make your films authentic" offered an incentive to upgrade the credibility of the topic with narrative techniques. Documentary mobilized public opinion through dramatization of fact. Described by many professional cinematographers in the pages of *American Cinematographer*, documentary expressed ideas through sequential stories. Pre-planning visual ideas curtailed more spontaneous on-the-spot shooting.[15] According to these essays, the difference between Hollywood narrative films and documentaries resided in the relationship between story and technique: all components in Hollywood narratives propped up the story, whereas technique and story in documentaries bulwarked abstract social ideas.

These attitudes regarding compositional harmony were not limited to Hollywood cinematographers. Writing in *American Cinematographer*, British documentary producer John Grierson advanced the idea of dramatic elements beyond the actuality footage. He was more concerned with documentary effectivity than with shot composition or editing style. In "Documentary Films in War Time," published in *American Cinematographer* in 1942, Grierson decreed:

> We have the more difficult duty . . . of shaping from our war observations on every front—both military and civilian—the strategic pattern of highly complex events . . . *in simple dramatic patterns of thought and feeling.* (Emphasis added)[16]

Even Joris Ivens, a pioneer of combat shooting in the center of action in *The Spanish Earth*, concurred. A piece in a 1942 *American Cinematographer* illustrates his position: "Only as long as your subject is firmly connected with dramatic

reality, can the film you are making develop you and your co-workers artistically."[17] Although Ivens embraced the visual power of on-the-spot filming, he
had no reservations when it came to reenactments to deliver "an emotional
presentation of fact" in documentary.[18]

Richard Meran Barsam has noted that Hollywood professional and independent documentary filmmakers produced combat films. However, he ignores
the infusion of amateurs.[19] Barsam praises the realistic shock value of war
scenes but also compliments their gradual improvement in technique, organization, and narrative, largely a result of the influx of Hollywood theatrical-film
technicians.[20] According to the official military history of the Signal Corps,
combat motion picture training reiterated the need for "story coverage" on as-
signments. As part of their instruction, trainees scripted potential news stories.[21] Darryl F. Zanuck, vice-president of Twentieth Century Fox and an officer
on the Research Council of the Academy of Motion Picture Arts and Sciences,
reorganized the training-film division of the Corps along Hollywood lines. In
a military report, he commented that training films needed humor and professional actors.[22] For the 1942 North African invasion, Zanuck organized special
photographic detachments to document assault landings and land action. They
shot over five thousand feet of film. Zanuck responded to the invasion footage
like a Hollywood producer: "I don't suppose our war scenes will look as savage
and realistic as those we usually make on the backlot, but then you can't have
everything."[23] In the early stages of the war, combat cinematographers envied
the Germans' staged battle scenes. They felt those scenes sustained greater
authenticity than their own documentary footage. They complained that the
American shots were taken from the worst angle because the enemy occupied
the better shooting position.[24] Rather than mirroring an unmediated "reality,"
military documentary and even some combat films conversely pined for Hollywood narrative style.

The connection between newsreel companies and the military was particularly close. In 1941 at the Fort Monmouth Training Film Production Laboratory
of the Signal Corps School, the March of Time initiated a course in movie filming and editing.[25] Many professional cinematographers and newsreelers were
exempted from the draft due to age. Consequently, the Signal Corps experienced
difficulty finding inductees with previous professional photographic experience
to meet the military's increased demands for war coverage.[26] Although in 1941
and 1942 many of the camera operators in the Army Signal Corps and the Navy
received their initial training from the March of Time and Fox Movietone, most
newsreel companies were not autonomous from the government during World
War II. The government provided a majority of combat footage. Newsreels from
different companies resembled each other and often utilized the same footage.

Washington censored film. Raw-stock shortages reduced reel length. Controversial issues disappeared. Nearly 75 percent of newsreel footage during this period depicted the war or some aspect of it furnished by the Signal Corps. Rather than prompting a more realistic technique, newsreels relied on reconstructions, absurdities, or unique news occurrences—in short, sensationalism.[27]

Broadcasting, too, imported narrative formats to news. War bond drives, insertion of war-related material into existing programs, and Office of War Information monitored news thrived. In fact, broadcasters enjoyed enormous financial gains during the war, paralleling the economic surge of other companies with military contracts like Bell and Howell. With newspaper shortages, advertisers turned to radio with its large audience for a more cost-effective media buy. However, a uniquely constituted realism crept into broadcasting. Like combat footage, it derived its immediacy from the development of new technologies: the miniaturization of components and live broadcasts from the battlefields. Once an anomaly, Edward R. Murrow's live broadcasts from the European theater became the standard. Radio news and specials comprised almost 20 percent of wartime network programming.[28]

While radio inaugurated a new visceral, documentary style, the still photography of *Life* and *Look* seemed static and inert in comparison; it resembled catalogs for war weapons and planes more than it did graphic combat realism.[29] Most World War II photos frame planes, tanks, trucks, and ships with dramatically composed angles.

These picture magazines more typically featured narrative stories about particular individuals dealing with the war on a personal level. Photographic sequences resembled storyboards for continuity scripts. One story adapted an "authentic" account of a homeless woman befriended by a hulking American marine in London. The marine departs for his tour of duty, and the authorities jail the woman for vagrancy. After the marine returns and rescues her, the woman marries him. Significantly, the form is docudrama: nonactors reenact the story, shot in a filmic narrative style with close-ups, medium shots, and long shots. Indeed, the piece could be a Paramount storyboard.

Unless supplied by enlisted amateurs or the Signal Corps, very few images of battles or the wounded graced the pages of *Life* and *Look*. More typically, the written text described battles at great length and in graphic detail, supplemented with drawings of explosions. *Life* and *Look* obtained the rare shots of sinking U-boats from enlisted amateur photographers. To meet the growing need for trained camera operators, professional news photographers from the *Daily Mirror*, the Associated Press, and the *New York Times* even volunteered to train recruits in proper compositional technique to improve the quality of their images.[30]

In his World War II study *V Was for Victory*, John Morton Blum outlined the violent and bitter policy conflicts among members of the Office of War Information over whether war efforts should stress facts or figurative persuasion.[31] This contradiction between factuality and emotion dispersed into several different areas. While print journalists opted for facts and sifted through government documents, advertising and communications researchers in the Department of War Information argued for fictionalized, persuasive propaganda. Concerned about government censorship, Hollywood followed the researchers and spent the remainder of the war cranking out patriotic narratives.

16mm Is Drafted

Within this overarching aesthetic context of narrative, the military snapped 16mm amateur-film technology into the war like rubber and nylon. Amateur-film technology's influence on the construction of realism was enormous. Ironically, an invocation of the scientific standards of industrial capitalism generated the less-controlled, more spontaneous shooting style of the era. At this point of departure, 16mm technology went to war with B-17s. As a scientific tool, it was used for experimental purposes, for training, and for reconnaissance. As necessary as radar, these small, portable cameras analyzed enemy equipment and recorded battles. These scientific procedures appended a discourse on realism to 16mm camera technology. Combat cinematographers encouraged the employment of lighter-weight, hand-held equipment. According to military sources, they found Bell and Howell's 35mm Eyemo and 16mm films easier to operate under adverse conditions and more durable in extreme climates than most other cameras. Because Bell and Howell and Eastman Kodak, whose Cine-Kodak Special was also used for combat, had converted to war production, the military was confronted with a camera shortage. Eastman Kodak had discontinued camera production for 1941 and 1942. The Signal Corps urged private owners to sell their equipment.[32]

Lacking a plan for prewar procurement of photographic equipment, subsequent camera shortages forced the Signal Corps to purchase cameras of substandard design.[33] The rapidly multiplying needs of the military for still and motion picture coverage of the war for reconnaissance, training information, and public relations, combined with the resulting raw-stock and camera shortages explain why amateur-cinema magazines and professional magazines shuffled their discourse from aesthetics to combat and the war.

This new articulation connected 16mm technology with guns. The technological and scientific capacities of amateur technology were cultivated rather than proper aesthetic execution and control. A 1938 *American Cinematographer* article demonstrating how a gunstock could replace a tripod perhaps most explicitly reveals the analogy between cameras and guns. With a Leica mounted on a rifle stock, the amateur could procure rock-steady shots.[34] An amateur motion picture aficionado in a 1942 *American Cinematographer* story, "Shooting Action Movies from a Gunstock Mount," even suggested that amateurs attach their Eyemos and Filmos to guns in order to pan more smoothly—like combat "sharpshooters" filming from foxholes.[35] These anecdotes evidence a discursive change from an artistic cinematic consciousness located in the filmmaker to an infatuation with technology as the locus of filmmaking activity. The training of combat photographers and cinematographers even duplicated these metaphorical alliances: Signal Corps training schools taught recruits to simultaneously shoot both cameras and guns, a task most Hollywood cinematographers did not need to master.[36]

Bell and Howell's advertising and marketing departments exploited this influx of amateur and professional filmmaking equipment into the war effort to increase legitimacy for their 16mm substandard equipment. In corporate ads in *American Cinematographer*, *Personal Movies*, newspapers, and other more national magazines, the Filmo and Eyemo performed against an ideal backdrop to foreground their superior manufacturing: World War II combat. The camera itself displaced thought and narrative and bloomed into an aggressive recording instrument that directly experienced the war, foreshadowing the participatory realism that would later surface in actual film imagery. The aesthetic linked with nuclear families perished from the primarily technological determinations of the war.

According to corporate ads Eyemos had "versatility and stamina on the front," "matched the war's lightning pace," were "the camera for men of action," "the aircorps super snooper," and ignored "falls, mud, jars, shocks and vibration." In another ad H. S. "Newsreel" Wong expounded on his preference for an Eyemo, because it was "rugged and always ready for action." These ads presented amateur cameras as possessing memories: "This Eyemo Remembers Pearl Harbor," "Eyemos Are Shooting Japanese," "Eyemo's War Began Years Ago." Passively recording family history in the 1920s and 1930s, Cine-Kodaks now were dubbed "the fighting Cine-Kodaks."[37]

In corporate advertisements for cameras, an ideology of technology replaced the previous discourse on amateur imitation of Hollywood style. These ads bragged that cameras secured images beyond normal human capacity—Japanese, Nazis, planes, classified information. Cameras evolved into thinking machines during World War II. This development not only further naturalized the technology, it also fancied 16mm cameras could supersede, if not improve upon, standard human attributes. Early amateur-film writers had fretted over whether professionalism and capitalism would turn people into machines and stultify them with a technocratic consciousness, but ironically World War II anthropomorphized cameras.

Scientific principles of observation and analysis also articulated the military's use of amateur cameras as empirical instruments: "We make movies of tests when the action involved is too fast, too complicated, or too remote for accurate observation with the human eye," explained a writer in the June 1942 issue of the *Journal of the Society of Motion Picture Engineers*.[38] The 16mm Filmos and 35mm Eyemos measured airplane takeoffs and landings, deciphered propeller problems, followed bombs, performed structural tests on planes, and, after the war, even studied the atomic blasts at Bikini Island with the largest film crew in history.[39] Of course, since the inception of photography, this observational component of film was congruent with scientific agendas. This scientism and elevation of the camera apparatus into an observational tool by the military discursively and practically legitimated the smaller 16mm technology by assigning it a political purpose—victory through technology. When amateur technology entered World War II via the military, capitalist principles of rationality and science reorganized its social relations and usage. The war merely amplified the technological dimensions of 16mm by dissolving its status as a consumer commodity.

Another case of this instrumentalizing of amateur film that dispelled individual, emotional artistry and expedited a less-controlled aesthetic was 16mm interactive training films. With over three hundred theaters, three distribution exchanges, and one thousand feature programs in circulation in both 16mm and 35mm as early as 1932, the Navy was well equipped to screen 16mm training films.[40] Some ships, nicknamed "floating studios," had processing and production facilities. Films of target practices trained gunners and spotters, substituting film for experience and reenacting battles with actuality footage.[41] These simulations scrambled together audience participation, realism, and recreation, much like contemporary computer war games.

In the 1930s the military screened historical war footage for tactical analysis and officers proposed a continuous recording of all divisions in future confrontations.[42] According to the official military history of the Signal Corps, film production was a low priority until World War II. At that time, most combat footage was slated for film updates on the war effort for public exhibition.[43] By 1943 an article in *International Projectionist*, "16mm vs. 35mm Projection in Army Training Camps," reported that the military had already anticipated how a surplus of trained camera operators and 16mm equipment would impact postwar civilian industry.[44]

While the simulations established visual chaos as the norm of realism, other military training films relied on tried and true Hollywood-style production methods—full crews, preproduction planning, scripts, emotional appeal.[45] The *Journal of the Society of Motion Picture Engineers* scrutinized these methods for military purposes. However, the smaller-gauge equipment had increased production efficiency. Carl Preyer, of the A.S.C., in his article "Movies Report on Defense Programs" in a 1943 *American Cinematographer* elaborated on the differences between Hollywood productions and combat filmmaking.

> The technical requirements of such a small production unit is rather confusing to those accustomed to Hollywood standards. The first requirement is absolute mobility, to travel cheaply and quickly under any conditions—plane, auto, boat. . . . Equipment must be reduced to a minimum, both as to camera equipment and lighting equipment for interiors.[46]

These cinematography units shot with Eyemos and Filmos rather than with large, cumbersome studio cameras.

These efficiency requirements of wartime film production extended to camera skills. The military needed a larger number of competent camera operators to record reconnaissance and combat footage and to maintain an effective organization. Skills not only had to be standardized but also interchangeable. In a June 1942 article called "Navy's Use of Motion Picture Films for Training Purposes" in the *Journal of the Society of Motion Picture Engineers*, Walter Exton reasoned that the training of military recruits and Signal Corps cinematographers fulfilled identical functions: "The interchangeability of men is of importance to the efficiency of the fleet."[47] For the smooth coordination and deployment of photography units, camera skills had to be interchangeable, standardized, and homogenized—the same as industrial machinery. This standardization of producers, a form of professionalism, temporarily instigated fluidity between amateurs and professionals, although the military and Hollywood controlled and commandeered it.

Despite their grand claims, newsreel companies did not train the majority of motion picture camera operators in the Army Signal Corps, although some of their younger, former employees may have joined. Hollywood mass-produced military camera operators, expanding its domination as it temporarily created more mobility for amateurs to achieve professional status. The Research Council of the Academy of Motion Picture Arts and Sciences, the American Society of Cinematographers, the International Photographers Local 659 of the International Association of Theatrical and Stage Employees, and technical experts from film-manufacturing companies taught intensive six-week cinematography courses to amateurs enlisted in the Army Signal Corps.[48] Ironically, trainees learned how to shoot in the field from studio exterior experts. These trainees learned only exterior techniques; the instructors bypassed lighting and interior shooting, which was not required for shooting in combat.[49] Perhaps more significantly, the course represented the first time the A.S.C. offered formal cinematography training of any kind. In a June 1942 *American Cinematographer* article, "A.S.C. and the Academy to Train Cameramen for Army Services," the A.S.C. claimed:

> Today, a motion picture section is an integral part of every military unit . . . unfortunately, this country has a great untapped reserve of capable cinematographic talent among *amateurs and semiprofessionals—men who though they may not have made a career out of photography, have yet attained great skill with their 16mm and 8mm cameras.* (Emphasis added)[50]

This assembly-line production of cinematographers was perhaps best exemplified in a 1943 picture of uniformed Marine camera operators in formation on a studio backlot, holding their tripods like guns, facing their Hollywood instructors.[51]

Many A.S.C. members served in the Army Signal Corps.[52] Wartime covers of *American Cinematographer* showed battle scenes being filmed by Hollywood-like crews. Consequently, this new form of realism may have been the residue of insufficient training, 16mm hand-held equipment, and war contingency. "We tried to obtain as much realism as possible, which required the fastest available film. Shooting army locations in wartime prevents the use of lights with the freedom associated with Hollywood," a Hollywood cinematographer named Ray Fernstrom serving in the Army Signal Corps explained in *American Cinematographer*.[53]

The concrete effects of this cinematic training on the technical and aesthetic capacities of recruits in the Army Signal Corps is difficult to ascertain. However, one film preserved from this period demonstrates the complexities of the social relations between recruits, the military, and the cultures in which these draftees were stationed. The film is simply titled "Hawaiian Hula Positions" in the Human Studies Film Archive of the Smithsonian Institution, but its actual title is "The Hula of Old Hawaii."[54] It was photographed in 1943 by George Bacon, an air force camera operator. On the surface, it appears to straightforwardly document various Hawaiian hula dances in medium long shot. Yet these simple im-

ages introduced by raised titles arranged on backgrounds of tropical flowers en-
twine a much more intricate set of social and representational relations.

The boundaries of culture are much more fluid and shifting than the discourse of *American Cinematographer* or *Amateur Movie Makers* would suggest; this
interpenetration between the ideologies of Hollywood, the military and indigenous cultures evidences the dialectical eruption of cinematic training and access to cameras. These cameras and their operators could slide between wartime
coverage during duty and ethnographic filmmaking during their leisure time.
In the hands of military men on leave in Hawaii, perhaps one of America's most
exotic territories, amateur film was cloaked in a more resistant armor, one that
used military privilege to the radical end of preserving native dances on film.
This odd mixture of military skill, ethnographic documentation, and cinematic
romance can perhaps provide some insight into the interstices of the impact of
actual 16mm technology during World War II. The Hula film evidences the visual contours of this training and its use for slightly different goals than military
reconnaissance.

The Human Studies Film Archive collection actually contains two versions
of "Hawaiian Hula Positions." Both films were shot in color, a significant historical feature since the World War II period ushered in the first use of color
film for documentary. John Ford's *Battle of Midway* set this new standard. The
first film is three hundred feet of silent, edited footage. The second film is actually full-documentation footage rather than a completed film, although it does
include intertitles and some cuts from long shot to medium shot of the dancer.
The longer version features a voice-over annotation of an interview conducted
by the staff of the Human Studies Film Archive with George Bacon and his wife,
Pat, who explain the film's history and the nature of the hula dances.

Their comments are extremely significant for this discussion of the intriguing liaison between amateur film and the military during World War II, because they highlight how the minutiae of interpersonal and social practices
constantly interrupt and challenge the domination of seemingly impenetrable
and highly codified discourses. Their annotation also explicates on a micropo-
litical level the complexities of these cultural exchanges between the military
and the "exotic" and between whites' particularly potent imagery of the racial-
ized South Pacific and the urge of indigenous cultures to insulate themselves
from complete homogenization.[55]

Pat Bacon (the former Patience Wiggins, the featured dancer in the film)
explains that native women amused GIs at the USO in Hawaii with their hula
dances. Their entertainment extended to special trips to army and navy bases
to perform these various traditional dances, accompanied by a woman who ex-

plained the meaning of the movements and the story of the dance to the male audience. Pat further interjects that although the film shows only one dancer, this was highly unusual. She comments that Hawaiians always performed these dances in a group, first to the gods, and then to the chiefs.

While the annotation does not mention the reception of these dances by the GIs, it is not difficult to imagine the way in which soldiers stranded in a nearly all-male world would respond to these dancers with a highly charged, eroticized gaze. The context of the dance, then, reconfigured it from community ritual to performance as erotic consumption in this white, military audience. Pat contends that the nature of the dances changed as a result of the economic exchange relations of tourism in Hawaii and the stereotyped notions of natives as spectacle held by tourists. She explains that the dances Bacon filmed represented the revival and perseverance of traditional Hawaiian culture. In effect, this film of these dances opposed the more accessible and showy dances tourists and GIs demanded of Hawaiian dancers, an example of cultural practice blending in and accommodating ill-informed conceptions of the "other."

> These dances were not very popular because the tourists were not interested, so most of the dancers were into the kind of dances that they could be entertained and be paid for [in the background, her husband George disgruntling mutters "Hollywood stuff"]. Nobody would pay to look at a dancer like that.

These filmic representations, then, constitute both a preservation of traditional culture and a backlash against the influx of tourists and GIs to the Hawaiian islands. These were dances outside, on the border, of the trivialization induced by economic exchange. George's offhanded interjection of "Hollywood stuff" is particularly potent. With traditional dances relocated within the horizons of white conceptions of spectacle, the comment evidences George's identification with the dancers, as a fellow traveler rather than as a complete cultural voyeur who repositions religious ritual as erotic enticement. His expression of allegiance with the Hawaiians—through the museum, his subsequent offer of help, his filming of these more traditional, more obscure dances, and his subsequent marriage—interestingly illustrates fluidity and hybridity between various cultural spheres, their constant washing against and modification of each other.

The production history of "Hawaiian Hula Positions" illustrates in microcosm the historical trends of access to 16mm film, training in film technique, and shortages in 16mm raw stock. In this configuration, amateur film moves into a more subversive and even romantic position, an oasis protected from the horrors and losses of war. While traditional dancers journeyed to USOs and various military bases as a traveling show of Hawaiian exotica and romanticism, George inverted this move. He ventured off the base to the Bishop Museum of Anthropology in Honolulu. Bacon recounts that he had shot a training film for the air force that was screened in a course taught by a Dr. Emory. Unfortunately, he does not mention the content of this course nor Dr. Emory's specialty in the annotation. Bacon, grateful for his invited guest lecture and screening at the museum, claims he approached Emory:

> I asked him if there was anything I could do for the museum. He said, "Well, we have this girl here who knows more of the ancient dances than anyone living—we'd like to record it." Well, one thing led to another and I finally married her.

Bacon offered to record these dances. Due to wartime shortages and rationing, the museum was not able to purchase 16mm film. Almost altruistically, Bacon shot the film entirely in one afternoon with a Cine-Kodak Special, the top of the line amateur motion picture camera he no doubt "borrowed" from the military. He used one-hundred-foot rolls and kept the camera on a tripod.

Visually, the film (and the footage included in the one-thousand-foot record) resembles early Lumière films with its static camera and full-body shots. The constructed nature of the filming is revealed in the full-frontal photography and the evidence that the dances are quite literally performed for the camera. It is only through the subsequent annotated voice-over nearly forty years later that we learn the dance for the camera was also an intricate mating ritual mediated by both the camera and the jungle for the camera operator's loving gaze. In this sense, this film suggests a shared and reciprocal gazing, negotiated through two distinct symbolic languages: George Bacon's camera employs the cinematic language of filming in wide shots to record the complete movement of the dance, while the dancer and eventual Mrs. Bacon converses through the gestures and movements of the traditional hula. However, these languages communicate only tangentially and allusively as they graze each other in this jungle: white cameraman armed with amateur technology and Hawaiian woman disarming with movements descended through the centuries.

In the beginning of the film, raised white titles in English on a blue background announce the film: "The Hula of Old Hawaii. Dances by Mrs. Mary Kawaema, Palenu Wiggins, and Pele Pukui." A title marking the dance to follow appears next: "Kaulilua I Ke Anu Waialeale," with the English translation, "Very Cold is Waialeale." This pattern of Hawaiian title, English translation, and dance repeats throughout the entire three hundred feet of the film. The camera pans a luxuriant, densely green jungle of gigantic ferns and palms; in the clearing, a young woman dances in a grass skirt, carefully executing the moves of this hula, while an older woman raps a drum. On occasion, the dancer's eyes dart to the camera. The shot is an extremely long take, without a cut or change in camera angle.

Several dances follow, featuring hulas performed by two young women kneeling on the grass; others with the young women are adorned with leis. The titles specify the hulas: "I Was at Hilo," "The Hill Kalalea" "In Honor of the Turtle God," "Hold Fast to Your Heritage Oh Child," "Let the Sun Rise." The obscured narrative progression of the titles moves from locations, to gods, to an invocation of history, to the hopes for the future, and, perhaps, to the survival of the hula signified in sunrise.

Each dance is photographed with an identical strategy: long takes in long shot, with a continuity cut to a medium shot of long duration, and then a return to the long shot. However, to anoint this editing pattern a narrative strategy would be highly overstated claim, for the film lacks point-of-view shots or any changes in angle that would aid in spectator identification. Indeed, it emits a rather complicated point of view: Is the film itself the point of view of the museum, the dancers, or Bacon's camera? The point of view, then, shifts and is overdetermined by context. Instead, the film "The Hula of Old Hawaii" traces the strain between the codified and controlled language of cinema that Bacon no doubt learned in the military and the pressure to preserve the ancient cultural practice of the hula as a usable ethnographic record.

If this film were not dated and if the annotation were not available, "The Hula of Old Hawaii" would seem remote from the battlefields of Pearl Harbor, the South Pacific, and Japan. Only the color film and the amateur 16mm camera insinuate the United States military's tenancy in Hawaii. The jungle setting occupies multiple discursive positions—positions that resist the presence of the war.

While it resonates as the appropriate mise-en-scène for the ancient hula, the jungle frames the dances as a "pure" cultural practice not contaminated by encroaching white tourists. The lush, green jungle suggests the primordial origins of the hula, yet the performance for the camera alone removes and separates the hulas from the social and tribal relations in which they were danced. The green leaves, grasses, and laserlike sunlight in these shots situate the dancer's cultural geography as unified with nature, but they also represent a rejection of the hula as staged performances for white tourists and GIs. The film's distance from the subject, full-body shots, and long takes of complete dances conform to the observational requirements of ethnographic film. However, the shooting itself was only made possible through the United States military and World War II, which deposited cameras and men on the sandy, seductive shores of Hawaii.

Camera Rattling

What factors explain the association of shaky, moving camera work with realism during World War II? Subjected to the uncontrolled conditions of war, combat field photography redefined realism. The combat film unit performed three military tasks: to aid in saving the lives of men, to expose any technological weakness of the enemy, and to reveal the enemy's war machines.[56] The unit's work was primarily tactical and operational. Using 16mm cameras on B-17s, camera operators were also trained as gunners so that they could "drop their cameras for a gun" if the press of battle demanded it. Otherwise, they were ordered to "shoot to preserve the war."[57]

As early as World War I, simulation gunnery training employed actuality footage. The conflation between cameras and guns strengthened when cameras were inserted on machine gun mounts in bomber planes and operated by pilots.[58] The war also propelled Hollywood camera designers to create 35mm and 16mm hand-held cameras in gun-stock forms with pistol grips—the Cunningham Combat camera with studio-type pilot pin registration movement is an outstanding example.[59] Other technologies were also developed for combat photography: an innovative continuous-step printer could churn out one thousand prints per hour,[60] and camera remote controls (first developed by an amateur) were improved.[61] Remote-control mechanisms for cameras signified the ultimate scientific application of World War II film activity; more efficient technological designs severed thoughtful planning from narrative. In fact, by May 1942 an A.S.C. cinematographer writing in *American Cinematographer* recommended 16mm Filmos over Akeley, Debrie, or studio Mitchell 35mm cameras, because they did not require any setup time.[62] These suggestions were clearly the end result of location field experience. Darryl Zanuck, for example, realized that the massive motion picture crew mounted for the North African invasion was completely overdrawn and inefficient. He reduced crews to one motion picture and one still photographer to increase their mobility.[63]

These lightweight hand-held 16mm and 35mm cameras—more flexible than tripod-mounted 35mm DeVry cameras—bounced, shook, and quivered during turbulence, antiaircraft fire, or fierce combat. James Wong Howe in Howard Hawk's *Airplane* even simulated this turbulence in the interior plane shots by shaking the camera. This "camera rattling," formerly an amateur transgression against Hollywood conventions of unified composition and organization, was reinterpreted as experiential, audience-directed, participatory realism when employed in commercial films. For example, in a 1944 *Journal of the Society of Motion Picture Engineers* article, "Cinematography Goes to War," W. R. McGee lamented:

> I might add that flak (anti-aircraft explosions) is the cameraman's nemesis. Its concussions bounce the ship so that the resulting films are jerky. It's difficult enough to shoot good films from a flying ship with a hand held camera, but when flak enters the picture the hazards are multiplied.
>
> Sometimes these concussions result in a "jump." An excellent example of this appeared in *The Battle of Midway* film. . . . You may recall one scene in which the film jumped an entire frame. This was probably caused by FLAK.[64]

In fact, John Ford's *Battle of Midway* was shot entirely in 16mm with a Filmo by Ford alone, earning him an Academy Award despite, or perhaps due to, the many jumpy shots of explosions.

Personal accounts of combat camera operators in *American Cinematographer* reveal the genesis of this chaotic composition. Camera operators constantly reacted to the battle and the enemy to save their own lives and thereby justified "cinematic mistakes," omissions, and less than stable camera work by vaunting their daring and courage. All these accounts heralded the camera operator's speedy cinematic response to the enemy's advances. They disregarded studio technique. No story or preplanning could survive bullets and bombs; the point was to "capture the enemy on film," to make a record, not a narrative film with emotion appeal. Armed with their compact Eyemos and Filmos, camera operators could instantly spring into action.[65] Small and light, 16mm equipment could be comfortably hand-held under the most severe conditions—an inconceivable activity with larger, 35mm professional cameras. The rigid and disciplined cinematic preconsciousness of aesthetic discourse dictated to amateurs before the war collapsed under combat expediency. The camera, the battle, and the operator were contiguous; split-second responses eclipsed planned and controlled cinematography. Some Hollywood technicians even wondered how to execute these stupendous "special effects." Lieutenant Arthur Arling, U.S.N.R., A.S.C., in his October 1943 *American Cinematographer* piece "Cameramen in Uniform" justified less than perfect camera work:

> The first screening of the 16mm film revealed a very disturbing fault: the violent concussion of the exploding bombs had caused the film to jump out of frame in the camera aperture, but fortunately it regained its normal frame after a few feet. At first the film didn't seem usable, but since no other film of the explosions were to be had we put them in just as they

were and the result, as seen in the public release of *The Battle of Midway* caused considerable comment by several Hollywood technicians who thought we had done this optically just to produce this effect.[66]

World War II altered the cultural position and discourse of amateur film-making: it revised its earlier aesthetic definition to a more technologically located identity. Scientific attributes—observation, analysis, recording, effi-ciency—expelled any lingering notions of composition, artistry, or individual-ism in amateur filmmaking. The scientific use and the small size of cameras and the lack of trained camera operators shooting in combat situations un-locked codes of realism to move toward a more spontaneous, less-controlled style usually reserved for professionals. Although the war opened up possibili-ties for fluidity between amateur- and professional-film technology, style, and producers, Hollywood and the military dominated.

Socialization and Education: 16mm Style as a Paradigm

When you pan or tilt a camera on a tripod, as we do today with the 35mm, it is quite different from panning or tilting by hand. Hand tilting and pan-ning is more sensitive. Such movements are often very important to the story and they should never be obvious as they often are. . . . The more we keep artificial and obvious movements out of the camera in telling a story the less disturbing it is to the audience. The spectator should never be con-scious of the mechanics of a movie. . . . *Jimmy's arguments in favor of the 16mm camera's more natural and realistic documentation of its subject matter is borne out by the vivid combat photography that slashes across the nation's news-reel screens everyday.* (Emphasis added)[67]

This quotation from a postwar article called "The Documentary Technique and Hollywood" by James Wong Howe in a 1944 *American Cinematographer* boldly marks how postwar narrative submerged the more reflexive element of "realistic" camera technique. The effects of the war on 16mm and commercial filmmaking were far-reaching. The widespread usage of this amateur gauge during the war legitimated 16mm through increased standardization and con-tributed to the further professionalization of amateur equipment. It launched a move toward location, rather than studio, shooting; it provided film for the es-tablishment of a war archive for Hollywood studios; and it instituted more re-alistic simulations in narrative style by recuperating combat technique into an invisible, mechanically induced spectatorship.

This postwar period inverted Hollywood's earlier twenty-year contain-ment of amateur film. Narrative film incorporated technologies and style from amateur film. The public exhibition of military combat films during World War II prepared audiences for imagery that simulated experience. Although this adaptation of smaller technologies and hand-held style slightly edged Hollywood style away from pictorialist compositional standards, it contributed little to the legitimacy of amateur filmmaking. Hollywood cinematographers ransacked the more mobile equipment and stylistic innovations of combat cinematography but then encircled them with the dominant structures of Hollywood narrative and technical expertise, consequently professionalizing them. The hand-held style possible with 16mm gear was beyond the reach of amateurs themselves; only Hollywood professionals could "perfect" this more realistic and intimate technique through study, duplication, and even improvement of combat footage. In professional hands, the spontaneous, efficient shooting style, clearly endemic to 16mm, metamorphosized into an expression of professional technical manipulation and control.

Standardization ushered in this co-optation of amateur film; interchangeability expanded access to commercial filmmaking. Before the war, only 16mm film gauge perforations were standardized. Confronted with the military's enormous photographic requirements, 16mm manufacturing accelerated similar to the tooling-up in the radio and electronics industries. To facilitate equipment production and to further standardize filmmaking training, the equipment needed to be as interchangeable as the combat photographers who operated it. Because equipment broke down more easily in wartime situations, standardization of parts was crucial. On 15 December 1943, the Society of Motion Picture Engineers, together with the Signal Corps, the Army Air Force, Army Engineer Corps, and the Navy and Marine Corps, created the War Standards Committee. Experienced motion picture engineers who formerly solved Hollywood technical problems now answered military needs.[68] 16mm was advancing into professional quarters.

This standardization of 16mm opened up the vast educational-film market, an area that Kodak, Bell and Howell, and Victor Animatograph had tried to instigate since the 1920s. Although the history of educational film and 16mm technology provides an intriguing example of the twilight zone of film activity called semiprofessional film, its rich and ideologically complex development extends beyond the scope of the articulations of amateur film explored in this study. Yet this semiprofessional territory—loosely defined as filmmaking that used the substandard 16mm gauge for commercial filmmaking outside of the Hollywood narrative-film market—did, in fact, decenter filmmaking from Hollywood.

The availability of surplus 16mm cameras after the war impelled both experimental and regional filmmaking. Although very few archives have preserved these films taken of family businesses, local parades, and regional industries, such as dairy farming in Wisconsin or ranching in Arizona, Northeast Historic Film, a film archive in Maine, has amassed a wide and impressive collection of these shorts, all produced by residents of the Northeast.[69] Evidencing the diffusion of 16mm, the films document not only family activity but also logging, paper mills, ice cutting, and fishing in Maine and its neighboring states in the Northeast. Lacking spectacle and often narrative, these films are extremely significant, because their regional visual vernacular circumvents the nationalization and homogenization endemic to Hollywood films. These films testify to the political effects of standardization: alternative forms of production and distribution began to sprout around the country.

A more specific example of this postwar regional filmmaking with a more radical and oppositional viewpoint is a 1947 16mm color/sound film called "Hopi Horizons," produced by Mary L. DeGive, Ph.D., and Margaret Cussler, Ph.D.[70] Scripted and photographed by these two white women anthropologists, the film promotes a very antigovernmental, pro-Indian sympathy. As an advocacy film for Hopi autonomy and participation in government planning, "Hopi Horizons" applies a rather standard voice-over narration over medium shots of Hopi daily activities: in school, on their farms, in the desert, making bread, weaving baskets. While the camera evades intimate close-ups, the voice-over exposes a much more urgent political message.

The film opens with traditional Hopi chanting and the narrator proclaims, "Here, for the first time, the Hopi Indians themselves use the new medium of film to speak to the world beyond the reservation." The film does not clarify how the Hopis made the film; the opening credits suggest it was produced by the anthropologists, so this narration may indeed refer to a more collaborative process between filmmaker and informants. Most of the narration conforms to the 1930s elegiac tone of a government-sponsored Pare Lorentz film as it explains the problems of Hopi ranching (less land, fewer sheep), the history of Hopi arts and crafts (we learn one man is a Guggenheim fellow), and the issue of Hopi assimilation into white culture (we see Indian children roller-skating, playing stickball, learning English). The narrator asks, "Should they be educated for the world outside?," as the camera pans Indian teenagers cooking in the pristine, modern kitchen of a home economics class. The narrator delivers some compelling evidence to answer this query. A white teacher believes the Hopi should learn white ways to be able to attend formal dances; there is only one dentist for thousands of miles. The film concludes with a Hopi man's plea, "We Hopi people want to decide our own economic problems, to decide where dams go . . . give us a voice in the plans."

While "Hopi Horizons" is photographed in a very conventional and by this time traditional 1930s New Deal government documentary style, its appearance in this postwar period and its regional and minority content suggest a radically different argument and politics from its more formal documentary ancestors. Not only did the standardization and increased availability of 16mm disperse cameras and producers to these visually underrepresented areas, but it facilitated an alternative distribution for films like "Hopi Horizons." Bypassing 35mm commercial theaters, films such as this could be screened in private homes, churches, museums, and other more local venues, helping to build a new, different, and, at times, even oppositional distribution system.

Hollywood also adapted amateur technology for testing, and as early as 1942 Hollywood studios experimented with 16mm beyond preproduction testing. Because the second processing phase, the reversal Kodacolor process, washed away the larger silver-halide grains, studio special-effects departments saw the advantages this lack of graininess offered for blowing up matted background scenes from military films. In a bomber plane, the 16mm camera operator was positioned for shots that the size and bulk of 35mm equipment would have prohibited. However, special-effects departments warned that these 16mm shots needed to be photographed "with the professional precision" of 35mm, which entailed critically sharp lenses and flat lighting.[71] Attempts were also made to improve the focusing system of 16mm Bolexes by installing a throw-over, ground-glass focusing screen with magnifying system.[72] By 1946 16mm had gone Hollywood. Cinematographers modified cameras by adding focusing systems and shot several features in 16mm for 35mm blowup.[73] The 16mm film cut production costs and reduced grain. However, it remained primarily a production format rather than a distribution medium. Eventually, the expansion of television and advertising and industrial films in the postwar period intensified demand for 16mm.[74]

The Signal Corps application of 16mm also influenced more realistic Hollywood sets. With wartime restrictions of $5,000 worth of new material per picture, many studios moved to location shooting and implemented more documentary rear-screen projection. Set designers and directors hailed this change from elaborate sets to pared-down productions as more "realistic." Maximizing the camera's "suggestive" capabilities, location shooting elevated cinematography to a vital narrative service. Directors craved "down-to-earth" camera work. According to a 1945 *American Cinematographer* article's assessment of postwar narrative films, several contingencies forced cinematographers to eliminate complicated lighting schemes and to light in a flatter style: shooting in actual towns, factories, or battlefields; time constraints; and an impulse to employ documentary style.[75]

This trend toward more realism and authenticity in Hollywood films reached its apex with the formation of the Academy War Film Library in 1945. Collecting 16mm and 35mm battle films culled from various governmental, military, and international sources, this library loaned studios films to aid in

checking the visual accuracy of their representations of war. If the project required actual war footage, the studios obtained rights from the military unit
that had produced the original footage. This combat-footage archive functioned
as a touchstone for the new realistic standard.[76] Films like *Mission to Moscow*,
which intercut large amounts of documentary footage, constructed their entire
narratives around match cuts and point-of-view shots to connect studio scenes
with actuality footage.

While many World War II era Hollywood features were shot on destroyers
or in military camps in cooperation with the United States government, the
most convincing evidence of this 16mm-induced realistic surge into Hollywood
films may surface as the most seemingly trivial: the shaking camera in studio
shots. Howard Hawk's 1943 *Air Force* stands as but one example of a Hollywood
film where this technique creates a more intimate and a more sensory spectator experience. In this film shot by James Wong Howe, virtually all the interior
plane scenes evidence this camera turbulence to simulate the bumpy ride in a
B-17 bomber. When antiaircraft flak escalates, so do these slight camera rattles.
This realistic technique exhibits how 16mm amateur technology and war-con-
tingency shooting seeped into more dominant Hollywood film. Rather than
narrative exposition, these movements induced audience participation in the
represented experience. Hollywood cinematographer James Wong Howe attested:

> In some of the most spectacular explosion shots, say, in bombed ships at
> sea (in *Air Force*), I directed an operator to shake his camera as if from
> concussion, let the actors blur out of focus, and tip the camera sharply as
> the decks tipped high in the air. *This gave the audience a sense of real partici-
> pation—an effect, difficult, even impossible to get with a big camera.* (Emphasis
> added)[77]

Postwar Hollywood film transposed the empirical link between camera and
subject established in and on the battlefields of World War II. While 16mm
equipment immersed spectators into narrative space, the professional means of
production remained even more naturalized, more invisible, and more remote
from the amateur. The standardization of 16mm would eventually allow independent filmmakers in the 1950s limited access to art-house distribution and
limited public exhibition, yet Hollywood cornered these new, hand-held, aesthetic codes of realism. While within the scope of amateur resources, Hollywood positioned hand-held shooting as an advanced and complicated expression of its technical prowess. In the 1950s the position, function, and definition
of amateur film shifted from aesthetics and technology into a social configuration exclusively administrating bourgeois, nuclear-family ideologies.

5

Do-It-Yourself

1950–1962

IN AN 8MM home movie made in Chicago in 1956 with a Revere camera, a young mother in a red-velvet, sleeveless blouse with a cowl neck and a tight-fitting black skirt holds up a naked baby boy to the camera. She seductively, yet innocently, smiles at the camera operator, obviously the proud father. A small square of white cloth drapes the baby's genitalia. The camera tilts up and down between the mother and the baby boy as she displays him to the camera like a religious offering, a prize, a treasure. A few shots later, the baby boy silently sleeps on his back in a wooden bassinet. The camera swirls up and down his body, then glides up to the mother at his side who motions down to the baby with her eyes and her hands. The baby boy is a spectacle of paternity, of patriarchy, of the phallus, of the beginning of family.

Later on in the fifty-foot reel, a two-year-old girl with curly red hair poses with her Christmas toys—dolls, stuffed animals, a rocking horse, a red firetruck—in a green dress with a flouncy petticoat. Buttressed by the kneeling mother's hand and legs behind him, her baby brother is nestled between the girl and the toys, as if he were also a Christmas present. A few jump cuts later, the girl straddles a stuffed horse and pretends to ride it. Her dress rises to reveal her underpants. The mother nervously glances at the camera, then yanks down the dress and resumes her kneeling position among the toys and the children. The camera presents a high-angle shot, clearly from the point of view of the tall father, pointing down at this scene of overflowing family, commodities, and holiday leisure.

The angle of the camera, its mobility, and its control over representation unfurl patriarchal prerogative. The woman and her children are immobilized by the camera, yet blissfully and almost self-reflectively participate in its representation like a game of charades or a pantomime of *Parents Magazine* covers. They all seem to be having fun: the camera explores with moves and pans; the woman and her children look quizzically at the camera and periodically sprout small smiles that give away the ruse. Several more shots ensue: the same Christmas scene repeats with two grandmothers on either side of the frame, removed from the children and mother, trussing the edges of the frame like pillars. The father is absent from all of these images, strung together in jump cuts like shaky, almost volatile, tableaux of family life. Yet the camera imprints his presence and control over the actors. It traces his leisure, his time away from work, his experiments with family and technology.

By the 1950s popular discourse in magazines and instruction books accentuated the social functions of amateur filmmaking as a commodity for use within nuclear families rather than its aesthetics. The relationship between amateur and professional equipment translated into a graduated scale of product lines based on the coordination of price, technical gadgetry, and a simulation of professional gear. With an increase in leisure time and disposable income, amateur-film discourse articulated Hollywood narrative style as a natural, filmmaking version of common sense. It also refracted professionalism into private life as an end in and of itself—a mirror image of the disciplined, skilled, coordinated world of work, enveloped and ameliorated by the leisure activities of the nuclear family. "Togetherness" situated amateur filmmaking as "home movies"—private films as a confined diversion for the home. This domestication of amateur filmmaking as a leisure-time commodity erased any of its social, political, or economic possibilities.

Do-It-Yourself: Economic Boom, Leisure, and Simple Cameras

In the 1950s the photographic and mass-market press located amateur film as a hobby. Yet, unlike the two previous periods of 1897-1923 and 1923-49, this hobby facilitated acquisition of professional technical standards for a price. Although World War II had standardized 16mm film into a semiprofessional medium with limited commercial possibilities, the skyrocketing growth of the postwar leisure market provided a powerful marketing incentive and social context in which to slide amateur-film technology into the home as simply another "do-it-yourself" ideology.

The extraordinary growth of consumer photographic hobbies propelled three distinct technological trends. First, camera companies differentiated product lines to capture a more diverse consumer market. Second, this differentiation instilled an idolatry of Hollywood's and network television's technical wizardry. And ultimately, the vigorous entry of formidable foreign camera manufacturers with their even simpler automatic cameras displaced American firms. Technology, technical control, and expertise marked the shifting boundaries between professional film and amateur film.

America's postwar economy rapidly expanded to gratify consumer demands truncated by World War II shortages. American industry increased its production capacity, spurred in large part by automation developed during the war. With postwar affluence, advertising inducted precise sociological analyses and pointed psychological predictions of market needs, desires, and demographics. Banks extended credit to the middle and lower classes, igniting an economy based on prolific spending rather than on thrift and saving. As Marty Jezer has pointed out in his *Dark Ages: Life in the United States, 1945-1960*, concentration and nationalization of major industries such as beer, oil, and automobiles accelerated. Big business invested in overseas markets and manufacturing plants, conglomerated, and diversified as a direct result of huge profits generated from this excessive consumer spending.[1]

The leisure-and-recreational-goods market swelled at astonishing rates. According to a 1955 *Fortune* magazine study, $30.6 billion was spent on leisure and recreational activities. This figure represented 50 percent of the average consumer clothing and housing expenditures. And it was twice the amount spent on new cars and home goods, a significant shift from the wartime economy of scarcity.[2] Sociological research to pinpoint leisure patterns for more efficient target marketing exploded.[3]

Concrete changes in management and worker relations initiated this rise in leisure: the reduction of the workweek, making the three-night, two-day weekend the norm for a majority of Americans; industry's growing policy of paid vacations to offset worker boredom; increasing reliance on automation; and increases in wages and disposable income.[4] Corporations targeted a substantial amount of this leisure-goods marketing at the suburban nuclear family. A pervasive and somewhat idealized popular ideology, this advertising construct of the family grafted intimacy and togetherness to consumerism. A 1953 *Business Week* essay titled "Leisured Masses" explains:

> Take a serf who works 12 hours a day, seven days a week. What kind of
> life is that? He's a mole. All he needs is some burlap to clothe him, some
> potatoes, a pair of brogans. Now think of a family spending its leisure on
> the beach or gardening. The slave hasn't time to consume anything. The
> family on the beach has time for everything.[5]

As leisure time increased, social and cultural discourses idealized free time and the nuclear family. Cold War politics, the ideology of homogenity, and white-collar worker identification with employers circumscribed the political potential of leisure.[6] Business writers hitched prosperity and leisure to industrial and economic productivity. *Business Week* marveled, "Prosperity has done extraordinary things to our leisure habits. And for this we are in turn indebted to increased productivity—the value of a worker's output in a given time—which has made the prosperity and leisure possible."[7] A 1958 study published in the *Monthly Labor Review* explained that increased productivity and labor union pressure contributed to reducing the workweek to forty hours. Quoting a University of Michigan study, the report optimistically projected a 60 percent rise in real wages and a 40 percent increase in leisure expenditures.[8]

This rapidly expanding leisure market propelled Bell and Howell into a strong position in the photographic market, second only to Kodak. According to a 1956 Arthur D. Little audit of Bell and Howell, the company's net profits more than tripled from 1947 to 1956.[9] Bell and Howell's sales accounted for 36 percent of the entire photographic industry.[10] Like other major corporations, more efficient, streamlined production methods designed for wartime production increased profit margins. Bell and Howell's cumulative wartime-high, net-sales total of $21,930,971 by 1945 fell to $13,238,116 by the end of the 1946-49 period. In 1948 and 1949, due in part to a wartime 25 percent excise tax on all photographic equipment, sales for the entire photographic industry in the United States dropped 40 percent. After this tax was reduced to 10 percent in 1949, sales escalated.[11] From 1949 to 1952, the cumulative net-sales total more than doubled the $13,238,116 of the 1948-49 period, peaking at $28,665,915 by 1952.[12]

Bell and Howell initiated more aggressive marketing based on research surveys of family photographic needs. According to the 1952 Annual Report, only 6 percent of American families owned amateur-movie equipment. Families cited high prices and difficulty in operation as the two greatest inhibitors of camera ownership.[13] By 1952 Bell and Howell had established a record high in sales as a result of these research efforts, a gain of nearly 19 percent over the previous year. Following the nationwide trends toward more efficient and more automated production, Bell and Howell expanded its Chicago camera-manufacturing plant by 26 percent, instituted straight-line production methods, and, through a reorganization of their camera-casting process area, effected a 50 percent reduction in process time.[14] By 1956 general sales had increased 125 percent over 1947, with an 80 percent increase in total photographic-industry shipments.[15]

Bell and Howell's extreme financial success with product diversification tilted its manufacturing emphasis away from professional motion picture equipment toward amateur, educational, and institutional markets.[16] This diversification depended on the development of new product lines and the acquisition of existing firms. The company purchased other firms in the information industry in 1949: the Three Dimension Company, a leading manufacturer of slide projectors; the Burroughs Corporation, a sales and distribution outlet for microfilm equipment; and the DeVry Corporation, the largest supplier of 16mm sound projectors to the military.[17] By 1956 professional motion picture equipment represented less than 3 percent of Bell and Howell's total company sales, with amateur 8mm and 16mm cameras constituting 27 percent of total sales. Sound projectors garnered 22 percent of all sales and military products 18 percent. Military, industrial, and educational equipment comprised 73 percent of all sales.[18] Military products accounted for the largest growth. The production of military items had beneficial consequences for Bell and Howell. With the development of the space program in the late 1950s, the company emerged as a prime contractor for space instrumentation.

Many camera companies in this postwar period actively positioned 16mm as a semiprofessional medium for educational and industrial films; they remolded 16mm as top-of-the-line semiprofessional equipment and 8mm as amateur. For example, the number of projectors in schools increased by more than tenfold after World War II.[19] This educational market spread like wildfire, accounting for the professionalization of amateur 16mm equipment. By 1955 the nonluxury markets of business, science, industry, government, and education constituted 61 percent of all camera sales, according to a Bell and Howell press release issued that same year.[20]

This diversification was most pronounced in new product lines for amateur motion pictures. Many writers attributed the evolution from spectator sports to individual recreation to the restoration and resurgence of the importance of the family unit. Historian Richard Pollenberg contends in *One Nation Divisible* that this fetishization of the family was largely based on enormous population shifts away from more public, communal, ethnic urban living patterns to isolated, homebound suburban living.[21] For example, Bell and Howell's 1954 Annual Report noted that the rising birthrate and the increase in travel indicated major increases for the family photography market.[22]

Business Week noted that $1.5 billion were spent on spectator sports in 1952, compared with $8.4 billion spent on individual recreation.[23] Americans spent nearly eight times more money on private and individualized creative activities than on more public and community-oriented ones. In his famous 1957 essay "The Suburban Sadness" David Reisman described how this decentralization of leisure pivoted on the suburban-family home. The home, rather than the neighborhood, was the focus of leisure and fun. Reisman attributed the homogeneity of suburban living to this diminished contact with differentiated people. Yet he also noted that this increase in leisure expressed a rather neutralized rebellion against the increasing workplace automation and the resulting paucity of meaningful work.[24] Consumption compensated for lack of control and creativity at work.

Similarly, the rise of home ownership, largely as the result of easy credit and mortgages (nearly 55 percent of all Americans owned their own homes in 1955, compared to 40 percent in 1946), precipitated what the United States Department of Commerce dubbed the "do-it-yourself" movement—young suburbanites lavishing time and money on home improvement.[25] This do-it-yourself cultural discourse idealized the home and nuclear family as more "creative" labor sites. Even a 1954 article in *Fortune* observed that most Americans preferred "active fun" to onlooking.[26]

Bell and Howell responded to the expansion of working and middle-class leisure markets and the cultural fascination with meaningful hobbies by diversifying its amateur-movie cameras. This equipment stratification targeting specific income groups changed Bell and Howell's corporate profile. Previously identified with the relatively small, professional cameras and upper-class amateur luxury cameras, the company transformed into a formidable presence in the mass marketing of amateur equipment. Although Bell and Howell depended on the growth of the luxury camera market, which hinged on high levels of disposable income, its diversification provided a hedge against sudden economic downturns in amateur photography and cinematography.[27]

Bell and Howell amateur motion picture equipment had occupied the enviable position of a top-of-the-line item for a wealthy clientele. By the late 1940s the company had initiated a powerful marketing strategy of "trading down"—producing less-expensive lines of goods to attract a lower-income market. Between 1947 and 1954, demand for 16mm equipment decreased as lower-priced and more competitive 8mm equipment, many from foreign manufacturers, captured a larger share of the amateur-cinematography market. Camera shipments increased 45 percent, evidencing the market effectiveness of this diversification scheme.[28] Lower-priced 8mm cameras, reintroduced by both Kodak and Bell and Howell in 1952, substantially widened the market for amateur-movie equipment. The 8mm equipment was simpler to operate and much cheaper. From 1947 to 1954 8mm camera sales increased by 62 percent, while 16mm camera sales decreased by 43 percent.[29] Ultimately, 8mm developed into the new substandard gauge for families.

Bell and Howell's main competitors in the amateur motion picture market were Kodak, Revere, Keystone, and Bolex—a Swiss camera manufacturer.[30] All of these companies offered an extensive line of amateur cameras from a full range of 16mm cameras to technically simplified and cheaper 8mm cameras. Elaborated in corporate ads, the ideological and technical contours of "trading down" map how amateur-movie technology was designed for hobby rather than commercially competitive usage.

Manufacturers differentiated amateur cameras according to how much technical skill, expertise, and manipulation their operation required. The amateur-consumer market, then, was divided according to technical classifications of skill. This stratification by film producers manifested the social inscription of professionalization; hierarchies based on consumption of technically complicated machines like 16mm translated to hierarchies of class in the workplace. The more professional an amateur was, the more the equipment appropriated the professional technical standards, format, and technical control of 16mm film. The Revere Company specialized in 8mm. Its most expensive camera, the Revere 84, used three lenses and retailed for $122.50. Its least-expensive camera, the Revere 50, featured drop-in loading and cost $49.50, less than 50 percent of the Revere 84.[31] In comparison, the Bell and Howell 70DL sold for $365.00. Its ad copy proclaimed, "The cameraman's 16 and the choice of advanced amateurs and professionals." Bell and Howell's magazine-load 16mm cameras cost only $174.00, with its 8mm inexpensively priced according to market fluctuations.[32] Kodak's cameras, on the other hand, spanned a broad price range: $898.00 for the Cine-Kodak Special—capable of dissolves and multiple exposures—to $192.50 for magazine-load 16mm, to $47.50 for the Brownie 8mm.[33]

Most manufacturers differentiated amateur cameras through film-gauge reductions and technological simplification. The cheaper the camera, the less control over image production. The top-of-the-line cameras simulated professionalism—they required technical control. The bottom-of-the-line cameras were consummately amateur—they were technically simple. Corporate advertising in photography magazines identified the top-of-the-line luxury cameras like the Bell and Howell Filmo 70DL and the Cine-Kodak Special as professional cameras, because they had more controls than 8mm models. Shooting standard 16mm roll film, the Filmo 70DL and Cine-Kodak Special required hand threading rather than a preloaded cartridge magazine. As camera price declined, simple operation replaced technical control. The distinctions between professional and amateur filmmaking equipment resided in the degree of technical control over exposure, focusing, and effects. Manipulation of technology, higher cost, and technical complexity denoted professionalism, and conversely, ease of operation, lower cost, and simplicity defined amateurism.

As ability improved, consumers could "trade up" to a higher status by purchasing more expensive and complicated equipment. On the social and ideological level, this hierarchy of camera designs positioned filmmaking expertise as a passport to further professionalization of leisure usage with more and more expensive equipment and gadgets. The Revere 50, the Bell and Howell 172B, and the Kodak Brownie 8mm functioned as training cameras; they eased the amateur moviemaker into film technology and aesthetics. The demarcation between professional and amateur here was almost exclusively financial, if not illusory: consumers could possess the trappings of professionalism through purchasing an expensive camera. Although manufacturers designed these camera lines to lure the disposable income of the middle and working classes, this diversification also instituted a technological class structure defined by cost, technical control, and film gauge. Note Bell and Howell's description of the Filmo 70DL in an August 1953 *Photography* ad:

> Precision equipment . . . worthy of your experience. This is the 16mm camera that will take you just as far as you can go in photography. . . . These . . . innumerable built-in features . . . make the 70 the master of all 16mm cameras.[34]

Professional standards of technical control and manipulation also filtered into amateur cameras with the mimicking of Hollywood special effects. The advent of television and the postwar decline in movie attendance emboldened Hollywood to change its marketing emphasis from a belief that good pictures would attract audiences to a conviction that modern audiences desired technical novelties.[35] Hollywood experimented briefly with 3-D movies in 1952.[36] In 1953 Bolex introduced a camera that could make 3-D movies as well. In 1953 Twentieth Century Fox unveiled a wide-screen process called CinemaScope that produced an image wider than the usual 35mm aspect ratio.[37] Two years later both Bell and Howell and Vitascope introduced wide-screen apparatuses with anamorphic lenses to produce an image three times as wide as it was high. Bell and Howell's Filmorama sold for $760, while the Dutch-manufactured Vitascope sold for $125. These amateur wide-screen imitations resembled and evoked the dimensions of CinemaScope. A 1955 *Popular Science* article on wide screen explained, "You get the sense of three dimension."[38]

By the late 1950s the amateur could re-create television aesthetics at home with zoom lenses. A 1962 *Popular Photography* advertisement for DeJur cameras proclaimed that even the lowly amateur could obtain "professional style pans" and "television style zooms."[39] Amateur-film technology and its array of special attachments squeezed hobby production into a rehash of technical spectacles. This trend framed amateur cameras as do-it-yourself gadgets and sophisticated technical toys reminiscent of the period 1897–1923.

The infusion of foreign-made cameras demonstrated the effectiveness of this ideology of professionalism in attracting consumers. The definition of amateur film assumed an even more technical character. In response to foreign competition, camera operation became increasingly more simple. This hierarchy

based on technical control eventually dissolved into a spontaneous form of amateurism, because it required minimal technical manipulation and control. Increased automation of amateur cameras also eased its way into the homes of
nuclear families.

From 1950 to 1955 Bell and Howell's principal competition came from
Bolex, holding an 80 percent market share of all amateur-movie camera and
equipment imports. German amateur-camera manufacturers' export volume
also increased tenfold.[40] According to a specially commissioned Bell and Howell
study, European income levels did not sustain a broad-based market for luxury
leisure items.[41] These European demographics had two important effects on
amateur-film technology. First, they created an incentive for German and Swiss
manufacturers to export. Second, because the European amateur market was
primarily tooled up for upper-class markets with disposable leisure incomes,
their cameras appealed to the advanced amateur and semiprofessional. Unlike
American mass-produced amateur cameras, imported models were assembled
by hand. Their finish, precision, and craftspersonship—traditional attributes of
professional cameras—contributed to their mechanical excellence.

However, Bell and Howell and Kodak dominated mass-distribution channels in the United States. Their long, successful history of retail distribution
outflanked the more specialized foreign competition until the late fifties. Prod-
ded by the expanding leisure-goods market and the emergence of outlying suburban shopping centers, Bell and Howell gradually redirected its camera distribution from major metropolitan specialized photo dealers toward more general
retail trade in photo departments of national retail stores such as Sears, Roebuck
and Company and Montgomery Ward.[42] Specialty stores carried advanced amateur cameras in declining downtown areas; market retail chains that captured
the largest volume of suburban leisure dollars sold lower-priced lines.

Bell and Howell's reorientation toward outlying malls reflected the national
trend toward the suburbanization of retail trade in the 1950s, where suburban
stores recorded higher profits than central-city shops.[43] Unlike its foreign competition, Bell and Howell was able to distribute its diversified, traded-down
camera lines through mass-market retail channels located in the areas of the
most dramatic demographic expansion—the suburbs.

Despite this retailing strategy, foreign-import amateur cameras undercut
Bell and Howell and Kodak by the late fifties: their lower prices, increased automation of filmmaking technology, and greater ease of operation outdistanced
American cameras.[44] In 1959 foreign-camera sales in the United States increased
by 5 percent in one year.[45] This influx of foreign-made amateur cameras rode
the tide of an economic upturn in the photographic market. By 1961 researchers
estimated the photographic-goods leisure market at $700 million per year.[46] Be-
tween 1950 and 1958 the amateur-photo market exploded by 112.5 percent; 8mm

film camera use swelled by 41 percent; and 8mm camera shipments increased by 201 percent.[47] Japanese automatic cameras secured a large share of this exponential growth of the photographic market. In response, Bell and Howell once again switched its manufacturing emphasis from technical control to semiautomatic devices: the remote-control Explorer slide projector; the three-lens, turret, electric-eye Perpetua 8mm camera; the self-threading, auto-load projector; and the Infallible electric-eye still camera.[48]

By 1961 amateur-camera sales accounted for less than 50 percent of Bell and Howell's total sales. To offset this drop, the company diversified into microfilm and the expanding audio-visual educational market to cushion against declining amateur-movie camera sales.[49] The company also initiated a number of offshore licensing agreements to take advantage of lower labor costs in other countries, most notably with the J. Arthur Rank Organization in England. To neutralize their losses, Bell and Howell acquired a 49 percent equity of Japan Cine Equipment Manufacturing Company (formerly a wholly owned subsidiary of J. Osawa and Company Limited, a Japanese distributor of Bell and Howell products) to compete in the Japanese retail market.[50] This plan achieved limited financial success however. Foreign competition drove Bell and Howell to produce more automatic and less mechanically controllable amateur cameras and pushed the company more and more into international manufacturing. It also stimulated Bell and Howell's diversification into the lucrative and growing business-information market. The entry of Japanese manufacturers with even more mass-produced, automated 8mm cameras terminated American domination over the manufacture and marketing of amateur-film technology. The limited technical capacities of these cameras abolished any fluidity between amateurs and professionals. Bell and Howell disengaged from the amateur-camera market in 1962.

The expanding leisure market, the do-it-yourself movement, product differentiation based on technical control, increased automation, and the substandard gauge of 8mm assigned amateur filmmaking to the home. These discourses and practices impeded amateur access into other more significant forms of media production. Technology masqueraded as a route to professionalism and creative labor, yet it only marginalized amateur filmmaking as an innocuous, frivolous hobby.

Hollywood, Home Movies, and Common Sense: Aesthetic Control

She: And just who is it in this family that handles the camera like a garden hose?
He: Don't interrupt, please.[51]

This exchange between a husband and wife amateur movie-making team registers common motifs of family-oriented amateur filmmaking in a circa 1950 Kodak home-movie instruction manual entitled *How to Make Good Movies*. It also insinuates how amateur-movie practice slipped into the interstices of the 1950s nuclear family and was christened home movies—private movie production of and by the nuclear family.

By the 1950s photography and family-magazine writers inscribed technical manipulation and a slavish conformity to Hollywood narrative visual logic as the goal of amateur production. Hollywood style, as a natural and innate form of common sense, inoculated home movies, protecting them from chaos. Just as suburban golfers practiced drives and putts to lower their scores, family filmmaking continually veered toward the illusory adoption of Hollywood professional expertise. Amateur filmmaking's vestigial articulation of residual craft, implying total control over production, transformed into practice sessions for the dedicated cultivation of the visual grammar and story-telling logic of Hollywood. Subject choice, style, continuity, editing, audience reaction, and theories of film aesthetics homogenized amateur film, dissipating cultural diversity. Industrial norms of control, skill, and expertise standardized and managed private life.

With labor increasingly less diverse and creative and the workplace more organized and fragmented, David Reisman observed that leisure had surrendered its creative, emancipatory potential and its role as an integrator of communities. In an important 1950 essay called "Leisure and Work in a Post-Industrial Society," Reisman defined leisure as the site where workers could satiate untapped creative energies. However, Reisman also cynically recognized the futility of this claim; efficiency and boredom had permanently ruptured the delicate equilibrium between work and leisure. Reisman's conclusions evidence the class dimensions of leisure: the more professional, executive-level, higher-educated groups engaged more actively in leisure-time technology than less highly educated or working-class people.[52] Home-movie demographics support this contention. This new, class-bound articulation of leisure manifested itself in amateur-film production. As an essentially private activity cloistered in the home, home movies propagated the value of proficient skill rather than community interaction.

The familialist ideology camouflaged the private sphere's adoption of workplace values. Familialism describes the transference of the idea of the integrated family unit as a logical social structure onto other activities. Familialism, then, delineates how other social, cultural, or aesthetic formations organize in family patterns. The popular discourse on home movies expressed familialism by mixing professionalism with emotion and family ties.

In this context, children constituted one of the most pervasive amateur-film subjects. With earlier marriages, increased birthrates, and a decline in the number of single people, the statistical presence of nuclear families rose. As the family shed its productivity in the industrial economy and was retooled as a consumption unit, the role of the family increasingly concentrated on "production" (and reproduction) of children. A tertiary ideology sprung forth: families and children, like hobbies, were ends in themselves. In one study, 81 percent of all respondents named a better environment for their children as the main incentive for moves to the suburbs.[53] Movies chronicled children as a visual homage to familialism. Roy Pinney's 1956 *Parents Magazine* article "Tell a Story with Your Movie Camera" subscribes to this position:

> You'll find that material for a motion picture abounds in everything a child does from the time he first opens his eyes until the reluctant lids close. . . . You have material aplenty for an interesting storytelling sequence.[54]

As further demonstration of the cultural potency of familialism, discussion on amateur film not only appeared in cinematography magazines for amateurs and general photography magazines but also was published in family-oriented magazines like *Better Homes and Gardens, House and Garden,* and *Parents Magazine.*

Bell and Howell's internal marketing studies confirmed that photographing children compelled families to purchase amateur-film equipment; typical consumers who had one or two children at the time of purchase shot movies most frequently.[55] Amateur-cinematography production reinforced the patriarchal character of nuclear families. The father produced twice as many movies as the mother, according to a company report issued in 1961.[56]

Magazine writers also suggested family-travel films. The travel industry expanded after World War II, aided by the shorter workweek, paid vacations, the availability (for white, middle-class people) of easy credit to purchase cars, and the development of the superhighway system that effectively obliterated mass transit.[57] In 1956 the auto and highway industry lobbied Congress for passage of a federal law authorizing the construction of the 41,000-mile interstate highway system. Abundant, cheap gasoline further supported the production of large cars and long car trips.[58] These economic factors contributed to an increased emphasis on amateur travel films to document a family's affluence. In his book *The Tourist: A New Theory of the Leisure Class,* Dean MacCannell observes modern society's lust for expanding and accumulating experiences. Tourism manifests this overconsumption of diverse knowledge by the white middle class.[59] The differentiation of experience and scenery offered by car travel in the

United States offset the homogenizing of suburban life through rigid socialization and standardization. In 1951 an *American Photographer* column title "You
Need a Plan for Your Movies" outlined a plan for superb travel movies:

> Naturally, one of the delights of any trip is the unexpected. These shots
> will have to be included, but they will be more easily edited into a smooth
> film if they fit into a general framework planned ahead of time.[60]

Esther Cooke of *Popular Photography* also feared that the chaos of the open
road would sabotage continuity and comprehension in home movies. She advocated that mothers, who she reasoned had more spare time than overworked
fathers, busy themselves with preproduction research, planning, and plotting.[61]
A shooting script offered in Kodak's *How to Make Good Movies* exemplified this
obsession with continuity for travel films.[62] A section on vacation films asserted
that the narrative fulcrum of travel films depended on a buildup from work, the
anticipation of the vacation through fantasy, and the visual payoff of interesting
scenery and unexpected family interactions on the trip. Narrative and planning
thwarted travel films from reaching beyond the boundaries of leisure as a potent
antidote to worker boredom.

Composition also betrayed the discursive rivalry between control and mobile camera work. Photography magazines aligned less-controlled hand-held
shooting with "intimate" film production. A hierarchical dispersion eventually
blunted these antagonistic strategies. Writers assigned compositional stability
to amateurs while they marveled at camera mobility in professional cinema
verité films. Articles in *Popular Photography*, for example, preached tripods, no
panning, details, and close-ups.[63] Naturalism and uninhibited action manipulated spontaneity, viewed as the more accurate record of family activities and
emotions. The following directives published in a 1960 *Better Homes and Gardens*
article, "Shooting Script for Christmas Time Home Movies," chart the techniques of this controlled realism.

1. Shine the lights in the direction of the subject for several seconds before actually beginning to shoot the scene.
2. Don't encourage your subjects to look at the camera. They will look
   much more natural if they simply continue to do what they were doing before you started to shoot.
3. Grown-ups will be much less self-conscious if they are engaged in
   some activity with a child while you are shooting.[64]

Photography magazines also counseled the amateur in special effects. The
mystification of Hollywood-like special effects enlivened "spontaneous" footage

and intrigued audiences. While these apparatuses opened up markets for film-making accessories, they also fostered an idea of trading up to technology that included mechanisms for rewinding, split frames, frost, and soft-focus gels.[65] Spontaneous filming—whether through a static camera or special effects—controlled, overpowered, and manipulated the subject. Amateur special effects distorted professional filmmaking through an imitation of technical control.

However, during the late fifties and early sixties, moving-camera documentary-production methods focused this contradiction between the stability of tripods and the flexibility of lightweight equipment. In this provocative aesthetic, subject and camera movement probed unscripted "real life." This catalytic style directly challenged almost thirty years of amateur filmmaking aesthetics; controversy spilled over the pages of amateur-photography journals. To position the audience as an active participant rather than as a passive spectator, the moving camera swerved into intimacy with subjects. The camera metaphorically and visually metamorphosized into a spontaneous participant, gradually shedding its obtrusive, objective technological demeanor through a disguise of human characteristics. A 1954 *Photography* article titled "Ringlight Your Next Party Film" illustrates this more relaxed, participatory cinematography:

> Hand-hold your movie camera so that you can move around quickly. Move in for close-ups, out for wide shots.
> Don't direct attention to yourself by asking a subject to do something. If you missed an interesting bit, relax and catch it the next time it comes up. Remember you are out to catch real life movement, not direct a fictional movie.[66]

Although articles promoting this rather radical style did not represent the norm in the fifties, the camera was not left unchallenged. By 1962 this argument for the moving camera accrued additional credibility and legitimacy through the television distribution of independently produced cinema verité films. Moving-camera advocates coached amateurs to use their bodies like crab dollies and to always shoot with a wide-angle lens. A 1962 *Popular Photography* article, "Liberate Your Camera," converted the camera into a body appendage: "I think of the camera as my 'eye.' Once it starts rolling, the camera is part of me . . . I *see* with it."[67] The fluidity of the moving camera disengaged narrative conventions, point of view, and spectator passivity, according to advocates like Ed Corley:

> "Why Move?" If you want to look at the world through a rectangular window, the passive camera is fine. But if you want to escort your audience *through* that window, your camera must join in the life outside its encasement.[68]

To unleash the camera from the tyranny of the tripod, the amateur filmmaker was first required to unpack the narrative sequences of the event. The camera then attempted to duplicate its emotional and phenomenological dimensions through sensory simulation.

Contradicting this moving-camera aesthetic, writers continually and pervasively stamped narrative continuity as logical common sense. The characters in *How to Make Good Movies* responded to continuity with an almost religious fervor:

> She: This is the chapter I've been waiting for.
> He: Right! I've a feeling that this continuity idea is going to be good for our souls.[69]

This emphasis on Hollywood-continuity style dominated and restricted amateur-film aesthetic discourse; it naturalized its own codes and reined in the flexibility and spontaneity inherent in lightweight equipment. In a 1953 *Photography* article, "Three C's for Movie Makers," writer James Dobyns agitated for narrative order as the penultimate amateur goal:

> A movie attempts to create the illusion of reality. In real life the things we see during the course of a day bear a definite relationship to one another. . . .
>   If we were to describe the day's events to someone, the recital would be a narrative of what we saw and heard and recorded with our senses.[70]

Photography magazines revealed that conventional Hollywood-narrative rules—the relationships of shots to one another in a sequential and thematic order—were essential for complete audience enjoyment. This vociferous advocacy of narrative style for amateur filmmakers colonized reception; the private exhibition of these home movies copied the etiquette and structure of more commercial theater attendance. Any form of running commentary from the filmmaker transgressed the hallowed privacy of the audience, whose cinematic pleasure was derived from a quiet, individual immersion into the logic of conventional continuity. These polite techniques erased the producer—style overrode content. These formal conventions of narrative composed a cinematic Esperanto of universal truths accessible to the lowest level of spectator comprehension. In his 1952 *American Photography* article "Let's Make Movies" Carlyle Trevelyan pronounced: "How it is filmed is even more important than what is filmed."[71] A 1955 *Parents Magazine* piece, "Better Home Movies," stressed that "in our lexicon a mediocre movie is one that only your family can enjoy. A good movie can entertain an audience that doesn't know the actors."[72] This logic of continuity inflated from a technical and visual aspect of a Hollywood technique to an almost metaphysical expression of the natural as narrative grammar. In 1953 Roy Creveling expounded in *Photography*:

> Actually, motion picture technique, in spite of its high sounding name and Hollywood parentage, is little more than the application of *good common sense*. Anyone can apply it, once he is aware of its importance to the enjoyment of his films by others. (Emphasis added)[73]

Narrative organization and common sense united to stave off chaos, confusion, and incomprehensibility.

With narrative continuity underpinning all filmic organization, popular photography magazines strategically positioned editing as the scalpel to surgically repair haphazard and confusing amateur shooting to narrative norms. Editing could be performed indoors during inclement weather. From a marketing viewpoint, editing reconstituted home movie-making as less of a summertime seasonal activity and as more of a wintertime, bench-type hobby. While editing rejuvenated home movies with coherence, the underlying goal of editing was, according to Carlyle Trevelyan in a 1952 *American Photography* article, to produce a "logical, smooth, understandable flow of the actions and situations."[74] Articles elaborated shooting methods such as titling or shooting a person flipping through a book of snapshots—all of which could be completed indoors and out of narrative sequence.[75] When inexpensive sound recording became available to the amateur market in the midfifties, some amateur columnists redeemed audio tracks as yet a further extension of narrative continuity. A family could narrate the images and further integrate and control the action.[76]

Perhaps the most unusual articulation of this editing cult was the enterprise of Ralph Eno. His story provides a good example of how editing enhanced home-movie aesthetics. Eno, president of the Metropolitan Motion Picture Club, ran a home-movie editing service, described at great length in a 1956 *American Mercury* magazine. For a fee, Eno would "transform the jumble of unconnected frames into a coherent and interesting story of a family's life" and would even offer pretrip continuity consultations.[77] Of course, Eno's service was no doubt mainly utilized by an upper-class clientele. These edicts on editing injected Hollywood-narrative technique into home movies.

Ideologies of the nuclear family and Hollywood continuity did not totally eclipse the possibilities of amateur equipment. By the midfifties television camera operators covered news stories with Bell and Howell Filmo 70DLs, available to both amateurs and professionals. With access to television, amateurs had the remote possibility and opportunity to become quasi professionals. Amateurs selling news footage were encouraged to cultivate local television stations and to follow breaking community stories. In a 1955 *Popular Photography* article, "Cover Your Town for TV," Chester Burger advised:

> What they [the stations] need are stories which their own cameramen haven't covered. . . . This is where you come in. Your best chance of shooting saleable stories comes when you shoot what you know best—your own community, when things are happening, in the early stages before they reach their climax.[78]

Burger instructed potential amateur news cinematographers to avoid panning. News directors would deem the footage unusable and reject it.[79] It is nearly impossible to precisely document the success rate of amateur news footage sales to television stations. However, articles on strategies for selling footage are extremely significant, because they broadened amateur territory.

The standardization and availability of 16mm amateur filmmaking equipment contributed to the emergence of what experimental-film historians have termed the second avant-garde in the postwar period from 1945 to 1954 and in its continuation in art filmmaking through the late 1950s. The appearance of discussions of more experimental filmmaking practice directed to amateurs presents a rather fragmentary, but nonetheless important, rupture into the dominant aesthetic discourse of narrative and engenders the cultural association of amateurism with art as an oasis from capitalism.

Historians of this second wave of American avant-garde filmmaking attribute the production of these films by filmmakers like Maya Deren, Marie Menken, Gregory Markopooulos, Kenneth Anger, James Broughton, and John Whitney to the availability of 16mm amateur cameras in the consumer market, which significantly lowered the cost of producing films.[80] Historian Robert Sklar has noted that a surplus of 16mm camera equipment following World War II increased its availability to these filmmakers.[81] During the early wave of American avant-garde filmmaking in the late 1920s, most filmmakers worked in the more expensive and cumbersome 35mm format. By the 1950s both amateurs and the avant-garde employed the 16mm technology. Although a wide range of cameras with graduated technical features were offered, the less-expensive 8mm occupied a large market share. The context of the semiprofessional film market, the fact that these filmmakers shot for 16mm educational and industrial films, may better explain the production and distribution of experimental 16mm work. The growth of 16mm educational films and the influx of 16mm projectors in schools and universities aided the distribution of these films on the college circuit.

Popular photography and literary magazines translated the filmmaking work of these avant-gardists to amateurs as a representation of freedom and creativity. However, family magazines (e.g., *Better Homes and Gardens, House Beautiful,* or *Parents Magazine*) did not publish these rebellions against Hollywood narrative. These pieces appeared in photography magazines emphasizing technical sophistication and in literary magazines cultivating artistic appreciation—discourses resurfacing from the nineteenth century.

While amateur-movie writers in more mainstream venues instructed home moviemakers to reject content for formal imitation, photography and literary writers reversed the formula. They agitated for content over proper composition and valued form for its own plasticity rather than for its narrative exposition. Their call was not lost on amateurs. Maya Deren even wrote an article for the *First Popular Photography Movie Making Annual.* She asserted that the most important part of filmmaking equipment was the "mobile body" and an "imaginative mind"[82] rather than a static camera on a tripod, a mind rigidified with rules of continuity or technical gadgetry.

Filmmaker Maya Deren's writings on amateur film evoke some of the philosophical contours of amateur film. Her writings constitute some of the only advocacy for amateur film in both popular photography magazines and in specialty publications geared toward experimental filmmakers. In a series of short articles and addresses published over a fifteen-year span from the mid-1940s to the late 1950s, Deren proclaimed the unique status of amateur filmmakers. Deren viewed the amateur filmmaker as democratic, as intervening into the professionalization of a film industry dependent upon the division of labor, standardization, and large amounts of capital for production.

P. Adams Sitney in *Visionary Film: The American Avant-Garde, 1943–1978* views Deren as an apologist and propagandist for the avant-garde.[83] Sitney discerns that Deren emphasized realism over artifice, an integrated artistic vision combating scientific fragmentation and a rejection of all forms of cinema inhibiting imagination.[84] In *Experimental Cinema* David Curtis asserts that Deren's 1946 monograph *An Anagram of Ideas on Art Form and Film* was one of the "most complete statements by any film artist of their total position" until Stan Brakhage's 1963 publication of *Metaphors on Vision.*[85] Within the discourse of cinema, the terms *avant-garde* and *amateur* often collapse into each other, with *amateur* connoting creative freedom.

In an essay called "Planning by Eye: Notes on 'Individual' and 'Industrial' Film," Deren advanced the idea that commercial filmmaking form is not innovative because of a division of production into specialists: "They have been most carefully standardized in order, precisely, to insure a certain type of product. They have been carefully checked and rechecked to eliminate any risk of deviation."[86] Because the commercial-film industry commanded tremendous resources, Deren warned amateur filmmakers not to imitate it. Instead, she urged amateurs to exploit their minimal budgets through exploration, experimentation, and risk taking.[87]

In a pointed essay entitled "Amateur versus Professional," Deren developed this opposition. The freedom the amateur achieves, according to Deren, is both artistic and physical: artistic freedom results from private financing, and physical freedom is prompted by the portability of equipment, lack of trained actors, and location shooting. Of course, the expense of even low-cost amateur gear could be a prohibitive luxury, available only to middle- and upper-middle-class consumers. Deren postulated a definition of amateur film embodying two separate economic relationships: first, as individual artisanal work is removed from market relations, amateur filmmaking is peripheral to the social hierarchy of specialization. Second, its privatized, marginalized status preserves the mythicized ideals of democracy—risk, freedom, participation, personally meaningful work—ideas no longer expedient in more rationalized work situations.[88]

From the late 1940s through the late 1950s, literary and art magazines such as the *Saturday Review, Magazine of Art*, and *Theatre Arts* published two categories of articles on experimental films: glowing reviews of more conventional films on artists and dance for home consumption and energetic essays on abstract film as a new and vibrant art form. In general, these magazines cultivated middle-class appreciation of the high arts of literature, painting, and theater. They nostalgically and naively amalgamated noncommercialism with art. These magazine articles discussed the amateur 16mm gauge in two distinct ways. First, they queried home distribution for films on art. This discourse articulated a view of art films as consumer edification, repeating the exportation of the effect of classical plays on the working class and children in the early stages of the amateur-theater movement. Second, they cast experimental filmmakers as the pinnacle of noncommercialism, because they deployed art to stretch the limits of film representation. This discourse on experimental art recapitulated distinctions between artistic amateurs and hobbyists and constructed art as an amateur domain.

These art-film reviews for home consumption appeared in *Theater Arts, Saturday Review, Magazine of Art*, and the *Nation*. In general, they functioned as consumer guides to uplifting films pictorializing such diverse topics as Renaissance painting, Jackson Pollock, or dance. Most of these articles promoted the suitability of theme films for home projection. They highlighted particularly "artistic" films that could educate the consumer in the traditional art forms of painting, music, or dance.[89] Although these high-art educational films did not explore innovative visual styles, they nonetheless set the tone that appreciably elevated one's cultural sensibilities.

Another category of articles on experimental or abstract films concentrated on the material aspects of the medium rather than on narrative. Various articles described the work of John Whitney and James Whitney, a three-hour program of abstract-art films screened at the Museum of Modern Art in 1952, and the animated films of Norman McLaren. They focused on how these formal experimentations expanded all film practices, from amateur to Hollywood.[90] In a 1950 *Saturday Review of Literature* essay, "Self-Expression," Arthur Knight reviewed the work of East and West Coast experimental filmmakers working in nonobjective and subjective styles. He cited their difference from more bureaucratic Hollywood films: "Each of these films is a completely personal expression by the artist who made it."[91] Knight urged spectators who owned equipment to produce experimental films but reasoned only a few talented amateurs could master these strange visual forms and join the ranks of true art filmmakers. He suggested that amateurs might be better off renting these films for intensive study on their home 16mm projectors.[92] Knight's observations echo traditional attitudes initially formulated during the pictorialist photography movement distinguishing between artistic amateurs and more frivolous hobbyists. This differentiation of artists from amateurs can also be found in Cecile Starr's article on animation in a 1962 *Saturday Review*. She disdainfully remarks that students and individual experimenters often copy the techniques of more experimental animators.[93] Despite the snobbery and elitism percolating throughout these articles, they do constitute an alternative discourse and a counterpoint to Hollywood-narrative style.

A 1962 obituary of Maya Deren published in *Popular Photography* implicitly recognized the latent potential of amateur film to oppose and even topple the dominance of professional filmmaking standards. Containing a critical point on amateurism, this piece heralded the individuality of the filmmaker articulated in both personal vision and total control over the filmmaking process. In this presentation of the avant-garde aesthetic, amateur filmmaking's individual control over all phases of the filmmaking process resisted the dehumanization of mass production and bureaucratic organization typified in Hollywood filmmaking. A *Popular Photography* posthumous salute to Maya Deren's work established her amateurism and individual expression as goals for the amateur producer. Deren's aesthetic sensibility diverged dramatically from family magazines' home-movie rules, which conversely mediated familialism with quasi-professional techniques:

She was the epitome of what an amateur should be. . . . Her films were made not with the resources of a professional studio but with simple equipment and at a cost comparable to many amateur productions. They were not made by a highly trained staff of technical experts but by Maya herself as a writer, director, cameraman, and editor. This was their strength, for they were very personal expressions of an artist who had very definite ideas to express.[94]

Rather than a liability, amateurism could be reinvented as an asset and a resource for the filmmaker. It countered big-budget productions with high barriers to entry with low-cost films. It displaced expertise with imagination. It replaced professional equipment with simple cameras. And it abolished the division of labor with the total integration of the individual in the filmmaking process.

While clearly a tertiary discourse, these discussions on the avant-garde demonstrate first, how other forms of filmmaking sifted down to amateurs. Second, this discourse on the art of film reproduces long-term cultural trends situating amateurism as a refuge from commercialism and as a haven for a pure art not sullied by market relations. This discourse also conforms to earlier expressions of a caste system between artistic amateurs and hobbyists. Third, on the ideological level, art-cinema and avant-garde-film discourse suggests an alternative, although certainly nascent, view of amateurism as a liberated zone. Regardless of these utopian and sporadic ruptures, the ideology of familialism motored the social relations of amateur film.

Home Movies and Barbecue Grills: Familialism as a Filmmaking Force

In the 1950s the expansion of leisure time and the naturalization of Hollywood style deactivated the definition of amateur film after its standardization during the 1940s. The renewed fervor of familialism, an ideology and social practice that emphasized family relations above other kinds of social or political interactions, wedded amateur film to the blissful domain of the home.

This weaving together of amateur film as a hobby and familialism as an ideology of social interaction permanently displaced any other production possibilities for families to such a degree that any distinction between amateur film and home movies collapsed. The two terms functioned as synonyms. As a consequence, the idea that "home movies" implied family activity flourished. Children replaced nature as the prime subjects of amateur film, at least in popular discussions. The home-movie style zeroed in on and celebrated the family. Narrative codes negotiated universal audience comprehension, translating the extremely isolated, idiosyncratic activities of the nuclear family to a wider audience. Professional-film techniques aggrandized the representation of the family. With leisure-time expansion, the nuclear family's most important recreation was itself. Home movies conscripted "togetherness," family harmony, children, and travel into a performance of familialism.

Popular ideology resurrected the family as an invention signifying the quest for fulfillment of subjective needs and the satisfaction of desires for meaningful social interactions. The popularized notion of togetherness epitomized this ideology of the family as an emotional lifeboat in an automated, efficient, and distant society. Discussed in women's magazines, sociological studies, and the mainstream press, togetherness promoted the bourgeois nuclear family as the only social structure available for the expression of common, shared experiences that could shore one up against alienation and isolation.[95] This togetherness myth had several social consequences. With a distinct antifeminist bias, it entrenched and isolated women within the home, and it nestled family security, comfort, and happiness firmly in consumption.[96] In this cultural gridlock, home movies preserved and evoked a residual social formation of families as important cultural and social agents through idealizing, indeed worshipping, its cloistered interactions. The movie camera and projector, as yet a few more indispensable recreational devices, facilitated and produced family happiness through consumption. Quite tellingly, Ben Williams observed in a 1954 *House and Garden* article: "Many families now consider a good projector, preferably 16mm sound, a standard part of their recreation equipment, like the charcoal grill, scrabble set, or ping pong table."[97]

As Margaret Mead noted in 1957, the home "has now become the reason for existence, which justifies working at all."[98] Another sociological study in the late fifties by Ernest Mower titled "The Family in Suburbia" showed that most of the suburban family's recreation was centered in the home.[99] Women's magazine articles on amateur movie-making paralleled these findings. A series of articles in a 1955 *Woman's Home Companion* entitled "How You Can Make the Most of Family Leisure" listed photography, music, and home movies as ideal choices for family recreation, because they included the entire family.[100] If previous periods had girdled amateur film with pseudo or authentic ambitions of upward mobility and entrance into professional filmmaking, the 1950's discourse on "home movies" assigned upward mobility exclusively to the private sphere through a professionalization of leisure time.

Why were these cultural activities of consummate importance? The family could launch into them as a unit, rather than as discrete individuals. The Richard E. Rylands family, the family selected by the editors of *Woman's Home Companion* in 1955 to illustrate home movies as a hobby, proudly asserted: "Shooting movies isn't a hobby with us—it's even more important. It's our way of remembering . . . we record our memories in motion and color and store them in film cans for the future."[101] Home movies for memory documentation veered into the family equivalent of bomb shelters for civil defense—insurance against the insecurities of the future. Home movies instigated and documented family togetherness. A 1953 *Parents Magazine* writer summarized these trends: "They [home movies] can be an animated, living album of family good times, of all the playing and working together that make up successful family living."[102] Home movie-making, then, synchronized with the elevation of the nuclear family as the ideological center of all meaningful activity in the fifties.

Familialism socialized, redirected, and controlled the function of amateur film. Vance Packard's lengthy account of his "conversion" to home movies appeared in a 1952 issue of *American Magazine*. He described his consumer journey in purchasing his home-movie equipment. After his son complained that all their neighbors owned home-movie cameras, Packard initiated a rather thorough investigation into amateur filmmaking. Admitting he was "afraid of bungling," he contacted the American Cinema League in New York for advice, consulted camera stores, read numerous instruction books, and, finally, unspooled his films for a former MGM employee to obtain an expert critique on his shooting.[103] Packard then filmed a family feast and his children working and playing in the garden, with every reel in a narrative style that idolized naturalism and surveillance.[104] He contended, "It is important that the people acting in your movie be so deeply absorbed with what they are doing that they seem to be taken unawares. They break the spell if they yell, wave or stick out their tongues."[105] This institutionalization of the family as a natural construct preserved the ideology of the patriarch in total control of his family, if not his work life. Typically, the father (in this case Vance Packard) was the primary filmmaker.

Children, too, represented crucial components of family togetherness. The ideology of excessive child nurturance as the ultimate goal in life and in recreation infused amateur film. As the birthrate increased in the 1950s, sociologist Martha Wolfenstein observed that popular-magazine writers colored parenting as fun, promising parents "that having children will keep them together, keep them young, and give them fun and happiness."[106] This cult of child rearing increasingly associated amateur movies with the preservation of the images of children and with the cultural production of the myth of parenting as a leisure-time hobby. According to Roy Pinney in a 1955 *Parents Magazine*, home movies were not designed for children but for parents. With their reels and projectors, they could prolong the duration of the prototypical nuclear family. " 'If only they wouldn't grow up so fast,' that's a common complaint. . . . But you can make a permanent record of their childhood—an investment of time that will pay dividends in pleasure for decades to come."[107] A 1951 *Parents Magazine* article described one family who mailed home movies of their children to friends and relatives as a modern form of letter writing, elevating this cult of imaging children to social exchange and communication.[108]

The discussion on travel films correlated with familialism and the marginalization of home movies as leisure. While on the road, the family was together for longer periods of time than during the working year. Vacations signaled the total integration of family play as togetherness. Travel home movies were not prized for their pictorialist exuberance as in the twenties nor for images of unusual and exotic sites as in the thirties. Their most esteemed representations were portrayals of the family reacting to different experiences. A 1956 *Parents Magazine* article entitled "Better Vacation Movies" verifies this claim: "Whether you spend your vacation at the beach or in the mountains, it isn't the beauty of the place that makes the picture good—it's your family's response to it."[109] By the 1950s travel home movies, at least in the eyes of journalists, unmasked the penultimate expression of family togetherness.

Images of family, children, and travel coalesced into the ideology of togetherness. The nuclear family drafted amateur film as a self-conscious and self-reflective activity, glorifying the solitary activities of the private home. Previously, the discursive relations of amateur film promoted private life as a place where one could practice skills and techniques that would aid advancement into commercial gain. Togetherness and its adjunct, familialism, directed filmmaking to the pristine suburban backyard. As an end in itself, the family was reduced to a pure commodity consumed with measured abandon. With the cultural definition of amateur film quarantined in the secluded and supposedly idyllic sphere of the nuclear family, its relationship to larger political issues was modified into a marketing ploy against declining sales by American manufacturers like Bell and Howell.

To See the World and Bring It Home

The scene unfolds in a jittery medium shot of an African village in the Belgian Congo crammed with circular thatched huts, the sun piercing like an atomic blast. A large huddled mass of Pygmies engulf a middle-aged white woman in a belted pink dress and heels, a still camera draped around her neck like a necklace. The Pygmies are very short; they barely reach the woman's shoulders. They crowd around the woman with a curious reverence and an inquisitive, yet somewhat bewildered, distance. They nudge each other. They whisper into each other's ears.

The white woman frantically motions to her camera, pantomiming instructions for them to perform a traditional tribal dance for the camera. Fifty-one shots of half-naked Pygmies ensue, all photographed in medium shot, all very short and choppy, their composition canted. The Pygmies dance in a circle and some blow reed pipes. Occasionally they peer at the camera. The film is unedited and visually congested, a bottleneck of close-ups of Pygmies and wobbly camera work; the shots unspool in rapid, machine-gun-fire succession. The dancers swarm around the filmmaker, overwhelming the camera. A black man in Western khaki enters the frame. He stands next to a Pygmy man who reaches his hip. He pats the Pygmy on the head and smiles knowingly at the camera.

This excerpt is from a 1,600-foot, 16mm amateur film shot by Ethel Cutler Freeman on a family tour of Africa during the winter of 1949–50. Freeman, a wealthy East Coast woman, mother of three grown children and a recent grandmother, embarked on a grand tour of Africa from South Africa up through Kenya, the Congo, and Egypt with her invalid husband, Leon. Many discourses wrap around Freeman's touristic view of Africa, destabilizing her gaze, her footage, and her presence with multiple subject positions: wife, nurse, anthropologist, tourist, collector, filmmaker, and socialite.

Ethel Cutler Freeman's hobby and life passion was anthropology, perhaps as an energetic antidote to her enervated husband. The scenes she shot form an unedited sequence of film recording her various encounters with white colonials and African tribes up and down the continent, a trip she had meticulously planned for two years. The footage is provocative: it invokes many of the discourses enveloping amateur film during the 1950s. These discourses on productive leisure, science, technology, travel, the Third World, family, professionalism, education, class, and the position of women as active image-makers overlap, crisscross, and often contradict each other. They mingle together as a pastiche of the themes emerging from amateur film. They mark off a territory outside of commercial film; yet ideas referencing professional production and exhibition curiously intersect.

While Freeman fancied herself an anthropologist and ethnographic filmmaker, her footage contains scenes quite typical of travel home movies. Early in the footage, Freeman films the people on board a cruise ship as it enters a South African port. She shoots several close-ups of the captain intercut with shaky long shots of mountains photographed from the deck of the ship. This sequence features several close-ups of women passengers, then more shots of mountains, then the crew. After this berserk montage of wealthy tourists at leisure and distant exotic terrain as a backdrop to their antics, a sequence begins with the captain and his mate in full uniform. The captain ambles toward the camera with his arms extended as though he intended to hug the filmmaker. A woman dressed in a fur coat approaches the camera with a coy smile. Several more short close-ups of the captain, other male passengers, and the woman follow. The camera is close to these subjects, but the subjects obviously feel comfortable hamming.

The scene then jumps abruptly to a pan of white tourists on the beach sunning themselves. Then, without transition or warning, the camera pans a row of black children in a shantytown. For the next thirty-seven short takes, various black children and women pose for the camera, frozen by its gaze, intimidated perhaps by this white woman cruising their neighborhood searching for interesting specimens of Zulus. This sequence slides between the luxury of the upper-class cruise ship and the poverty of the South African shantytown. Her mobility to slip in and out of various social structures, never trapped in one, denotes her class privilege. Her trips in the field concluded with lovely continental dinners at the finest hotels.

These two sequences suggest the slippery lines between amateur filmmaking, home movies, ethnography, science, and vacation footage. Obviously, Freeman did not engage in long-term immersion in a culture, learning its language and its traditions. Her tourism offered only a surface view, typified in her cinematography that aims for examples of "types" of tourists, indigenous people, and the spectacle of dances. The intimacy conveyed in the footage of white friends—their modeling for the camera and their nearly equal participation in the performance of filmmaking—is absent from footage of indigenous peoples.

Freeman's voluminous diaries elaborate her encounters with "these natives," as she dubbed them: she paid or bribed them to perform dances or to pose for her cameras. The images of various tribes masquerade as ethnography, but in actuality record imperial exchanges. Freeman often journeyed to these villages with colonial officials or landowners. Despite these visual articulations, her own diary displays her disdain for the mere tourist:

> The lounges, dining room and bar are all charming and decorated in simple good taste. The passengers look unusually attractive. There is nothing to attract a cheap, newly rich crowd. They do not look like tourists and sightseers, but like people traveling for a purpose.

Most intriguingly, the film is coupled with copious notes and diaries by Freeman, providing insight into the intentions and attitudes of its maker.[110] The Freeman material provides a rare record of amateur filmmaking and its professionalization as pseudoethnography. Although most of her "ethnographic filmmaking and field work" was conducted with the Florida Seminoles, the African footage is particularly potent, because it drifts between tourism and ethnography. While the footage itself is quite repetitive, duplicating the shaky, skewed medium shots of the Pygmy scene with various other tribes, animals in game preserves, or wealthy friends posed in front of Lake Victoria or hamming on the patios of colonial mansions, Freeman's almost obsessive record keeping constructs a less-formalized, more specific, and confused discourse on amateur filmmaking than more codified, popular-magazine articles. Of course, her social and economic position afforded her both time and money to embark on such ethnographic and writerly expeditions, to manufacturer a personna as a scientist. The diaries and endless assortment of clippings pertaining to filmmaking, Africa, and anthropology yield a production history of one particular obscure amateur film. These documents and the film itself demonstrate how the discourses on amateurism, professionalism, and education sifted down to a localized site. They affirm the inability of these aesthetic, leisure, technological, and Hollywood discourses to completely contain and control the work and representations of amateurs. The specific, almost quirky, instance of filmmaking in Africa by a woman of leisure juts against the unified manifestos of amateur-advice writers.

Freeman did not take filmmaking lightly. She regularly clipped articles on amateur filmmaking out of the *New York Times*, underlining passages on composition and editing. Although her films do not evidence much "cinematic aesthetic control," she nonetheless pursued filmmaking as a research project. She wrote film reviews for *Films in Review* and *Natural History*, assessing the veracity of Hollywood films about Africa and the Seminoles. Prior to her African trip, she consulted with Eastman Kodak to determine how to protect her films from the heat and humidity of the tropics. She maintained a file of film reviews of Hollywood narratives about Africa, such as the *African Queen*.[111] She attended a class in effective public speaking and kept notes on how to use films to illustrate lectures. Freeman energetically engaged with these discourses on film, borrowing from amateur-advice columns, Hollywood reviews, and course work, molding these discourses for her purposes. Her footage, unfortunately, did not improve.

The African footage reverberates with the technology, practices, and ideologies of amateur film in the 1950s. It uses Kodachrome color film and 16mm equipment. It parades as a scientific, professional educational film and investigates the Third World through the eyes of First World technology. It is a family-travel film recounting homey details of markets, tribes, friends, and exotic African animals. Probing the visual manifestation of apartheid in South Africa, the film explores the conditions of indigenous people. Freeman's footage invents an image of Africa of elegant hotels for whites, primitive peoples dancing, and elephants and hippopotamuses rambling the wild terrain. These unedited reels accompanied her lectures to garden clubs, various upper-class societies, and other suburban functions. The footage chronicles a travelogue of a wild adventure and verifies scientific purpose. Produced by a woman who energetically engaged the world of science, high society, and intellectual life, the film drifts easily between scenes of "primitives" dancing or walking and scenes of white colonials sipping tea on lovely mansion terraces. Freeman considered herself a liberal on "tribal affairs" but disdained the manners of the black Africans and preferred the more refined, polite company of cultured whites.

A world traveler, filmmaker, wealthy benefactor, and amateur anthropologist, Ethel Cutler Freeman spawned a meticulous, lengthy diary of her trip to accompany her 1,600 feet of film and many sheets of still photographs. The three hundred-page, typed diary entitled "Africa 1950" was probably intended for book publication as a combination anthropological study and travel literature, but it was never published. Bulging with details of conversations and gossip with other American and European travelers in Africa with regard to food quality, hotel service, and car and plane travel in Africa, the diary also erupts with dense ethnographic descriptions of "encounters with the primitive." Hiring cars and penning endless letters to various colonial magistrates, imperial mining interests, and anthropologists in the field, Freeman uncovered the location of "pure primitive tribes, untouched by European contact." She encountered Zulus, Pygmies, Masai, always lusting for pure primitives isolated from European restraints to locate an ethnographic experience not contaminated and complicated by outside interaction. She hired planes and cars to transport her to these villages for one-day field trips, amassing contacts with various tribes as though they themselves were artifacts. She always carried hard candies, claiming that sweetness lured "natives" into contact with her. Yet her liberalism seeped through in many curious ways: the trip objectives written in her diary assert that

> this field trip to Africa was inspired by a desire for knowledge that may help to rectify injustices and practices that lead to the deterioration of peoples and their culture who are themselves unable to cope with the encroachments and pressures of a dominant civilization.[112]

The diary reveals many complex, disturbing, eerie dispositions; it demonstrates how Freeman wafted in and out of ruling-class privilege with hotels, servants, and cars and into the world of anthropology and field notes. Her amateurism is not easy to locate or define. She was an amateur anthropologist with professional pretensions, intentions, and connections. She considered herself an amateur travel writer, even enrolling in classes at the Breadloaf Writers' Conference in Vermont to improve her writing skills. An amateur filmmaker and photographer, she produced abundant images under the solemn mantel of scientific recording. Her diary entry for 10 March 1950 on the Pygmy scene unravels these contradictions:

> As I wondered how far we could go on and whether it was possible for the air to become increasingly humid, the forest opened into a small clear-

ing and I saw a row of five miniature grass bee-hive huts and doll-like men and women and lilliputian children who scampered into the bush when they heard our car. The government man got out of our car and called them and they came from their hiding places, shyly, meekly. He talked to them in their language and lined them up in a row. There were about 30 or 40 of them.[113]

Freeman's description of these Pygmies belies her condescending attitude toward Africans in general, one that is repeated throughout the diary. However, her anthropological curiosity mitigates her racism and colonialism. Repeatedly Freeman analyzes the problems of cultural change and remarks on the serious problems of assimilating these cultures to the "white man's ways." In effect, she advocates preserving these cultures from any white dissemination to safeguard their "purity." As she traveled through the African continent on this seven-month journey, she went to great lengths to locate tribes not adulterated by intercommunication with whites. She maintained a scientific voyeurism to see and to comprehend through amateur filmmaking, yet she participated minimally in these cultures. She departed to these villages for less than one day as a tourist collecting disassociated, unconnected images and artifacts. Her film lacks social or historical content. Her contact with the indigenous peoples primarily consisted of exchanges based on candy, money, and filming. Later in the same entry, she notes:

We had bought 4 packets of cigarettes and salt at Beni for 20 francs. That was what Serwanga had told us we should do. We now gave them to the government man for the Pygmies. He talked to them for some time and there seemed to be an argument. Then he came over to Serwanga and told him he relayed the message to me that if I would give them 5of which was $1.00 as well as the cigarettes and salt they would get their musical instruments, their native made flutes, and drums and dance for me and I could take pictures.[114]

Her attitude toward her subjects reveals a peculiar combination of awe, wonder, abhorrence, and pseudoscientific exploration. She describes the size of the Pygmies as "quite appalling." She elaborates her own feelings toward this encounter: "I felt as though I were in Alice through the Looking Glass and these people had eaten the piece of cake that made them grow small."[115] The home-movie camera served as Freeman's "looking glass."

Her ethnographic filmmaking pretensions plaster over these perspectives. The camera quite literally collects images as one might accumulate primitive artifacts for display in a museum or for home study. The camera deifies the encounter, bestows it with ethnographic significance and scientific importance and verifies the scientific status of the filmmaker. The camera supplies as well an incentive to travel by car to remote, inaccessible villages. The 16mm camera legitimated Ethel Freeman's concocted self-creation as a scientist.

> I was so disappointed that I have to leave tomorrow that I could sit down and cry, for with a little more time and planning, I could get a wonderful sequence of their daily life and culture and make a good documentary film of their ceremonies, for it was obvious that unless one was very stupid and unsympathetically trod on their toes, the Pygmies would do what the government asked of them.
>
> I took 100 feet of 16mm cinema Kodachrome and some 35mm color film, so that now I at least have some record of my visit to the Pygmies in the Ituri Rain Forest of the Congo.[116]

Freeman's autobiography chronicles how she circulated through the outskirts of professional ethnography and became acquainted with the intellectual skills required for field work. Her filmmaking functioned both as a scientific record for analysis and as home movies to screen for New Jersey garden clubs. Bored with her social life of clubs, teas, and benefits, she began graduate course work in anthropology in 1934 at the age of thirty-eight, studying exclusively with Ruth Benedict, whom she greatly admired. Notwithstanding, she never received a formal graduate degree.

By 1938 Freeman was a field associate of the American Museum of Natural History as a benefactor with anthropological affectations, which the various curators cultivated. She became a member of the American Anthropological Society, wrote a few scholarly papers, attended conferences, and corresponded with a wide variety of ethnographic and anthropological scholars. For a period of nearly thirty-five years, she conducted field trips to study "primitive people," beginning with the Arapohoe and Shoshone of the American West and branching out to the Florida Seminoles, who became her life's work. From 1939 to 1944 she spent every winter with the Florida Seminoles, writing copious notes, making sketches of various dances, foods, and housing arrangements, and producing 16mm films. No mere dilettante, her research was a serious hobby, an obsession with anthropology, science, and indigenous peoples.

In subsequent years Freeman ventured on solo field trips to New Mexico to study the Pueblo and Navajo. She traveled to Arizona, the Bahamas, Haiti, and Oklahoma to investigate various tribes with her home-movie camera and notebooks. Her scientific interests can be marked by her trusteeship of the American Institute of Anthropology. Her representation of the American Civil Liberties Union (ACLU) on the National Coordinating Committee for Indian Affairs connotes her liberal, if not patronizing, intentions. These positions suggest an involvement extending beyond the boundaries of the amateur, yet her continual lack of any permanent, full-time affiliation with any museum or university stations her as an upper-class protagonist indulging in anthropology and ethnographic filmmaking for excitement and intellectual stimulation. It was certainly not her career.

However, as Freeman's film and diary drift between travel, ethnography, science, and elaborations of upper-class leisure time in Africa, her sensibilities were not as conservative as her attitude toward the indigenous people might imply. Throughout the diary she mourns for South Africa, worried about the recent development of apartheid. After her trip she corresponded with a white South African friend who mailed her newspaper clippings on apartheid from the white South African point of view. She maintained a file of articles from *U.S. News and World Report* and the *New York Times* on political upheaval in South Africa. Although framed within upper-class privilege, her trip to Africa enlightened her to the struggles of indigenous people on that continent. Her abhorrence of apartheid contradicted her racist attitudes concerning the proficiency of the black servants in the finest African hotels. Her film, then, represents a process of learning about Africa rather than a finished statement.

Ethel Cutler Freeman's footage and diaries of Africa do not contain much theory or interpretation. Both remain on the level of almost excessive description and superfluous itemization. Overloaded in details referencing hotels, Leon, friends, and various tribes, the diary erases subjectivity, analysis, insight, or interrogation. Because the film is completely unedited, structural analysis through documentary or narrative theory is questionable. Lacking any postproduction, the film is stuck as a record of production. Its montage replicates a stream of consciousness not rearranged through the intervention of editing. Instead, it traces the dimensions and narrative order of the trip. The footage does not expose ethnographic content but rather an unprocessed mediation between one wealthy white woman and the Africa continent. The diaries and the film present the textual overproduction of the self: the self devolves into the ethnographic document through home movie-making.

Reduced to a few narrow components, the discursive definition of amateur film incorporated the very limited, almost claustrophobic territory of the suburbanized private sphere. The socialization pressures of consumption, leisure, the family, and the Cold War created an ideological construct of amateur film as sterile, passive, apolitical, and an inconsequential commodity. These discourses dissipated amateur film into an atrophied, impotent plaything, a toy to endlessly replay repressive ideologies.

6

Reinventing Amateurism

A T THE 1989 Academy Awards broadcast, famous Hollywood couples, friends, families, and comrades presented Oscars: Goldie Hawn and Kurt Russell, the Douglas family, Lucille Ball and Bob Hope, Dustin Hoffman and Tom Cruise, Jeff Goldblum and Geena Davis, Don Johnson and Melanie Griffith. They cracked insipid jokes about their cozy "familial," intimate ties. While many articulations of families unfurled—couples now back together, those who live together, on-screen buddies, pairs from movies, married couples—they were all draped in familialism—the contours of the patriarchal nuclear family their ideological wardrobe.

Bruce Willis, with slightly spiked hair, and Demi Moore, wearing a tight dress that ballooned out over black pedal pushers, walked onto the stage—an exhibition of the chic ultramodern couple. They said good night to their new baby and directed the audience to a television insert on-screen next to them. A shaky, hand-held amateur video materialized: one long take from eye level of Demi delightedly feeding their infant daughter in their roomy kitchen. Willis is obviously the camera operator. He swirls around them. Clad in a sloppy, over-sized shirt, Demi smiles hurriedly at the camera, wielding a spoon dripping baby food. The entire awards ceremony audience cried out "Ah" in an adoring chorus. Demi and Bruce proudly gazed up at the screen and then at each other.

This rather sentimental public spectacle of Hollywood family life tenders a 1989 version of amateur-film history. It reverberates, reworks, and updates discourses on technology, aesthetics, Hollywood, families, socialization, and professionalism. With new video technology, families can shoot in longer takes with less light, continuing the trend of technological simplification. The Willis/Moore video contrasts sharply with the technical and formal superiority of the films nominated for Academy Awards. It lacks special effects, editing, spectacle, smooth camera work, a script. Its imperfect control over formal aesthetics and the subjects' self-conscious hobnobbing with the camera register its emotional authenticity.

This domestic scene of an ordinary detail of everyday life—feeding an infant in a high chair—is wedged into one of the largest, self-congratulatory Hollywood spectacles of the year. The mawkishness of the video and its record of the daily operations of new parents authenticates Willis and Moore as a down-to-earth, average, likeable young couple who feed their baby themselves rather than as media-industry millionaires. It jettisons class, prestige, and privilege with a media carnival of reproduction. As it snaps images of the private sphere and amateur production into a Hollywood extravaganza, this home video sweetly, alluringly affirms Hollywood narrative as the quintessence of professional film. In Hollywood, narratives, technology, expertise, and execution triumph; in home video, the interpersonal relations between an unskilled camera operator and the friendly subjects and the preservation of fleeting, perishable moments of family history prevail.

In this context of network television, the home video passes as an aside, a reversion to a media-produced nostalgia for prototypical family values. Unlike Hollywood-narrative film or commercial television sitcoms, the Willis/Moore video demands spectator interaction; without the gaze of Bruce and Demi and the sentimental outbursts of the audience, the video would be reduced to disengaged, inconsequential surveillance. With these accouterments, it realizes its role as a negotiator and preserver of valued, precious leisure time floating in a social and political void. The stars tape home movies, reminiscent of stars of the 1920s and 1930s who peddled amateur cameras in magazines. Moving from the private sphere to the nationally broadcast, mass-mediated public sphere (with one of the largest international audience shares of any program except perhaps the Superbowl), the video validates emotion, family interaction, reproduction, and sentiment as leisure, as sites exempt from capitalism, commercial filmmaking, or the burdens of working as a famous star.

This same affinity between amateur video as a more authentic, less-warped, more truthful, and less-manufactured representation with a beeline to nostalgia and emotion erupts in many films and videos. It occurs so frequently as a reworking of idealized paraphrases of childhood and as a more raw, less-mediated record of private history that it almost seems a projection of fantasy or the last relic of resistance to the enervation of the mass media. In some music videos by John Cougar Mellencamp or Bruce Springsteen, the old amateur-movie footage embroiders the excesses of raucous rock and roll sound with the tranquility of the ordinary. These old home movies from the 1950s and 1960s resonate with the familiarity of white, suburban middle-class America: barbecues, baseball games, family picnics. In other music videos, the amateur footage coaxes smugness in the spectator; it diminishes into merely hokey sentiment, because it is so boldly out of fashion and fashionless. Its capricious family sentiment and the quirky awkwardness of the subjects in their retro fashions of pedal pushers and crew cuts amplify the surface style of the musicians and their audiences through the naive lack of style. The home movies in these music videos juxtapose the modern and the postmodern, the record and the pastiche of it. Family history becomes a museum of surface style.

In some recent Hollywood films like *Down and Out in Beverly Hills* (1986) or *Cousins* (1989) (both remakes of French films), the male child of an emotionally dysfunctional couple wields the camera like a scalpel, surgically opening up and exposing family secrets of illicit love affairs and wounds of misfired interactions as a form of revenge. As an assertion of autonomy, these home videos ensconced within Hollywood narratives fashion a rather brutal, but innovative, form of amateur video, as though Hollywood narrative was incapable of disclosing the more uncomfortable interstices of family life. As the family collapses on screen, the child records it.

Recent AT&T commercials feature testimonials by various middle managers who extol how AT&T communication systems increased their corporate efficiency and productivity. The cinematography musters home movies: the camera jerks around the frame in one long, thirty-second take like a father "firehosing" a newborn. This lack of composition wraps their testimony in anxiety; it labors as a visual correlative for their corporate problems. Its sloppiness signifies in a negative statement the urgency of a professional communication system. It visually replicates anxiety and confusion much like World War II films, but this time for the expansion of a communication monopoly.

These various images all refract the history of amateur film—a history that reflects structural changes in the relationships among discourses on technology, aesthetics, social uses, and political ends. Initially identified through its substandard technology and entrepreneurial economics, amateur film eventually moved into a primarily aesthetic territory by the 1920s, where any deviations from Hollywood were trivialized as amateur. By the 1950s amateur film married the nuclear family after the standardization of 16mm during World War II. Amateur film progressed from an economic definition to an aesthetic deviation to a social function. Its definition narrowed from a utopian hope of upward mobility to a consumer practice zone for perfecting Hollywood pictorial composition and narrative techniques to a nonserious, leisure-time activity bolstering family solidarity and consumption. The role of amateur film in economic, social, and political life diminished as leisure time expanded. Amateur film translated, deflected, and mediated larger social and historical constructs on craftspersonship, social mobility, creativity, professionalism, Hollywood, efficiency, naturalism, technical control, pictorialism, and private life. Through these historical transformations, the wide discursive components of amateur film tapered down to a limited, privatized, isolated site: the nuclear family. These discourses ultimately positioned amateur film within rigid social hierarchies of work and leisure, commerce and art, professionalism and consumerism. Ama-

teur-film discourse marginalized amateur filmmaking as a hobby to fill up leisure time and as a retreat from social and political participation.

While journals, magazines, distributors, camera manufacturers, and capitalist culture may have reinforced the isolation of amateur filmmaking, its
spirit, if not its makers, nonetheless trespassed into contemporary experimental,
narrative, and documentary film. These films rouse the political struggles of
amateur film. They attempt to analyze the structures of media production by
foregrounding the problem of power relations among professionalism, amateurism, family, aesthetics, neurosis, and work.

Since the 1950s, with filmmakers such as Stan Brakhage and Jonas Mekas,
the American avant-garde has appropriated home-movie style as a formal manifestation of a spontaneous, untampered form of filmmaking. Filmmakers working in super-8 as an inexpensive, artistic medium express this liberated amateurism. This "home-movie" style does not execute the rigid standards of
composition, narrative, and the erasure of the filmmaker characteristic of the
ideological discourse on amateur filmmaking. It does not conform to prescriptive formats: subjects interact with the camera as friends and openly pose, the
camera firehoses, and scenes from daily life unroll unedited or in no particular
narrative sequence. Experimental films in this style explore, publicize, and, in
a minimal way, legitimate this spontaneous, untrained, unskilled technique—
the violent underside of the polite grid of narrative rules for amateurs. In these
avant-garde films and common home movies, this style unleashes a contradiction between the ideology of the dominant professional codes of narrative and
classical, pictorial composition and the contingencies of amateur production.
While amateur filmmakers usually photograph familiar subjects in everyday
contexts, these situations can be aleatory and uncontrolled, contributing to a
less-organized visual style. Three films negotiate and interrogate these hierarchies between professional and amateur filmmaking: *Nissan Ariana Window*
(1972), an experimental film by Ken Jacobs; *Peeping Tom* (1960), a commercial feature film by Michael Powell; and *Demon Lover Diary* (1980), an independently
produced documentary shot by Joel DeMott.[1]

Ken Jacobs's *Nissan Ariana Window* (1972) is a short, silent, 16mm film of his
wife and child. It shows scenes from home life. The compositional style and
static camera work of the film correspond to amateur directives to use a tripod.
Yet this almost photographlike compositional aesthetic with an absolutely
immobilized camera underscores the spontaneity, intimacy, and interaction
with the subjects of a typical amateur, which exceeds formal control. The film
includes shots of Jacobs's pregnant wife, a shot of her holding up baby clothes
for the camera, a shot of the child sleeping, a shot of the wife clothing it, a fast-
motion shot of some cats. These images are mundane. There are no spectacles

or technical tricks. As familiar, everyday scenes, they are within anyone's reach. A revealing scene deconstructs patriarchal domination through camera placement and pictorial composition. Using a high-angle shot, Jacobs shoots down at his baby positioned on the middle of a rug. The baby persistently crawls off the rug, requiring Jacobs to enter the frame several times to return her to center-stage position. *Nissan Ariana Window* deploys home-movie content—spontaneity, intimacy, subject interaction, and lack of soundtrack—as a formal strategy. It critiques a static camera on a tripod with the lack of control over subjects, one of the social hallmarks of home movies.

Michael Powell's commercial narrative film *Peeping Tom* (1960) also disinters the tyranny of the camera and the consequences of the privatization of amateur film. The plot revolves around a professional-film studio focus puller named Mark Lewis who moonlights photographing models for pornographic views. He murders the young women with a pointed tip from his tripod leg as he films their horrified faces with a 16mm Filmo. This film is a probing and disturbing analysis of the parameters of filmmaking. It traverses through voyeurism, the domination of women and children with cameras, and the range of film practice extending from professional filmmaking to home movies, surveillance, pornography, documentary, and finally to science.

The son of a biologist who studied the nervous system, Lewis archives his father's home movies. When we see these films, which he projects for a young woman neighbor in his room, their abusive content suggests the ideology of scientific empiricism and the camera's domination over subjects. *Peeping Tom* exposes these two discourses in their most extreme psychological manifestations: the child as scientific specimen and the dementia of camera control. The father's home movies show Mark as a child awakened and stunned by a bright light flashed in his eyes. He screams as his father drops a salamander on his stomach. A series of home-movie scenes of his dead mother lying in bed and his new stepmother cavorting with his father follow. The amateur camera does not idealize the nuclear family but rather fetishizes its malfunctions, its breaks and fissures. Mark explains that as a consequence of his father's excessive shooting, he had "no privacy in [his] childhood. He [his father] was interested in the reactions of the nervous system to fear." While presenting the psychological groundwork for Mark's murder of women, these home movies interwoven with the narrative also expose how camera domination and control expresses, in its most demented form, the perverse rationality of science and its mutation into voyeurism and deadly misogyny.

In his professional film career, Mark is a noncreative functionary; in his private life, he exerts total control over women through his amateur-film camera that records their brutal deaths as he kills them. Through the police investigators who track him, to the director who terrorizes an actress who cannot get her lines right, to the home movies and the murder film, *Peeping Tom* insinuates that no form of filmmaking is exempt from the power relations of voyeurism, control, domination, and a scientific mode of distanced observation. Lewis's "private" use of his amateur-movie equipment congeals all of these components in their most excessive and terrifying articulation—the murder of sexualized women.

This struggle between professional and amateur filmmaking and access to media production explodes in Joel DeMott's independently produced documentary *Demon Lover Diary* (1980). DeMott's film chronicles the production of a low-budget horror film called *The Demon Lover*. It was financed by two Michigan factory workers: Don, who mortgaged his furniture for $3,000, and Jerry, who self-amputated his finger for an $8,000 insurance settlement. DeMott's film follows the developing tensions between the professional crew and Don and Jerry as they produce the horror film that chronicles the many women who lust after a demon man.

The film tracks the way in which Don and Jerry's visions of upward mobility and total creative control over their work attract them to independent feature filmmaking. Enroute to pick up their rental film equipment in Chicago, Don tells Joel and Jeff, "I can work on this movie twenty hours a day and not be tired. It's what I've wanted to do for twenty years." Later, while Don shoots super-8 films of the crew picking up its professional gear from a rental house, Joel comments in voice-over on the soundtrack, "I think Don would really like to shoot the movie himself, but he's too afraid, so he shoots home movies instead." The construction of media expertise limits and intimidates producers as inexperienced as Don.

At several other points in the film, the ideology of professionalism invades the interactions between Don and Jerry, the factory workers, and Mark and Jeff, the professional crew. When Mark and Jeff try to arrange who will haul the gear to locations, Don exclaims, "A director shouldn't be carrying anything, I'm carrying the weight of the film." Talking to a reporter, Don explains that *Demon Lover* will be a success because he spent all of his time reading film magazines and film books and preparing his "preproduction planning." He hopes to demonstrate the efficiency of his production to potential investors. He even informs the reporter, "Film is unlike any other medium—it costs a lot to participate." Don and Jerry exemplify how the ideology of professional filmmaking permeates dreams of upward mobility and poses as a form of unalienated, meaningful work over which one can have control.

But the most volatile conflict in *Demon Lover Diary* centers around the problems between the inexperienced working-class producers with a vision of join-

ing the "big time" and the professional crew. Don and Jerry's lack of organization and direction finally infuriates Jeff. At one point Don bribes Jeff and says,
"I'll pay you double if you work the f-stops and light it." Ray, Don's cousin and
another factory worker, later tells the crew, "You're doing something you enjoy;
I don't enjoy my work, but I make good money and I have good fringes." When
the personnel office at Don's firm inquired about his absence, he tells the camera
and Joel that he answered, "I know what's wrong with me; I have film fever."
Later he says, "The company and the union are trying to figure out how to fire
me even though I'm on sick leave. They're going to try to fire me because of the
fact that I made a movie." Their ineptitude at imitating professional standards
leads Jeff, the camera operator, and Mark, the sound technician, to comment on
Don and Jerry's filmmaking "stupidity." Finally, the bewildered Don and Jerry
become so enraged with the film, with the production, and with Jeff and Mark
that they fire at them with guns. The crew and Joel exit Michigan, worried that
Don and Jerry are chasing them.

Shot by one person, *Demon Lover Diary* focuses and pinpoints crucial issues
of amateur-film discourse. In this film the question of access to media production turns on ideologies and practical expressions of professionalism based on
organization, technical control, and money. Professional film and the appropriation of its aesthetic, technical, and narrative standards present a myth of upward
mobility and meaningful labor. The film also explicates, in a very real and extremely personal way, the political potency of the whole ideology of filmmaking. These working-class producers are so desperate for participation in media
and for less-monotonous labor, they mortgage their possessions, mutilate themselves, and engage in armed struggle with the crew. The tensions between Don
and Jerry, as imitators of professionalism, and Mark and Jeff, as working professionals, graph in personal terms this historical battle between control and
spontaneity, corporate organization and personal freedom, the myth of professional filmmaking and the actuality of shooting, enervating work and radical
creativity.

This inquiry into the power relations imbricated in the accessibility of inexpensive movie technology is not confined to historical discourse, primary evidence, and commercial films. The struggle between professionalism as a region
of technical control, rationality, and expertise, and amateurism as a territory of
freedom, spontaneity, and individualism disperses into many sites of media
production: communication education, cable television, the question of access
for independent filmmakers to the Public Broadcasting Service and the net-
works, and home video.

From *Newsweek* to *Video Review* to *Esquire* to *Popular Photography*, journalists
have disposed of super-8 amateur film as a mute technological dinosaur lacking

audio or stereo sound. Kodak has not manufactured a home-movie camera since 1981. Home movies are too cumbersome and pricey to make nonstop shooting of a birthday party or wedding affordable.[2] In place of this outmoded technology abandoned in the heap of cameras discarded by market or art, these writers lionize home video. For them, home video presents the technological solution to the expensive, hard to operate, and even more difficult to exhibit amateur film. As it advances toward ever-increasing miniaturization and automation, the home-video camera emerges as a silent relative at family gatherings, never interrupting, never gossiping, never interpreting as it records hugs, kisses, hamming, and idealized memories of a contrived family harmony. The machine itself inches toward its own invisibility as it loses weight, as its tapes become smaller, and as it operates silently. In this popular discourse on home video, camcorders erase home-movie history as a technology too intrusive and too aesthetically complicated. Its images endure too permanently to have any use value at all in the ephemera of the end of the twentieth century. The floating signifier of Jean Baudrillard, the signifier that can be attached to anything, finds its technological articulation in home video, where family history can evaporate with the push of the button and a different, happier history can be encoded.

These death sentences on home movies are fairly recent. They began in 1981 with the initial appearance of home-video recorders after the introduction of VCRs for the consumer market in 1975.[3] As discourses that imagine they mark both the end of one historical era and the origin of a new, more perfect epoch of representing and mediating the family, they deserve analysis. Underneath these requiems lie many layers of marginality and history. The magazine articles draft home video in technological terms: they argue over format (VHS, BETA, or 8mm) and assess the auto focus, zoom, or automatic white cards of various cameras. Most articles concentrate on those aspects of the home-video discourse and practice that most directly translate into consumption: gadgets like auto focus or zoom weight, ease of operation, quality, and price. These technical concerns determine how one machine is constituted, analyzed, marketed, and sold over another. Like its ancestor amateur film, home video is entrenched within upper-middle-class respectability; although twenty million United States households have VCRs, only 10 percent own video cameras. Cameras are expensive: they range from $300 to $2,000 for a state-of-the-art 8mm system, with the average price for the home consumer who desires to shoot a child's birthday averaging $1,000.[4] This technological bent accents consumption over production.

Articles in the technophile and popular press concentrate almost single-mindedly on how effectively automation can efface technology. The camcorder operator is free to roam the family event unencumbered by technological control or aesthetic planning. Metaphorically, the machine approximates invisibility. On another level, the discourse on these machines positions videography as a labor-free pursuit, a pure phenomenological state of flux and integration with environment, requiring no involvement from the maker, only the noninterventionist mediation of technology. Like the microwave oven that condenses heating time and heats food without browning, the video camera eradicates labor and process. With a two-hour tape a fraction of the cost of comparable super-8 film, the difference between real life and tape recording is elided. On the surface both appear unmediated and exempt from the physical and mental work of media-making.

These absences further structure the politics of home-video discourse. Elaborations on technology and price eclipse a silent discourse on aesthetics. The technical specifications and the assessments on the ease of lightweight-camera shooting disperse the aesthetic, the social, the political. This equipment returns its users to a natural, primitive state of video pleasure. The glaring absence of aesthetic directives and the enforcement of naturalism and nonintervention suggest that self-consciousness, formalism, and interrogation of the relationship between the maker and the subject are not only unnecessary but are vestiges of an antiquated technology and a former era like that of the super-8.

One article in *Popular Photography* on Albert and David Maysles, known for their work in cinema verité, knits together the hand-held shooting style of the Maysles and home video. This article bares some interesting assumptions about home video. Cinema verité, first produced in the late 1950s, depended on small, lightweight technology to produce a greater sense of immediacy and intimacy through hand-held camera work, a style of camera work that emphasized the drama of an event rather than a voice-over analysis of its history or implications. Intimacy and drama were parallel concerns of amateur film as well. Inflecting its moving-camera technique with the visual signifiers of continuity (narrative, close-ups, and cutaways for dramatic effect and individual characters), the exciting visual style of cinema verité ideologically proposed the unification of the camera, the event, and the filmmaker.[5] In the late 1950s when amateur-film marketing and penetration had reached its zenith with the baby boom, many of the early cinema verité filmmakers offered technical tips to amateurs in various movie magazines. Their similarity to amateurs revolved on two aspects: first, they both used lightweight equipment; second, they both moved with their equipment rather than using tripods, investing the camera operator as the sole author of the film.

Nearly thirty years and several technological mutations later the discourse on cinema verité resurfaces and the Maysles continue to insist on the freedom subjects enjoy under the gaze of a hand-held camera. However, with the advent of home videotaping and its facility for continuous shooting, they worry about an inherent laziness in video practice, its jettisoning of care and precision in favor of shooting. They proclaim, "There must be some kind of moral equivalent to that kind of care and precision in the mind of the amateur, to appreciate every bit of tape. But because tape is so much cheaper and runs so much longer than film, the quality of video tends to be less than that of film, and it is more difficult for the amateur to edit."[6]

Like romantic modernist artists, the Maysles lament the degradation of craft and the diminution of editing for home video. Yet the technology itself champions production over editing and structure. As most of the articles on home video illustrate, home editing is anything but simple, requiring the borrowing of a neighbor's machine or editing in the camera.[7] This technological liability, of course, propels the home videomaker toward replicating the sequence of events rather than toward structure or analysis. In a recent issue of *Motion Picture*, experimental filmmaker George Kuchar appraises home video as an outlet for experimental filmmakers. In contrast, he contends editing limitations push the innovative, rebellious producer toward in-camera editing, its use of materials summoning painting or collage composition more than postproduction editing.[8] This procedure presents a dramatically different epistemology of media structure, more immediate and perhaps more dialectical than bench editing, a cinema verité of the mind and the edit.

Within these ideological constraints of technology and the family, home video, as Kuchar also attests, can be appropriated, its social and aesthetic use recaptured and reconfigured. Increasingly saturated by an avant-garde that appropriates and pastiches mass-media images, our postmodern epoch can easily forget that the means of production—not only representation—should also be appropriated. New use of amateur cameras could be reinvented. They could retaliate against the enervation of the mass media and intervene into its reproduction of aesthetic norms and unexamined familial ideologies. After all, technology itself does not impel political change; social relations determine its uses, deploy its technology, and strategize its boundaries. As with all new technologies, home video bursts with a dialectically loaded possibility. On the one hand, it is merely another leisure-time commodity for the bourgeois family. On the other hand, it may foment opportunities for media-production access, invention, and critique.

There is evidence that these latter possibilities of home video are not latent, only marginal and emerging. Since 1981 experimental film and video have experienced a significant increase in the amount of work collaging material from other sources. This process deconstructs the original footage to expose its concealed positions of domination, control, and resistance. This increased activity parallels the availability of consumer video and the accessibility of large collections of film and video in video stores, representing a congruence rather than a cause.

Some college-level film students have appropriated home-video cameras owned by their parents or neighbors. They shoot their families and then reedit the footage on film. With home video, more footage can be shot than in 16mm film. But this expansion of amateur screen time is perhaps too simple an analysis of the experimental and radical possibilities of home video. In this case the power relationship between camera owner and subject is inverted. Children shoot their parents, a practice never advocated in previous discourse on amateur film, where fathers controlled the means of production and family representation. Because the content crosses the border from video to film and is frequently intercut with family television shows, intertitles, or other live film footage in more critical pieces, the home-video footage sheds its naturalistic aura and its masquerade of unmediated humanity. It is positioned within a more forcefully articulated social and historical context; its voice interrogates rather than reproduces.

For example, during his college spring break, one film student at an upstate New York film school videotaped his dentist father lifting weights in a gym and talking at the kitchen table; he then intercut these images with scenes, nearly therapeutic, of television dads' idealized interactions with their kids from family-oriented television shows like "Family Ties" and "The Cosby Show." The home-video footage betrays the psychoanalytic conflicts between parents and children as small cracks, fissures, and tensions over power, whereas the television footage parades endlessly duplicated understanding fathers. During the videotape sequences, the student orders his father to behave more "naturally." He explains he is trying to make a cinema verité film in which the subjects are supposed to reveal themselves without acknowledging the camera. While home-video marketing adorns itself with fetished images of children and happy parents with cameras, this identical technology and content may decompose and decompress these fabricated fantasies of family life. Children can point the home-video camera in the opposite direction.

The current fascination with home video as a discourse and as a practice, as a marketing ploy, and as a technology is not without history, despite journalists' disengagement from home-movie apparatuses. While the technologies of celluloid and tape may differ, they share a discourse on amateurism nearly one hundred years old. They also share a social formation constructed out of consumerism, leisure time, aesthetic norms, bourgeois family life, the utopianism of new technologies, and corporate capitalism. By removing cameras from their traditional yoke of the home, nature, and travel, home movies and home video may break with naturalism and emotional bonds as aesthetic organizing principles. In the case of home video, public screening of these naturalized, emotional bonds in other exhibition contexts may defuse their dominance and open up critiques of representations of the private sphere, family life, and leisure.

Both home-movie and home-video discourse focus on technological gadgets to upgrade equipment and to create an aura of "professionalism." Harker, Potamkin, and others writing in the late 1920s refused the nostalgia of a preindustrial cinematic era debunking technical manipulation and gadgetrylike slow and fast motion. Instead, they scavenged ways in which these techniques could articulate a heightened social and aesthetic consciousness. With home-video manufacturers echoing the manufacturing trends of early amateur-camera makers through continued equipment upgrades, home video's emancipatory and experimental potential must be invented. These cameras and their technical features can be used critically. Again, history may offer a strategy but certainly not a blueprint. While home movies and home videos operate within the same discourse, their historical and aesthetic context and social relations differ dramatically.

In the early 1990s some gay and lesbian videomakers commandeered the radical potential of accessible amateur technologies, deploying it to dismantle the homogenization and massification of the media. Their work aggressively deconstructs the privileging of the bourgeois nuclear family and heterosexuality in previous historical formations of amateurism.[9] This work envisions the potentialities of amateurism for exploration of the self and the private sphere. These amateur formats exorcise familialism from the discursive construct of amateurism; they insist on specificity, difference, and voice. Home-video technologies have offered a means of communication by which marginalized and silenced voices can explore the tortured constructions of identity, the oppressiveness of social norms, and the ravages of AIDS. Deploying amateur formats, these gay and lesbian works sustain dispatches from the conflicted self, excavating complicated, private intimacies and pushing them into public scrutiny. These works collapse the contested, problematized borders between filmmaker and subject, between amateur and professional, between documentary and narrative, and between public and private. The amateur camera maps autobiography.

Sadie Benning used the Fisher-Price Pixelvision toy camera to construct video diaries exploring her identity as a teenage lesbian. Her camera plunges into the subversive and hidden cracks of family life, the places behind the closed doors of a teenager's bedroom, where sexual fantasies and social imaginaries are debunked and reinvented. Given the constraints of Pixelvision technology, her autobiographical tapes are shot in almost distorting close-ups, often within her own room. All of the tapes use voice-overs, which reflect on her life. The voice-overs function as a performance of young lesbian identity. Benning photographs her face, clothes, toys, and places she hangs out. The tapes often include handwritten words that flash across the screen describing her feelings or opinions. In *Jollies* (1989–91) Benning explores her own sexuality. The tape includes scenes of Barbie dolls kissing, Benning dressing up in men's clothing and shaving her face, and stories about her own sexual experiences with boys and girls. The Pixelvision camera unravels the psychic and political subject position of a lesbian teenager in the form of a video confessional. In Benning's work, from *Jollies* to *Leaving Normal* to *A Place Called Lovely*, the toy camera emerges as a device that liberates the sexual voice of the teenager from the confines of the home.[10]

Silverlake Life: The View from Here (1993) chronicles the relationship between Tom Joslin, a filmmaker, and Mark Massi, his lover, as they both are dying from AIDS. The tape assaults the very social construction of the home movie as the idealization of private life; here, private life is viewed in all of its complexities, ambiguities, and pain. Started as a video diary by Joslin, the tape presents an uncompromising view of the experience of AIDS on the body, the mind, and relationships. Shot from the point of view of the person living with AIDS, *Silverlake Life* explores AIDS from the locus of subjectivity and the body, not from science or medicine or political organizing. The tape shows Tom and Mark dancing with each other, discussing their relationship, and joking about AIDS.[11]

Yet the tape uncompromisingly plunges into the multiple ways the body with AIDS survives daily life, away from the spectacle of AIDS. This tape unravels AIDS as it enacts its devastation upon the body in micropractices: Kaposi's sarcoma treatments, meetings with family and friends, visits to doctors, alternative-medicine treatments, vitamins, anger and rage over the disease, death. The tape's narrative is the narrative not of a relationship's ups and down, but of AIDS and its inevitable progression toward death. In one scene in a grocery store Joslin, exhausted and weak, is unable to pry loose a plastic bin. He exclaims: "What a way to live. What a way to die." Later, a few days before Joslin dies, we see him lying in bed, camera on, talking about how his body has changed and how he feels. In another scene following Joslin's death, Massi sits on the floor of their apartment, his own body devastated by AIDS, talking about his lover's ashes and the urn that holds them.

After Joslin's death, Massi takes over the camcorder and attempts to finish the tape, but he too dies from AIDS. The tape was then finished by one of Joslin's former filmmaking students, Peter Friedman. *Silverlake Life* recaptures the radical potential of accessible technology by specifying AIDS from the voices of people with AIDS. The tape provides an implicit critique of home movie's visual iconography. Rather than idealization, it sustains materialization; rather than a nuclear family, it shows a loving gay couple; rather than surveillance of beatific family moments, it merges Tom and Mark's relationship with autobiography.

The early avant-garde home-movie liberators redeemed the excesses of production with the sculpting of montage, an ideological ordering to combat the naturalistic tendencies of the invisibility of production. For home video nearly fifty years later, editing is still problematic. Technical limitations impinge upon the amateur's resources. The absence of editing exalts spontaneity and shooting. Rather than implanting and consequently dehistoricizing prior editing resistances, the reassembling and recontextualizing dialectical strategy of montage may need to be more broadly applied. The proliferation of VCRs in the home, at libraries, and in schools and the increasingly high technical standards of amateur video may deflect montage from the text itself to the context of exhibition. Relocating the exhibition venue of home video may function as a montage strategy at the site of reception. In the student film on a real father and television dads, the deconstructive critique circulated in transferring formats, changing exhibition venues, and positioning the footage as "documentary."

On a more commercial level, the Cable News Network seeks amateur video for their Newshound project. They advertise a toll-free number amateurs can call to sell news footage to the network. The network typically buys only one amateur videotape a month, uses the footage only when their own crews did not cover an event, and retains editorial control. However, managing editor Earl Casey contends that the footage is generally technically comparable to professional footage because most automatic and electronic cameras are technically as good as professional gear. The problem, he maintains, is aesthetic norms; amateur footage evidences "bad" composition, swish panning, and framing not up to news standards.[12] Technical standards have traditionally limited the utopian potential of amateur gear for increasing independent access to the airwaves; the diminution of technical differences may provide opportunities for all kinds of independents to make significant inroads into alternative, commercial exhibition. As a 1985 *Newsweek* article noted, video's own social relations have transformed in the space of twenty years: "In the 1960s, video was an avant-garde art form, and not long ago a home screening room was the province of Hollywood moguls."[13] Video lost its high-art aura to become more reproducible and controllable in the private sphere; it moved from the obscurity of the art museum to the solitude of the home.

A notion of experimentalism that remaps territorial boundaries should be invoked, equally directed to aesthetic and political interrogation and the reinvention of reception. In a 1982 *Popular Photography* article, Leendert Drukker unknowingly expounds the experimental attitude of stretching the borders of expectation and common sense. He encourages videomakers to roam toy stores for gadgets like the Remco Sound FX machine, Casio's VL-Tone, Colorforms, Crepe Foam Rubber, and Make and Play Colorubs. These toys, he argues, will invigorate tapes by prodding "the imagination." He strangely echoes Potamkin when he asserts, "The distinction between toys and professional tools is largely a state of mind and sometimes a matter of distribution."[14] He's absolutely right. And if the discourse and practice of home video is not appropriated, we will all join the son in *Down and Out in Beverly Hills*, endlessly videotaping our family as a form of pseudoparticipation, forever trapped within a Hollywood narrative rented for our VCR. In 1991 George Holliday recorded Los Angeles police officers beating Rodney King. The amateur tape not only provided visual evidence in the trial of the police officers but, more importantly, served as counter-surviellance to the repressive tactics of the state. The King tape, replayed endlessly on national television, demonstrated how amateur technology could open up for full view the micropractices of racism, police brutality, and state violence.

This history of the discourse of amateur film has argued that its definition and cultural position was gradually squeezed into the nuclear family. Technical standards, aesthetic norms, socialization pressures, and political goals derailed its cultural construction into a privatized, almost silly, hobby. However, while Hollywood and corporate interests monitored, controlled, and sequestered them, these amateur cameras did, in a very minimal way, democratize media production. While the history of amateur-film discourse exposes its repressive discursive, its future may liberate it as a more accessible and meaningful form of personal expression and social and political intervention.

Notes

Preface

1. Hans Magnus Enzensberger, "Constituents of a Theory of the Media," in his *The Consciousness Industry* (New York: Seabury, 1974), 95–128.

2. Michel Foucault, "Lecture One: 7 January 1976," in *Power/Knowledge: Selected Interviews and Other Writings*, ed. Colin Gordon (New York: Pantheon, 1980), 81–82.

3. Richard Chalfen, "Home Movies as Cultural Documents," in *Film/Culture*, ed. Sari Thomas (Metuchen, N.J.: Scarecrow, 1982), 127.

4. Sol Worth and John Adair, *Through Navajo Eyes: An Exploration in Film Communication and Anthropology* (Bloomington: Indiana University Press, 1972), 18.

5. A sampling of anthropological research on visual communication produced by non-professional participants as an indicator of culture would include Ray L. Birdwhistell, *Kinesics and Context* (Philadelphia: University of Pennsylvania Press, 1970); John Collier, Jr., *Visual Anthropology: Photography as a Research Method* (New York: Holt, Rinehart and Winston, 1967); Margaret Mead and Rhoda Metraux, *The Study of Culture at a Distance* (Chicago: University of Chicago Press, 1953); Christopher Musello, "Studying the Home Mode: An Exploration of Family Photography and Visual Communication," *Studies in Visual Communication* 6, no. 1 (1980): 23–42.

6. Julia Hirsch, *Family Photographs: Content, Meaning and Effect* (New York: Oxford University Press, 1981), 102.

7. Susan Sontag, *On Photography* (New York: Farrar, Straus, and Giroux, 1983), 8.

8. Michael Lesy, introduction to *Time Frames: The Meaning of Family Pictures* (New York: Pantheon, 1980), xi–xxvii.

9. Photographic critics are in surprising agreement over the dimensions of these attributes of "innocent" image-making. Some critics consider Jacques-Henry Lartique's work the precursor of this aesthetic. For a good collection of his photographs, see *Diary of a Century: Jacques-Henry Lartique*, ed. Richard Avedon (New York: Viking, 1970), which also includes Lartique's comments. Janet Malcolm, in the essay "Diana and Nikon" in her *Diana and Nikon: Essays on the Aesthetic of Photography* (Boston: David R. Godine, 1980), notes that avant-garde photographers repudiated art-derived photos for this presumed innocence:

> The attributes previously sought by photographers (strong design, lucidity of content, good print values) have been stood on their heads, and the qualities now courted are formlessness, rawness, clutter, accident, and other manifestations of the camera's formidable capacity for imposing disorder on reality. (68)

Commenting on three different photographers and one photographic collection, critic A. D. Coleman also observes the "snapshot aesthetic" in the work of art photographers seeking spontaneity in their images. In his *Light Readings: A Photographic Critic's Writings* (New York: Oxford University Press, 1979), see "Bernadette Mayer: Memories," 98–99; "Robert Delford Brown on Introduction," 130–32; "Emmet Gowin," 163–66; and "Humanizing History: Michael Lesy's *Real Life*," 158–261.

10. In the special *Aperture* issue "The Snapshot" (19, no. 1, 1974), photographer Lisette Model comments:

The snapshooter disregards this problem (of structure and composition) and the result is that his pictures have an apparent disorder and imperfection, which is exactly their appeal and style. The picture isn't straight. It isn't done well. It isn't composed. It isn't thought out. And out of this imbalance, and out of this not knowing, and out of this real innocence toward the medium comes an enormous vitality and expression of life. The look of a snapshot is so similar around the world that it amounts to a universal style. (7)

Included in this book dedicated to investigating the snapshot aesthetic in art photography are photographers Walker Evans, Lee Friedlander, Emmet Gowin, Joel Meyerwitz, Paul Strand, and Garry Winogrand.

11. Jonas Mekas, "8mm as Folk Art," in his *Movie Journal* (New York: Macmillan, 1972), 83. Other studies that suggest a relationship between amateur film and the avant-garde include David Curtis, *Experimental Cinema* (New York: Universe, 1971), 38-44; Sheldon Renan, *An Introduction to the American Underground Film* (New York: Dutton, 1967), 46-51; and Malcolm LeGrice, *Abstract Film and Beyond* (Cambridge, MA: MIT Press, 1977), 52. See LeGrice, 52; Curtis, 49; and Robert Sklar, *Movie-Made America: A Cultural History of American Movies* (New York: Vintage, 1976), 306, for discussions on the rise of experimental film in the United States following World War II. P. Adams Sitney, in *Visionary Film: The American Avant-Garde, 1943-1978* (New York: Oxford University Press, 1979), remarks, for example, on Stan Brakhage's use of camera work to chronicle the vision of the filmmaker (136-45). This vision was often turned to everyday events, as in home movies.

12. Jonas Mekas, "On Law, Morality and Censorship," in *Movie Journal*, 132. See also Mekas, "Kuchar 8mm Manifesto," 166-68; and "On Film Journalism and Newsreels," 236, in *Movie Journal*.

13. See Michel Foucault, *The Archaeology of Knowledge and the Discourse on Language* (New York: Harper Colophon, 1972).

14. Hubert L. Dreyfus and Paul Rabinow, *Michel Foucault: Beyond Structuralism and Hermeneutics* (Chicago: University of Chicago Press, 1982), 67-72. See also Charles L. Lemert and Garth Gillan, *Michel Foucault: Social Theory and Transgressions* (New York: Columbia University Press, 1982), 129-30. For Foucault's own somewhat abstract and dense explanation of discourse, see chapter 1, "The Unities of Discourse," in his *The Archaeology of Knowledge*, 21-30.

15. Foucault, *The Archaeology of Knowledge*, 38.

16. Foucault's historical studies include *Madness and Civilization: A History of Insanity in the Age of Reason* (New York: Vintage, 1973, original printing by Random House, 1965); *Discipline and Punish: The Birth of a Prison* (New York: Vintage, 1979); *The History of Sexuality: Volume I: An Introduction* (New York: Vintage, 1980). For a discussion of Foucault as a metatheorist who seeks to account for phenomena as they are apprehended, see Robert Wuthnow, James Davison Hunter, Albert Bergeson, and Edith Kurzweil, *Cultural Analysis: The Work of Peter L. Berger, Mary Douglas, Michel Foucault and Jurgen Habermas* (Boston: Routledge and Kegan Paul, 1984). Chapter 4, "The Neo Structuralism of Michel Foucault," 133-78, was written by Kurzweil. For a discussion of Foucault's relationship to structuralism, see Lemert and Gillan, *Michel Foucault*, 4-18; and Dreyfus and Rabinow, *Michel Foucault*, 49-66. For a blistering account of the dangers in structuralist history, see E. P. Thompson, "The Poverty of Theory," in his *The Poverty of Theory and Other Essays* (New York: Monthly Review, 1967), 80-99.

17. Barry Smart, *Foucault, Marxism and Critique* (London: Routledge and Kegan Paul, 1983), 96.

18. Ferdinand Braudel, "History and the Social Sciences: The Long Term," in *The Varieties of History*, ed. Fritz Stern (New York: Random House, 1973), 404-11.

19. Gregor McLennon, *Marxism and the Methodologies of History* (London: Verso, 1981), 138-40.

20. Lemert and Gillan, *Michel Foucault*, 40-44.

21. Foucault, *The Archaeology of Knowledge*, 168–69. For a theoretical analysis of the historiographic issues of the relationship between media technology and media culture, see Raymond Williams, "Culture and Technology," in his *The Year 2000* (New York: Pantheon, 1983), 128–31; Stephen Heath, "The Cinematic Apparatus: Technology as Historical and Cultural Form," in *The Cinematic Apparatus*, ed. Teresa DeLauretis and Stephen Heath (New York: St. Martin's, 1980), 6–7.

22. For discussions of media and familialism, see Laura Mulvey, "Melodrama In and Out of the Home," 80–100; and Jane Feuer, "Narrative Form in American Television," in *High Theory/Low Culture: Analyzing Popular Television and Film*, ed. Colin MacCabe (New York: St. Martin's, 1986); Diane Waldman, "At Last I Can Tell It to Someone: Feminine Point of View and Subjectivity in the Gothic Romance Film of the 1940s," *Cinema Journal* 23, no. 2 (Winter 1984): 29–40; Julia Lesage, "Women's Rage," in *Marxism and the Interpretation of Culture*, ed. Gary Nelson and Lawrence Grossberg (Champaign-Urbana: University of Illinois Press, 1988), 419–28; Ellen Seiter, "Promise and Contradiction: The Daytime Television Serial," *Film Reader* 5 (1982): 150–63; Rosalind Coward, "The Mirror with a Memory," in *Female Desires* (New York: Grove, 1985), 49–54.

23. In contemporary film and video, amateur film has been used as archival footage of family life. Documentary compilation has a long history, particularly among radical filmmakers. For an excellent resource to critical issues for political documentary, especially in relationship to the debates between a more aggressively deconstructive compilation approach and the more realist, cinema verité approach, see *Show Us Life: Toward a History and Aesthetics of the Committed Documentary*, ed. Thomas Waugh (Metuchen, N.J.: Scarecrow, 1984). For an example of how these issues of compilation, deconstruction, and the interrogation of the realist text spill over into documentary photography as well, see Grant Kester, "Towards a New Social Documentary," *Afterimage* 14, no. 8 (March 1987): 10–14.

For a very thorough and exciting overview of the relationship between postmodernism and film, see a recent issue of *Screen* (28 no. 2 [Spring 1987]) entitled *Postmodern Screen*. Many of the articles in this special issue interrogate the question of the politics and power relationships in postmodernist aesthetic strategies. However, none of the articles discusses postmodernism in relationship to recent trends in compilation documentary film that play with the multiplicity of discourses and materials for a more pointed and complex political analysis less dependent on privileging the often naturalized relationship between filmmaker, camera, and subject. Many so-called critical postmodern films collapse the distinctions between professional and amateur film, as Rea Tajiri's *History and Memory*, Lise Yasi's *Family Gathering*, or Oliver Stone's *J.F.K.*

This issue of appropriating and reconstituting imagery, although an intervention, can obscure the larger political issue of access to media production and the public sphere, which is dependent on technology. In this way the issue of appropriation of imagery may maroon political discussions of media in an oasis of representation dislocated from actual political and social struggles. Access to the means of media production is still critical (see Paper Tiger TV or Deep Dish TV); amateurism, as a contradictory practice, which is both consumption and production, offers some limited access. The contradictory nature of amateurism has been argued by Enzensberger in "Constituents of a Theory of the Media," in *The Consciousness Industry*.

1. Pleasure or Money

1. Jean Bethke Elshtain, "Moral Woman and Immoral Man: A Consideration of the Public-Private Split and Its Political Ramifications," *Politics and Society* (1974): 453–73.

2. Jurgen Habermas, "The Public Sphere: An Encyclopaedia Article (1964)," *New German Critique* 3 (Fall 1974): 49–55.

3. Ibid., 51.

4. Raymond Williams, *The Sociology of Culture* (New York: Schocken, 1982), 91.

5. Jurgen Habermas, "Technology and Science as Ideology," in his *Towards a Rational Society*, trans. J. J. Shapiro (Boston: Beacon, 1970), 81–93.

6. Habermas, *Towards a Rational Society*, 97–104.

7. Jurgen Habermas, *Legitimation Crisis*, trans. Thomas McCarthy (Boston: Beacon, 1975), 84.

8. Williams, *Sociology of Culture*, 106–107.

9. Some of the recent research on the differentiation of skills in the workplace include an important work by Harry Braverman, *Labor and Monopoly Capital: The Degradation of Work in the Twentieth Century* (New York: Monthly Review, 1974); and Richard Edwards, *Contested Terrain: The Transformation of the Workplace in the Twentieth Century* (New York: Basic, 1979).

10. Adolfo Sanchez Vazquez, *Art and Society: Essays in Marxist Aesthetics* (New York: Monthly Review, 1973), 205–207.

11. Eli Zaretsky, *Capitalism, the Family and Personal Life* (New York: Harper and Row, 1976).

12. Habermas, *Legitimation Crisis*, 78.

13. Vazquez, *Art and Society*, 202–26.

14. Magali Sarfatti Larson, *The Rise of Professionalism: A Sociological Analysis* (Berkeley: University of California Press, 1977), 40–48.

15. Ibid., 40–41.

16. Janet Staiger, "Dividing Labor for Production Control: Thomas Ince and the Rise of the Studio System," in *Cinema Examined: Selections from Cinema Journal*, ed. Richard Dyer MacCann and Jack C. Ellis (New York: Dutton, 1982), 144–55.

17. Sklar, *Movie-Made America*, 34–41.

18. See, for example, Sklar, *Movie-Made America*; Stuart Ewen and Elizabeth Ewen, "City Lights: Immigrant Women and the Rise of the Movies," in their *Channels of Desire: Mass Images and the Shaping of American Consciousness* (New York: McGraw-Hill, 1982), 81–102; and John Ellis, "The Dominance of Hollywood Film," chap. 13 in his *Visible Fictions* (London: Routledge and Kegan Paul, 1982), 194–210.

19. Larson, *The Rise of Professionalism*, 40–41.

20. Alan Trachtenberg, *The Incorporation of America: Culture and Society in the Gilded Age* (New York: Hill and Wang, 1982), 60–65.

21. Ibid., 65–72.

22. For example, the Amateur Athletic Union began in 1880. The *Amateur Collector*, an organ that promoted amateur historical work, began publication in 1888. The *Amateur Gazette*, a more general magazine, assumed publication in 1873. The *Amateur Journal*, devoted to literary efforts, began in 1872. The *Amateur Press* began in 1878; *Amateur Work*, a scientifically oriented magazine, started in 1901; *Amateur World* in 1878; *Amateur Annual*, for amateur journalists, in 1872; *Amateur*, for music and literary pursuits, in 1870.

23. Larson, *The Rise of Professionalism*, 136.

24. Ibid., 137–45.

25. Ibid., 156–57.

26. Ibid., 140–42.

27. Ibid., 146.

28. Robert Wiebe, *The Search for Order, 1877–1920* (New York: Hill and Wang, 1967), 160–66.

29. David F. Noble, *America by Design: Science, Technology, and the Rise of Corporate Capitalism* (New York: Knopf, 1977).

30. "The Amateur Spirit," *Atlantic*, August 1901, 278.

31. Ibid., 276.

32. Ibid., 272–73.

33. John G. Cawelti, *Apostles of the Self-Made Man: Changing Concepts of Success in America* (Chicago: University of Chicago Press, 1965), 39–75.

34. Ibid., 165–99.

35. Ray Ginger, *The Age of Excess: The United States from 1877 to 1914* (New York: Macmil-

lan, 1975), 19–52. Ginger describes the growth of several major corporations from 1877 to 1892: Swift, Anaconda, Carnegie, Standard Oil. He comments that the development of these large organizations spurred many administrative programs in the delegating of decision making, and as a result, a system of specialists emerged. Ginger observes that these specialists within corporations were more inclined to conventional rather than to imaginative actions.

36. "Great Amateurs," *Living Age*, 22 April 1911, 248–50.

37. Ibid., 248.

38. From 1890 to 1910 a variety of popular magazines such as *Overland, Academy, Munsey's, Country Life in America, Argosy*, and *Strand* published articles extolling the virtues of amateur pursuits.

39. Anna Fuller, "An Amateur Gamble," *Scribner's Magazine* 14, 1893, 65–69.

40. T. J. Jackson Lears, "From Salvation to Self-Realization: Advertising and the Therapeutic Roots of the Consumer Culture, 1880–1930," in *The Culture of Consumption: Critical Essays in American History, 1880–1980*, ed. Richard Wrightman Fox and T. J. Jackson Lears (New York: Pantheon, 1983), 18–19.

41. John Berger, *Ways of Seeing* (London: British Broadcasting Corporation, 1972), 83–112.

42. See M. H. Spielman, "Amateur, Noble in Art," *Magazine of Art* 16, 1893, 62, as an example of the prejudice against this ruling-class dilettantism.

43. "Photography in Advertising," editorial, *Photo-Miniature*, June 1904, 57.

44. "The Amateur Spirit," 271.

2. Entrepreneurs, Artists, Hobbyists, and Workers: 1897–1923

1. Noble, introduction to *America by Design*, xxii.

2. C. W. Ceram, *Archeology of the Cinema* (New York: Harcourt, Brace and World, 1965), 141. See also P. L. Mannock, "The Father of Films Who Never Made a Halfpenny Out of Them," *Kinematograph Weekly* 28, October 1948, 6, 8, for an anecdotal account of William Friese-Greene's cinema technology. In addition, a document from the Bell and Howell Corporate Archive lists a similar assortment of inventors and machines, some of which are referred to in popular photography magazines of the period as amateur devices, like the Proszynski Aeroscope camera in 1910 and Birt Acres of England's "Birtag" combination camera and projector in 1898. For a description of this, see a letter from P. E. Phillimore to M. G. Townsley, 4 October 1954, Bell and Howell Corporate Archive, Bell and Howell Corporation, Chicago, Illinois. Kenneth Mac-Gowan, in his *Behind the Screen: The History and Techniques of the Motion Picture* (New York: Delacorte, 1965), 53–84, describes a similar study of competing inventors.

3. Ceram, *Archeology of the Cinema*, 141–53.

4. Sklar, *Movie-Made America*, 12–13.

5. Reese Jenkins, *Images and Enterprise: Technology and the American Photographic Industry, 1839–1925* (Baltimore: Johns Hopkins University Press, 1975), 276–79.

6. Jenkins, *Images and Enterprise*, 275; Mae D. Huettig, *Economic Control of the Motion Picture Industry* (Philadelphia: University of Pennsylvania Press, 1944), 11–12.

7. Jenkins, *Images and Enterprise*, 117.

8. Survey of *British Journal of Photography* from 1896 to 1924 and survey of United States Patents from 1896 to 1924.

9. See Dr. C. E. Kenneth Mees's two-part series on the Cine-Kodak in the *British Journal of Photography*. Part 1 is in *British Journal of Photography* (9 November 1923): 682–92, and part 2 is in *British Journal of Photography* (16 November 1923): 7, 020–26. Mees worked for Kodak's Research and Development Department. His leadership was directly responsible for the development of 16mm reversal film.

10. Sklar, *Movie-Made America*, 19.

11. Jeanne Allen, "The Decay of the Motion Picture Patents Company," in *The American Film Industry*, Tino Balio ed. (Madison: The University of Wisconsin Press, 1976), 122.

12. Lewis Jacobs, *The Rise of the American Film* (New York: Harcourt Brace and Co., 1939), 81–82.

13. William R. Johnson, "Albert Sumners Howell and Motion Picture Standards," n.d., 3–10, Bell and Howell Corporate Archive; and Jack Fay Robinson, *Bell and Howell Company: A Seventy-five-Year History* (Chicago: Bell and Howell Co., 1982), 15–23.

14. Johnson, "Albert Sumners Howell," 4–6.

15. "Bell and Howell 35mm camera," 18 September 1975, Bell and Howell Corporate Archive.

16. "Historical Data, Bell and Howell Equipment," 11 March 1949, Bell and Howell Corporate Archive. See also "Historical Data: Bell and Howell Equipment," 11 March 1949, Bell and Howell Corporate Archive; letter from John L. Peele, Patent Attorney, Bell and Howell Company, to John Caldwell, 16 June 1972, 1–3, Bell and Howell Corporate Archive; "Bell and Howell Motion Picture Film Printers," n.d., Bell and Howell Corporate Archive; and U.S. Patent no. 879,355 (18 February 1908) for Moving Picture Machine to Daniel Bell, U.S. Patent no. 1,038,586 (17 September 1912) for Moving Picture Machine to A. S. Howell, U.S. Patent no. 1,056,794 (25 March 1913) for Photographic Printing Apparatus to A. S. Howell, Bell and Howell Corporate Archive.

17. Johnson, "Albert Sumners Howell," 8.

18. Robinson, *Bell and Howell Company*, 27–31.

19. Memorandum from George Spoor to Bell and Howell Company, 19 April 1953, 1–7, Bell and Howell Corporate Archive.

20. Sales records of the Bell and Howell Professional Division, 1907–18, Bell and Howell Corporate Archive.

21. Sklar, *Movie-Made America*, 71.

22. Ibid., 50.

23. Raymond Fielding, *The American Newsreel, 1911–1967* (Norman: University of Oklahoma Press, 1972), 107.

24. Journals surveyed include *Lady's World, Ladies' Home Journal, Motography, Saturday Evening Post, Harper's Monthly Magazine*, and *McClure's*.

25. Photography and technical journals surveyed include *Illustrated World, Photographic News, Scientific American*, and *Popular Mechanics*.

26. Glenn Porter, *The Rise of Big Business, 1860–1910* (Arlington Heights, Ill.: ATTM Publishing Corporation, 1973), 88–92.

27. Noble, *America by Design*, xxii–xxiv.

28. See Glenn E. Mathews and Ralfe G. Tarkington, "Early History of Amateur Motion Picture Film," in *A Technological History of Motion Pictures and Television*, ed. Raymond Fielding (Berkeley: University of California Press, 1967), 129.

29. Ibid., 129.

30. Gordon Hendricks, "History of the Kinetoscope," in *The American Film Industry*, ed. Tino Balio, 35. The Kinetoscope's overall dimensions were 18 by 17 by 48.5 inches, including the base and the eyepiece. Although no systematic study of professional cameras has been executed to date, a survey of *Motion Picture World* equipment ads for 1900–23 supplies evidence that cameras during this early period had suitcaselike dimensions. Of course, by World War I the United States Government was shooting 35mm film on the fronts with cameras slightly smaller than a potato chip box.

31. Jenkins, *Images and Enterprise*, 276–89.

32. Allen, "The Decay of the Motion Picture Patents Company," 122.

33. See Reese Jenkins, chap. 3, "Some Interrelations of Science, Technology and the Photographic Industry in the Nineteenth Century" (Ph.D. diss., University of Wisconsin-Madison, 1974).

34. Jenkins, "Some Interrelations of Science," 287–95.

35. Jenkins, *Images and Enterprise*, 141–58.

36. Fielding, *The American Newsreel*, 130–31.

37. Ibid.

38. Tarkington, in *A Technological History*, ed. Fielding, 131.

39. See Martin Quigley, *Magic Shadows: The Story of the Origins of Motion Pictures* (Washington: Georgetown University Press, 1948).

40. Helmut Gernsheim, *The History of Photography* (London: Oxford University Press, 1955), 310.

41. "How to Build a Moving Picture Camera," *Scientific American*, 17 December 1910, 483. See also E. H. Williamson, "Building a Moving Picture Camera," *Scientific American*, 22 December 1917, 369–78.

42. "Two Pages of Interesting Pictures and Ideas for Children," *Popular Mechanics*, January 1917, 120.

43. "Interesting Ideas, Pictures and Toys for Boys and Girls," *Popular Mechanics*, June 1919, 920.

44. "Moving Picture Toy for Children," *Popular Mechanics*, December 1922, 981.

45. "A Homemade Motion Picture Camera," *Popular Mechanics*, December 1918, 969–74.

46. "The 1899 Cynnagraph," *Optical Magic Lantern and Photographic Enlarger*, September 1898, 138.

47. See discussion of Oskar Messter in Fielding, *The American Newsreel*, 109.

48. "Inventions New and Interesting," *Scientific American*, 14 June 1914, 554.

49. "Bringing the Talkies to Your Home," *Technical World*, August 1913, 813–18.

50. Patents published in the *British Journal of Photography*: "Prator Home Cinematographs" (20 March 1914): 235–36; "Home Cinematograph, No. 20, 365, 1913" (9 September 1913): 632; "New Apparatus" (6 November 1914): 287; "The Filmoscope Home Cinematograph" (26 March 1915): 213; "Home Cinematography, No. 18, 250, 1914" (29 August 1914): 513; "Home Cinematographs, No. 7, 524, 1914 (25 March 1914): 313.

51. "Motion Picture Projector in Compact Form," *Popular Mechanics*, September 1914, 348.

52. Fielding, *The American Newsreel*, 146.

53. "The Kammatograph," *British Journal of Photography* (9 March 1900): 147.

54. "Moving Pictures of the Amateur," *Technical World*, September 1912, 70–74.

55. For more specific descriptions of the Bettini disk system, see "Home Motion Pictures in Disk Form," *Scientific American*, 16 October 1916, 407; "Bringing Motion Pictures into the Home," *Scientific American*, 11 November 1916, 134–38; G. H. Dacy, "Tom Thumb of Movie Machines," *Illustrated World*, February 1921, 1,029–30.

56. "Bringing Motion Pictures into the Home," 134.

57. Joseph H. North, *The Early Development of the Motion Picture* (New York: Arno, 1973), 165–66.

58. "New Motion Picture Camera Has Unusual Features," *Popular Mechanics*, 23 February 1923, 253; and "Moving Picture Machine for Amateurs," *Popular Mechanics*, October 1913, 558.

59. "Novel Pocket Camera That Uses Movie Films," *Popular Mechanics*, September 1914, 403.

60. "Motion Pictures Portrait Photography," *Scientific American*, 13 July 1918, 28.

61. "A Novel Camera for Making Moving Pictures," *Scientific American*, 9 January 1909, 22.

62. "A Cinematograph Hand Camera," *Scientific American*, 1 November 1913, 346.

63. "Patent News: Home Cinematograph Camera, No. 14, 275, 1914," *British Journal of Photography*, (13 June 1914): 167.

64. "A Cinematograph Hand Camera," *Scientific American*, 346. See also "A Motion Picture Camera and Projector for Home Use," *Scientific American*, 24 February 1917, 206.

65. "The Latest Motion Picture Outfit for Amateurs," *Scientific American*, August 1923, 111.

66. For a brief account of this agreement, see L. Joseph Roberts, "Golden Anniversary for Bell and Howell Cameras," *International Photographer*, October 1979, 25–26.

67. "Bell and Howell—Age 45," Typescript (TS), n.d., Bell and Howell Corporate Archive.

68. U.S. Patents, Bell and Howell Corporate Archive; and letter from John E. Peele, Patent Attorney, Bell and Howell Company, to E. F. Bennett, 24 February 1975, Bell and Howell Corporate Archive.

69. Jenkins, *Images and Enterprise*, 188–89.

70. Ibid., 300–305.

71. For Eastman Kodak's explanation of why this reversal stock would stimulate the amateur-film market, see Malcolm G. Townsley, "Questionnaire Submitted to the Eastman Kodak Company," 8 February 1954, 1–8, Bell and Howell Corporate Archive.

72. Charles A. Bearchell, "Bell and Howell, the First Forty-Two Years," TS, Bell and Howell Corporate Archive.

73. Townsley, "Questionnaire Submitted to Eastman Kodak Company," 2.

74. Ibid.

75. "Bell and Howell 17.5mm Camera and Projector," Bell and Howell Corporate Archive. Also see U.S. Patent no. 1,417,523 (30 May 1922) for Motion Picture Camera and Tripod to A. S. Howell, filed 28 April 1918 for the specifications of this camera and tripod design.

76. Letter from R. J. Kittredge, President, Bell and Howell Company, to Board of Directors, 25 March 1921, 2, Bell and Howell Corporate Archive.

77. Bearchell, "Bell and Howell," 20–23. The Bell and Howell patents for the 16mm Filmo and projector are U.S. Patent no. 1,587,955 (8 June 1926) for Motion Picture Machine and the Like to A. S. Howell, filed 1 July 1922; U.S. Patent no. 1,620,726 (15 March 1927) for Motion Picture Camera and the Like to A. S. Howell, filed 13 September 1923; and U.S. Patent no. 1,620,727 (15 March 1927) for Photographic Camera to A. S. Howell, filed 12 August 1925.

78. See letter from John E. Peele, Patent Attorney, Bell and Howell Company, to E. F. Bennett, 24 February 1975, 2, Bell and Howell Corporate Archive.

79. "The Latest Motion Picture Outfit for Amateurs," *Scientific American*, August 1923, 111.

80. "Amateur Cinematography," *British Journal of Photography* (26 January 1923): 45.

81. Dr. C. E. Kenneth Mees, "Amateur Cinematography," *British Journal of Photography* (9 November 1925): 687.

82. J. H. McNabb, "How We Smashed Dealer Resistance for a New Product," *Sales Management*, 30 April 1927, 855, Bell and Howell Corporate Archive.

83. Ibid.

84. Ernest Dench, "Making Money with a Motion Picture Camera," *British Journal of Photography* (14 November 1919): 661–62.

85. Ellerslie Wallace, "Amateur Photography," *Outing*, May 1889, 102.

86. Gernsheim, *The History of Photography*, 312.

87. For a historical overview of this development, see Gernsheim, *The History of Photography*.

88. George H. Hepworth, "Amateur Photography," *Harper's Magazine*, August 1889, 454.

89. W. S. Harwood, "Amateur Photography of Today," *Cosmopolitan*, January 1896, 250. This article also situates industrial progress within amateur practice, which is formed as an area of invention. In current parlance, a free-enterprise zone.

90. Danny Guthrie, "Photography as Art" (Unpublished paper, January 1984, Ithaca College, Ithaca, New York).

91. Beaumont Newhall, *The History of Photography* (New York: Museum of Modern Art, 1982), 141–1,423.

92. Peter Henry Emerson, "Photography, a Pictorial Art," reprinted in his *Naturalistic Photography for Students of the Art* (London: Sampson Low, Marston, Searle and Rivington, 1889; reprint, New York: Arno, 1973), 278–84.

93. Emerson, *Naturalistic Photography*, 22–23. For a collection of Emerson's photographs from this period, see Nancy Newhall, *P. H. Emerson* (New York: Aperture, 1975).

94. Emerson, "Educated Sight," *Naturalistic Photography*, 229–36.

95. Peter Henry Emerson, *Death of Naturalist Photography* (Privately published, 1890; reprint, New York: Arno, 1973).

96. Newhall, *The History of Photography*, 146.

97. Abigail Solomon-Godeau, "The Return of Alfred Stieglitz," *Afterimage* (Summer 1984): 22.

98. Emerson, *Naturalistic Photography*, 18-22.

99. Solomon-Godeau, "The Return of Alfred Stieglitz," 22-23; Newhall, *The History of Photography*, 146-52.

100. See, for example, Mary Panzer, *Philadelphia Naturalistic Photography, 1865-1906* (New Haven: Yale University Art Gallery, 1982), 16-22; William Inness Homer, *Alfred Stieglitz and the Photo-Secession* (Boston: New York Graphic Society, 1983); Newhall, *The History of Photography*, 152-64.

101. Vicki Goldberg, "Pictorialism," *American Photographer*, May 1979, 58-62.

102. A. H. Wall, *Artistic Landscape Photography* (London: Percy Lund and Co., 1896; reprint, New York: Arno, 1973), 118.

103. Ibid., 127-52.

104. See A. J. Anderson, *The Artistic Side of Photography in Theory and Practice* (London: Stanley Paul and Co., 1910; reprint New York: Arno, 1973).

105. John Wallace Gillies, *Principles of Pictorial Photography* (New York: Falk, 1923; reprint, New York: Arno, 1973), 50-51.

106. Ibid., 60-71.

107. Ibid., 183-86.

108. For a discussion of straight photography, see Newhall, *The History of Photography*, 167-96. For historical overviews of these early twentieth-century art movements in painting, see H. H. Arnason, *History of Modern Art* (Englewood Cliffs, N.J.: Prentice-Hall, 1977): impressionism, 26-31; fauvism, 96-139; cubism, 201-19; expressionism, 162-74; futurism, 220-25; constructivism, 226-40; dadaism, 207-16.

109. W. S. Harwood, "Amateur Photography Today," *Cosmopolitan*, January 1896, 249-53.

110. Clarence B. Moore, "Leading Amateur Photographers," *Cosmopolitan*, February 1892, 421.

111. Ellerslie Wallace, "Amateur Photography," *Outing*, April 1889, 29.

112. Ibid. Another example of this movement toward discipline and duplication of residual cultural representations is Harwood, "Amateur Photography Today."

113. Margaret Biskind, "Photographing by Women," *Outing*, October 1890, 38.

114. See F. W. Crane, "Amateur Photographers: American Women," *Munsey's*, July 1894, 398-408. Crane claims that since women have more time and are more meticulous in the application of details, they are better photographers than men.

115. Wallace, "Amateur Photography," 29.

116. Biskind, "Photographing by Women," 40.

117. "Filming Adventures in Beauty," *Arts and Decoration*, 15 December 1921, 299.

118. Ibid.

119. "Painting Moods with a Motion Picture Camera," *Arts and Decoration*, September 1923, 44.

120. "Cinematography, a New Art for Amateurs," *Arts and Decoration*, September 1919, 230.

121. Ibid.

122. See Samuel Haber, *Efficiency and Uplift: Scientific Management in the Progressive Era* (Chicago: University of Chicago Press, 1964), 51-74, for an analysis of the general efficiency craze in American culture from 1905 to 1919. For a specific discussion of the exportation of principles of scientific management to the home, see Barbara Ehrenreich and Deidre English, *For Her Own Good: 150 Years of the Experts' Advice to Women* (Garden City, N.Y.: Anchor, 1978), 161-78.

123. See, for example, "Speeding Up Labor by Movies," *Current Opinion*, September 1913, 206.

124. Hirsch, *Family Photographs*, 3–46.

125. Sontag, *On Photography*, 8–9.

126. "Movies for Everybody," *Literary Digest*, 24 February 1917, 463.

127. "Filming the Family," *Literary Digest*, 5 June 1915, 1,346.

128. "Kinematography," *Photogram*, June 1899, 161, 166.

129. Mervin Delaway, "Make and Project Your Own Movies," *Illustrated World*, April 1917, 1,867.

130. H. H. Windsor, "Films for Families," *Popular Mechanics*, September 1911, 343.

131. "Filming the Family," *Literary Digest*, 1,347.

132. Fielding, *The American Newsreel*, 155–56.

133. See "Ways in Which Motion Pictures Are Playing a Big Part in the War," *Current Opinion*, June 1918, 403–40. See also Ernest A. Dench, "Military Air Scouting by Motion Pictures," *Scientific American*, 13 February 1915, 156.

134. "What the Camera Is Doing to Stimulate War and to Picture It for Posterity," *Current Opinion*, December 1917, 391.

135. Ibid.

136. "Secrets of the Motion Picture Camofleurs Are Revealed," *Current Opinion*, May 1918, 330.

137. See Oscar G. Brockett and Robert R. Findlay, *Century of Innovation: A History of European and American Theatre and Drama since 1870* (Englewood Cliffs, N.J.: Prentice-Hall, 1973), 182–83; and Bernard Hewitt, *Theatre U.S.A., 1868 to 1957* (New York: McGraw-Hill, 1959), 256–57.

138. See Brockett and Findlay, *Century of Innovation*, 183; and Hewitt, *Theatre U.S.A.*, 205. Brockett and Findlay trace the European influences on realist drama and describe playwrights and plays on pp. 34–180.

139. Charles Carey Waddle, "American Amateur State," *Cosmopolitan*, November 1890, 12.

140. Ibid., 25.

141. Ibid., 16.

142. Helena Smith Dayton and Louise Bascom Barratt, *The Book of Entertainments and Theatricals* (New York: Robert M. McBride and Co., 1923), 202–205.

143. A. Davies, "Society Amateur Actresses," *Cosmopolitan*, June 1905, 115–24. *Woman's Home Companion* published many articles explaining amateur theatrical practice for women. It is interesting to note that the site of this cultural resistance to the commodification of leisure and the isolation of the nuclear family circulates in a women's magazine devoted to the cult of true womanhood. For examples of the dissemination of administrative and cultural production skills to women, see Walter P. Eaton, "Outdoor Play," *Woman's Home Companion*, August 1910, 24; Scott C. Fauntleroy, "Amateur Dramatics: A Practical Talk on Getting Up a Play," *Woman's Home Companion*, April 1913, 28; E. H. Biefstadt, "Play Producing for Amateurs," *Woman's Home Companion*, December 1916, 14; and Cecil B. Casak, "Homemade Theater," *Woman's Home Companion*, February 1906, 40–41.

144. Davies, "Society Amateur Actresses," 122.

145. J. Barnes, "Amateur Theatricals," *Century*, March 1911, 671.

146. Corinne Robert Redgrave, "What Every Amateur Actress Ought to Know," *Ladies' Home Journal*, October 1913, 108.

147. Barnes, "Amateur Theatricals," 673. Advice centered on content choice as a way of dealing with audiences: for example, "Amateur theatricals, no matter how well done, can prove of interest only to those persons who are personally acquainted with performers," (Davies, "Society Amateur Actresses," 20).

148. "Amateur Theatrical Attempt to Improve the Dramatic Spirit," *Living Age*, 16 March 1907, 659.

149. Anne A. T. Craig, *The Dramatic Festival: A Consideration of the Lyrical Method as a Factor in Preparatory Education* (New York: G. P. Putnam's Sons, 1912), 7–13.

150. Brockett and Findlay, *Century of Innovation*, 228–29; Jay Williams, *Stage Left* (New York: Charles Scribner's Sons, 1974), 1–29.

151. Quoted in "Violation of Theatrical Neutrality by the Experimental Amateur," *Current Opinion*, May 1915, 355. This article provides a good synopsis and analysis of amateur theatrical activity as a center for experimentation from the perspective of the period.

152. Huettig, *Economic Control of the Motion Picture Industry*, 31–39; Sklar, *Movie-Made America*, 46–47; Balio, ed., *The American Film Industry*, 114.

153. MacGowan, *Behind the Screen*, 245–58. For an industry view of these economic developments, written in 1927, see Halsey, Stuart and Company, "The Motion Picture Industry as a Basis for Bond Financing," in *The American Film Industry*, ed. Balio, 171–91.

154. Sklar, *Movie-Made America*, 74–84.

155. See Elizabeth Stevenson, *Babbitts and Bohemians: The American 1920s* (New York: Macmillan, 1967), 74–84.

156. "Secrets of the Motion Picture Camofleurs Are Revealed," *Current Opinion*, 330–31.

157. A few examples of these magazine articles that stressed control and manipulation of nature as the mark of a true professional include B. Musson and R. Grau, "Fortune in Films: Moving Pictures in the Making," *McClure's*, December 1912, 193–202; Richard Harding Davies, "Breaking into the Movies," *Scribner's Magazine*, March 1914, 275–93; "Shooting Generals with a Movie Camera," *Literary Digest*, 8 December 1917, 78; Ernest A. Dench, "Amateur Photo Play Society," *Independent*, 1 December 1917, 428; and Lee Charles Miller, "Adventures of a Motion Picture Amateur," *Outing*, October 1921, 18–20.

158. Photoplay Research Society, *Opportunities in the Motion Picture Industry and How to Qualify for Positions in Its Many Branches* (Los Angeles: Bureau of Vocational Guidance, 1922), 7.

159. Aber Wycliffe Hill, *Ten Million Photoplay Plots* (Feature Photo-Drama Co., 1921; reprint, Los Angeles: Garland Classic of Film Literature, 1979). See also William Lord Wright, *Photoplay Writing* (New York: Falk, 1922); A. Van Buren Powell, *The Photoplay Synopsis* (Springfield, Mass.: The Home Correspondence School, 1919).

3. Professional Results with Amateur Ease: 1923–1940

1. A. P. Hollis, "Movies at Home," *Amateur Movie Makers* 2 no. 4, April 1927, 11.

2. Victor Animatograph Company ad, *American Cinematographer*, June 1929, 26.

3. Bell and Howell Filmo ad, *American Cinematographer*, June 1930, 29.

4. Ibid.

5. There is no existing documentation. This observation is based on inferential evidence derived from advertisements in amateur-film magazines and *American Cinematographer* from 1923 to 1933. I am assuming that the financial resources of these firms for national ad campaigns indicate a strong market position.

6. Herbert C. McKay, "The Amateur Kinematographer," *Photo-Era Magazine* 56 no. 3 March 1926, 169.

7. Herbert C. McKay, "The Amateur Kinematographer," *Photo-Era Magazine* 56 no. 2, February 1926, 11.

8. See, for example, *Photo-Era's* 1927 announcement of a special section of the magazine devoted to amateur cinema: "Our idea is to focus the attention of our readers on text-matter and advertising relating to motion picture equipment and accessories. We believe that this change will be of advantage to our readers and our advertisers" ("Our New Motion Picture Section," *Photo-Era* 57, no. 1, January 1927, 56). On the adjacent page, an announcement read,

Motion Picture Section featuring The Amateur Kinematographer edited by Herbert C. McKay, A.R.P.S., Dean of the New York Institute of Photography, author of several motion picture textbooks and the Announcement of Motion Picture Manufacturers and

Dealers in Amateur Equipment and Accessories, A Department Conducted For and By Photo-Era Readers and Advertisers, When Dealing with Advertisers Please Mention Photo-Era Magazine.

9. Annual Report (1944) of Victor Animatograph Corporation, "The 16mm Industry Comes of Age, 1912–1944," 6, Bell and Howell Corporate Archive.

10. Ibid., 7.

11. Alexander F. Victor, "The Portable Projector, Its Present Status and Needs," in the 1944 Annual Report of Victor Animatograph Corporation, 11.

12. Alexander F. Victor, "The History and Origin of 16mm," in the 1944 Annual Report of Victor Animatograph Corporation, 9–10.

13. Letter from G. Rose, President, Victor Animatograph Corporation, to Malcolm Townsley, 18 February 1954, addendum and pictures, Bell and Howell Corporate Archive.

14. "Eastman Kodak Company Patents Listing," TS, 1–104, Bell and Howell Corporate Archive.

15. "Bell and Howell—Age 45," TS, n.d., 3, Bell and Howell Corporate Archive.

16. "Bell and Howell Manufacturing Precision," *Photo-Era Magazine* 67 no. 1, July 1931, 56.

17. See *Selling Filmo*, 1927–32, Bell and Howell Corporate Archive.

18. "Historical Data—Bell and Howell Equipment," March 1949, Bell and Howell Corporate Archive.

19. Herbert C. McKay, "Popular Kinematography," *Photo-Era Magazine* 56 no. 1, January 1926, 50.

20. Ibid.

21. "A Solution to the News Kinematographer's Problem," *Photo-Era Magazine* 57 no. 4, October 1926, 218.

22. "Improved Eyemo Cameras," Form no. 6005, TS, n.d., Bell and Howell Corporate Archive.

23. See Filmo ads, Bell and Howell Corporate Archive.

24. See, for example, "Bell and Howell Announces a New, Lower Priced, Pocket Size Movie Camera," *Photo-Era Magazine* 64 no. 6, June 1928, 368.

25. J. H. McNabb, "The Amateur Turns a Penny," *Amateur Movie Makers*, December 1926, 19.

26. Dr. James Edward Rogers, "Recreation Annexes the Movies," *Amateur Movie Makers*, May 1929, 306–307.

27. "Industrial Efficiency by Amateur Movies," *Literary Digest* 17, January 1931, 26–27.

28. 1946 Bell and Howell Annual Report, 9; and Bearchell, "Bell and Howell," 25, both in Bell and Howell Corporate Archive.

29. John Markland, "More Home Movie Fans," *New York Times*, 17 January 1937, p. 10, sec. 11, C1. See also ad for Cine-Kodak 8, *New York Times*, 17 June 1934, 20, which states that this equipment is inexpensive.

30. Jenkins, *Images and Enterprise*, 317–18.

31. Dr. C. E. Kenneth Mees, *Photography* (New York: Macmillan, 1937), 145, 167–95.

32. Robinson, *Bell and Howell Company*, 161–62; see Appendix III, Sales, Earnings, and Employment.

33. Everett F. Wagner, quoted in Robinson, *Bell and Howell Company*, 47–48.

34. Bearchell, "Bell and Howell," 26–27; and Bell and Howell and Kodak Comparative Chronology, TS, n.d., Bell and Howell Corporate Archive.

35. Bell and Howell Company records on sales, profits, and employment, 1911–44, Bell and Howell Corporate Archive.

36. "Historical Data List of Bell and Howell Equipment," TS, n.d., 2, Bell and Howell Corporate Archive.

37. "Professional 16mm Camera," internal company document, February 1941, Bell and Howell Corporate Archive.

38. William Stull, A.S.C., "Bell and Howell's First Professional Sixteen," *American Cinematographer*, April 1941, 192.

39. 1946 Bell and Howell *Annual Report*, 3, Bell and Howell Corporate Archive.

40. Ibid.

41. See "Bell and Howell's Contribution to the War Effort, 1944," TS, n.d., Bell and Howell Corporate Archive.

42. Ibid., 1.

43. Ibid., 5.

44. Ibid., 5–7.

45. I. A. Williams, "The Importance of Doing Things Badly," *Living Age*, 16 June 1923, 671–73.

46. "The Amateur and the Dilettante," *Living Age*, 3 April 1926, 71.

47. Roy W. Winton, "The Amateur Cinema Camera Man," *Amateur Movie Makers*, March 1927, 28.

48. Phillip Sterling, "Sowing the 16mm Field," *New York Times*, 25 July 1937, p. 3, sec. 10, C7.

49. Reels 1–10, George Johnson Home Movie Collection, 1928–41, Wisconsin State Historical Society, Madison, Wisconsin.

50. "Home Movies," *Parents Magazine*, April 1929, 48; 1893, 65–69.

51. See Christopher Lasch, *Haven in a Heartless World* (New York: Basic, 1977), 22–44.

52. Eleanor King, "Let's Make a Movie," *Woman's Home Companion*, April 139, 48.

53. Herbert C. McKay, "Kinematography in the Home, *Photo-Era Magazine* 54 no. 6, June 1926, 343–44.

54. Gordon B. Wayne, "Pictorial Diary for a Lifetime: Home Movies for Christmas," *American Home*, December 1928, 266.

55. William Stull, "Amateur Movie Making," *American Cinematographer*, August 1929, 27.

56. See Society of Amateur Cinematographers ad, *American Cinematographer*, January 1937, 23. The society's executive board included John Arnold, president of the A.S.C. and executive director of photography, MGM; Karl Struss, A.S.C., director of photography, Paramount; Fred Jackman, A.S.C.; Dan Clark, A.S.C., director of photography, Twentieth Century Fox; and David Abel, A.S.C., director of photography, Fred Astaire Productions and RKO Studio.

57. Frederick D. Ryder, "Simple Ways to Improve Home Movies," *Popular Science*, May 1937, 96.

58. Frederick D. Ryder, "Home Movies: How to Take Them like a Professional," *Popular Science*, May 1934, 72.

59. Ibid., 85.

60. Stull, "Amateur Movie Making," 26.

61. Margaret Hutcheson, "Par Shooting," *Amateur Movie Makers*, January 1927, 20.

62. Hal Hall, "What Do You Photograph—Are You a Snapshooter or Do You Make Pictures?," *American Cinematographer*, March 1930, 33.

63. Ibid.

64. "Amateur Movie Making," *American Cinematographer*, June 1929, 27.

65. Ryder, "Home Movies: How to Take Them like a Professional," 72.

66. Paul Hugon, "Acting vs. Naturalness," *Amateur Movie Makers*, June 1929, 385.

67. Norman Phelps, "Putting Kick into the Home Movie: An Amateur's Viewpoint on Aerial Cinematography for Amateurs," *American Cinematographer*, December 1929, 34.

68. William Stull, "Amateur Movie Making," *American Cinematographer*, December 1929, 34.

69. "Amateur Movie Set," *American Cinematographer*, March 1937, 119.

70. William Stull, "Amateur Movie Making," *American Cinematographer*, October 1930, 34.

71. For example, see William Stull, "Cut Brothers, Cut with Care," *American Cinematographer*, October 1937, 437.

72. See "Amateur Movie Making," *American Cinematographer*, March 1936, 114: "Our world would be drab indeed if our mental capacity encompassed only bare truths and shut out hope, imagination, and the capacity to attribute to others rare and priceless qualities which may be visible only to our inventive eyes." See also Val J. Roper, "Everybody's in the Movies Now," *American Cinematographer*, March 1929, 27, which discusses the dramatic resources of the family album on film.

73. Karl E. Barleban, Jr., "The Cine-Amateur," *American Photography*, March 1932, 161.

74. Paul W. Kearney, "Summer Movies," *Parents Magazine*, May 1937, 100.

75. Karl E. Barleban, Jr., "Improving Your Game," *Amateur Movie Makers*, June 1929, 394.

76. Ibid.

77. William Stull, "Amateur Movie Making," *American Cinematographer*, November 1929, 27.

78. Sterling Gleason, "Amateur Movie Makers Use Professional Tricks," *Popular Science*, March 1933, 28.

79. William Stull, "Amateur Movie Making," *American Cinematographer*, August 1930, 28.

80. Ibid., June 1930, 28.

81. See, for example, William Stott, *Documentary Expression and Thirties America* (London: Oxford University Press, 1973).

82. Hutcheson "Par Shooting," 20; and Amateur Cinema League, *The ACL Movie Book: A Guide to Making Better Movies* (New York: Amateur Cinema League, 1940), 76–91. The chapter on direction stresses that the father/camera operator rehearse all family members when shooting personal movies, because then the films, ironically enough, would be more natural.

83. William Stull, "Amateur Movie Making," *American Cinematographer*, September 1929, 27; and Stull, "Amateur Movie Making," May 1930, 28.

84. Herbert C. McKay, "Making the Home Movie," *Photo-Era Magazine*, May 1928, 306.

85. Diana Rice, "Amateur Movies an Organized Sport," *New York Times* 17 June 1934, p. 12, sec. 8, C3.

86. Sterling, "Sowing the 16mm Field," p. 3.

87. Ibid.

88. Amateur Cinema League, *The ACL Movie Book: A Guide to Making Better Movies* (New York: Amateur Cinema League, 1932).

89. *The ACL Movie Book* (1940), 294–305.

90. Ibid., 38–75.

91. Ibid., 261–82.

92. John Markland, "Home Films Gain Scope," *New York Times*, 21 November 1937, p. 10, sec. 12, C1.

93. See "Coveted British Award Given for 'Sanders of the River,' " *New York Times*, 2 January 1926, p. 21, C1; "Amateurs Show Films," *New York Times*, 5 April 1926, p. 7, sec. 2, C4; "New Yorker Wins Film Prize," *New York Times*, 16 November 1936, p. 14, C1; Bosley Crowther, "Amateur Film Night," *New York Times*, 9 April 1939, p. 5, sec. 10, C7; Rice, "Amateur Movies an Organized Sport," p. 12.

94. I have not been able to determine the last publication date of *Kodakery*. *Kodakery* began advertising amateur-film equipment in 1923.

95. *Filmo Topics*, 1925–41, Bell and Howell Corporate Archive.

96. See William Stull, "Professional Amateurs: Lon Chaney Trains His Cameras on Celebrities and Cougars between Pictures," *American Cinematographer*, January 1930, 38; John W. Boyle, A.S.C., "Cine Kodak on Alaskan Location," *American Cinematographer*, September 1930, 46; Phil Townsend Hanna, "Exploring Mexico with a 16mm Camera," *American Cinematogra-*

pher, October 1930, 38–39; Stull, "Professional Amateurs: Eyemo Girdles the Globe with Claudette Colbert and Norman Foster," *American Cinematographer*, December 1930, 36–39.

97. Herbert C. McKay, "The Cine Amateur," *American Photography*, June 1932, 348.

98. Herbert C. McKay, "Vacation Cameras," *Photo-Era Magazine*, August 1931, 110.

99. Helen Lockwood Coffin, "A Twentieth Century Pilgrim's Progress," *Amateur Movie Makers*, July 1929, 442; Ruth Hamilton Kerr, "Movie Makers Paradise," *Amateur Movie Makers*, May 1927, 27; Emma Lindsay Squier, "Movie Making in Mexico," *Amateur Movie Makers*, April 1929, 226–27.

100. Herbert C. McKay, "Movie Making by Up-To-Date Travelers," *Photo-Era Magazine*, May 1931, 291.

101. See Gardner Wells, "Around the World with a Little Movie Camera," *Amateur Movie Makers*, January 1927, 7; and P. W. West, "Angles and Arches," *Amateur Movie Makers*, June 1927, 13, for discussions of how to find the picturesque and pictorial in foreign countries.

102. See "Close-Ups and Swaps," *Amateur Movie Makers*, May 1927, 36; Gardner Wells, "Mediterranean Movies," *Amateur Movie Makers*, May 1927, 20; and William Walker, "The First Movie Makers Cruise: A New Idea for a National Hobby," *Amateur Movie Makers*, September 1927, 26.

103. The Human Studies Film Archive in the National Museum of Natural History, Smithsonian Institution, contains over seventy-five different amateur films shot around the world by Americans. Each collection varies in length from fifty feet to over ten thousand feet of 16mm film. Amateur films span from the turn of the century to the present. Originally, curators collected these films for the anthropological content as evidence of cultures now materially altered or changed. All films discussed in this section are part of the Human Studies Film Archive.

104. Recently, poststructuralist anthropologists have interrogated this issue of the representatism of the "other" in ethnography, travel writing, novels, art, colonial documents, and museum exhibitions. However, none of these writers confront the thorny problematic of visual representatism. See, for example, Edward Said, *Orientalism* (New York: Pantheon, 1978); James Clifford and George E. Marcus, eds., *Writing Culture: The Poetics and Politics of Ethnography* (Berkeley: University of California Press, 1986); George E. Marcus and Michael M. J. Fischer, *Anthropology as Cultural Critique: An Experimental Moment in the Human Sciences* (Chicago: University of Chicago Press, 1986); and James Clifford, *The Predicament of Culture: Twentieth Century Ethnography, Literature, and Art* (Cambridge, Mass.: Howard University Press, 1988).

105. William Stull, "Professional Amateurs," *American Cinematographer*, July 1930, 31, 34.

106. William Stull, "Professional Amateurs: 'My Filmo Is My Easel and Sketching Outfit,' Says Wesley Ruggles," *American Cinematographer*, September 1930, 30.

107. Ibid.

108. Bell and Howell Filmo ad, *American Cinematographer*, October 1930, 35.

109. William Stull, "Professional Amateurs: Jackson Rose, A.S.C.," *American Cinematographer*, April 1930, 32–33.

110. Ibid.

111. William Stull, "Professional Amateurs: Cecil DeMille Goes Eyemo Camera Angling," *American Cinematographer*, October 1930, 36–37, 42.

112. For a discussion of the drop in disposable income for consumer items and the general economic factors contributing to the Depression, see Thomas C. Cochran, *The Great Depression and World War II, 1929–1945* (Glenview, Ill.: Scott, Foresman and Co., 1968), 1–33. For a discussion of the Depression's influence on the Hollywood motion picture industry, see Sklar, *Movie-Made America*, 161–67.

113. See David Curtis, *Experimental Cinema* (New York: Universe, 1971), 38–42; Sheldon Renan, *An Introduction to the American Underground Film* (New York: Dutton, 1967), 75–78.

114. Sklar, *Movie-Made America*, 86–100.

115. Curtis, *Experimental Cinema*, 43–44.

116. William Alexander, *Film on the Left: American Documentary from 1931 to 1942* (Princeton, N.J.: Princeton University Press, 1981), 9.

117. Curtis, *Experimental Cinema*, 92; Erik Barnouw, *Documentary: A History of the Non-Fiction Film* (London: Oxford University Press, 1974), 71–82; Malcolm LeGrice, *Abstract Film and Beyond* (Cambridge, Mass.: MIT Press, 1977), 44–62.

118. Curtis, *Experimental Cinema*, 44–48.

119. Bertolt Brecht, "The Popular and the Realistic," in *Brecht on Theatre*, trans. John Willett (New York: Hill and Wang, 1964), 108.

120. Ibid.

121. Brecht, "Two Essays on Unprofessional Acting: Is It Worth Speaking about the Amateur Theater?" in *Brecht on Theatre*, 149.

122. George W. Hess, "The Cine Analyst: *Thunder over Mexico*," *Personal Movies*, November 1933, 268.

123. Ibid.

124. Alfred Richman, "Technique of the Russians," *American Movie Makers*, September 1929, 56.

125. C. W. Gibbs, "Modernistic Movie Making," *Amateur Movie Makers*, August 1929, 505.

126. Gilbert Seldes, "The Intellectual Film," *American Movie Makers*, March 1929, 15, 38; see also Harry Alan Potamkin, "Tendencies in the Cinema," in *The Compound Cinema*, ed. Lewis Jacobs (New York: Teachers' College Press, 1977), 43–46.

127. Bruce Bliven, "Home Movies in Excelsis," *New Republic*, 11 June 1930, 101.

128. Ibid.

129. Ibid., 102.

130. Editorial, *American Movie Makers*, January 1927, 5.

131. "The Little Movie Movement," *Amateur Movie Makers*, December 1926, 18.

132. "Amateur Cinema League: A Close-Up," *Amateur Movie Makers*, December 1926, 7.

133. Leonard Harker, *Cinematic Design* (Boston: American Photographic, 1931), 3.

134. Gilbert Seldes, "Home Movies," *New Republic*, 6 March 1929, 71.

135. Ibid.

136. Herman Weinberg, "A Paradox of the Photoplay," *Amateur Movie Makers*, January 1929, 866–67.

137. Potamkin, "Tendencies in the Cinema," in *The Compound Cinema*, 43, 46.

138. Ibid., "The Montage Film," 70–73.

139. Ibid., "The Magic of Machine Films," 80–84.

4. Cameras and Guns: 1941–1949

1. Hal Hall, "Fighting with Film," *American Cinematographer*, September 1945, 324.

2. "While Camera Planes Win Wars," *American Cinematographer*, April 1944, 115.

3. A. G. Zimmerman, "War Standard for Photographer Equipment Speed Military Training," *Journal of the Society of Motion Picture Engineers* (August 1933): 115.

4. Editors of *Look*, *Movie Lot to Beachhead: The Motion Picture Goes to War and Prepares for the Future* (Garden City, N.Y.: Doubleday, Doran and Co., 1945).

5. *Movie Lot to Beachhead*, 58–59.

6. For a lively discussion of the collaboration between Hollywood studios and the Office of War Information in producing propagandistic, patriotic narratives during World War II, see Clayton R. Keppes and Gregory D. Block, *Hollywood Goes to War* (New York: Free Press, 1987).

7. James Wong Howe, A.S.C., "The Documentary Technique and Hollywood," *American Cinematographer*, January 1944, 10, 32.

8. Ibid., 10.

9. Ibid.

10. Barnouw, *Documentary*, 155.

11. See Stott, *Documentary Expression and Thirties America*.

12. Barnouw, *Documentary*, 112.

13. Barry Staley, "Documentary Film Patterned from Prizewinners," *American Cinematographer*, February 1937, 69.

14. William Stull, A.S.C., "Amateurs Make Defense Films," *American Cinematographer*, February 1942, 68; Byron Haskin, A.S.C., "Miniatures for 16mm Defense Films," *American Cinematographer*, March 1942, 116–17, 145; LeNelle Fosholdt, "Diary of a Defense Film," *American Cinematographer*, April 1942, 162, 176; W. G. Campbell Bosco, "Amateur Movies and the War Effort," *American Cinematographer*, February 1943, 62, 68.

15. See Edward H. Schustack, "Documentary Film in America," *American Cinematographer*, March 1939, 130; James A. Sherlock, "Documentary for the Amateur," *American Cinematographer*, September 1939, 414; John Grierson, "Maker of Documentary," *American Cinematographer*, October 1939, 442; George Blaisdell, "Documentary No. 1," *American Cinematographer*, August 1939, 342.

16. John Grierson, "Documentary Films in War Time," *American Cinematographer*, March 1942, 10.

17. Joris Ivens, "Making Documentary Films to Meet Today's Need," *American Cinematographer*, July 1942, 298–99.

18. Ibid.

19. Richard Meram Barsam, *Non-Fiction: A Critical History* (New York: Dutton, 1973), 180–81.

20. Ibid., 193–94.

21. George Raynor Thompson, Dixie R. Harris, Pauline M. Oakes, and Dulany Terret, *United States Army in World War II, the Technical Services, the Signal Corps: The Test (December 1941 to July 1943)* (Washington, D.C.: Office of the Chief of Military History, Department of the Army, 1957), 395–96. These volumes on the Signal Corps use documents from the Signal Corps historical files, correspondence, memos, and personal interviews.

22. Dulany Terret, *United States Army in World War II, the Technical Services, the Signal Corps: The Emergency (To December 1941)* (Washington, D.C.: Office of the Chief of Military History, Department of the Army, 1956), 225–30.

23. Quoted in Thompson et al., *The Test*, 398–400.

24. Thompson et al., *The Test* 402–403.

25. Terret, *The Emergency*, 224.

26. Thompson et al., *The Test*, 394–96.

27. Fielding, *The American Newsreel*, 288–303.

28. See Christopher H. Sterling and John M. Kittross, *Stayed Tuned: A Concise History of American Broadcasting* (Belmont, Calif.: Wadsworth, 1978), 200–245.

29. Random survey of *Life* and *Look*, 1938–45.

30. Thompson et al., *The Test*, 395.

31. John Morton Blum, *V Was for Victory: Politics and American Culture during World War II* (New York: Harcourt, 1976).

32. Thompson et al., *The Test*, 402, 408–11.

33. George Raynor Thompson and Dixie R. Harris, *United States Army in World War II, the Technical Services, the Signal Corps: The Outcome (Mid-1943 Through 1945)* (Washington, D.C.: Office of the Chief of Military History, United States Army, 1966), 565–69.

34. "Leica Gets Away from Tripod by Employing Gunstock for Platform," *American Cinematographer*, March 1938, 117.

35. Kenneth O. Hazzlewood, "Shooting Action Movies from a Gunstock Mount," *American Cinematographer*, October 1942, 444.

36. Thompson et al., *The Test*, 394–96; Thompson and Harris, *The Outcome*, 573–78; *Movie Lot to Beachhead*, 148–65.

37. Historical file on Bell and Howell equipment advertisements, 1940–45, Bell and Howell Corporate Archive.

38. G. G. Newhard, "Motion Picture Camera in Army Air Forces," *Journal of the Society of Motion Picture Engineers* (June 1942): 510.

39. See J. L. Boon, "Some Unusual Adaptations of 16mm Equipment for Special Purposes," *Journal of the Society of Motion Picture Engineers* (October 1938): 386–92; E. L. Gayhardt, "Model Basin High Speed Camera for Propeller Research," *American Society of Naval Engineers Journal* 49 no. 2 (May 1937): 174–83; Major Gilbert Warenton, A.S.C., U.S.A.A.F., "Greatest Photographic Organization in History Shot Bikini Blast," *American Cinematographer*, October 1946, 352; Lloyd W. Kenchtel, A.S.C., "Photographing the Underwater Atomic Bomb Test at Bikini," *American Cinematographer*, September 1946, 315.

40. C. E. Eraser, "Motion Pictures in United States Navy," *Journal of the Society of Motion Picture Engineers* (December 1932): 546–52.

41. Ibid., 550; and "Spotting by Film—Blenheim IV," *Aeroplane* 25 (October 1940): 460–61. Also see "Training Apparatus for Air Gunners," 158 no. 4,112, *Engineering* 3 (November 1944): 347.

42. F. W. Horn, "Military Training and Historical Films," *Journal of the Society of Motion Picture Engineers* (October 1933): 337–42.

43. Terret, *The Emergency*, 224–26; Thompson and Harris, *The Outcome*, 569–72.

44. A. Nadell, "16mm vs. 35mm Projection in Army Training Camps," *International Projectionist*, June 1943, 7–8, 18–19.

45. See O. Gouldner, "Problems in Production of U.S. Navy Training Films," *Journal of the Society of Motion Picture Engineers* (August 1943): 146–56; Frederick Heron, "U.S. Naval Photographic Services Depot," *Journal of the Society of Motion Picture Engineers* (October 1945): 294–96; Walter Exton, "Development in Use of Motion Pictures by Navy," *Journal of the Society of Motion Picture Engineers* (August 1943): 141–45; John G. Bradley, "Motion Pictures and the War Effort," *Journal of the Society of Motion Picture Engineers* (May 1943): 281–90; Les Carr, "Motion Picture in Service of Army Air Forces," *Journal of the Society of Motion Picture Engineers* (October 1943): 329–31; and Robert B. Konikow, "Motion Pictures in the Army," *American Cinematographer*, February 1942, 59, 84.

46. Carl Preyer, A.S.C., "Movies Report on Defense Programs," *American Cinematographer*, August 1943, 445.

47. Walter Exton, "Navy's Use of Motion Picture Films for Training Purposes," *Journal of the Society of Motion Picture Engineers*, June 1942, 504.

48. "A.S.C. and the Academy to Train Cameramen for Army Services," *American Cinematographer*, June 1942, 255.

49. "Uncle Sam's Cameramen Are Coming," *American Cinematographer*, September 1942, 418.

50. "A.S.C. and the Academy to Train Cameramen for Army Services," *American Cinematographer*, 255.

51. "Marines Learn Photography in Hollywood," *American Cinematographer*, October 1943, 364.

52. For example, "A.S.C. on Parade," *American Cinematographer*, July 1942, 306, lists A.S.C. members in Army Signal Corps positions.

53. Ray Fernstrom, A.S.C., "Solving Army Photo Problems," *American Cinematographer*, December 1944, 406.

54. The Human Studies Film Archive, National Museum of Natural History, Smithsonian Institution, contains many collections of film shot in Oceania. A bracketed title in the archive catalog indicates a full film record, that is, a chronological set of unedited rushes. "Hawaiian Hula Positions" is an example of this sort of ethnography of the progression of interactions between filmmakers and informants. Changes in the relationship between filmmakers and subjects, such as increased familiarity and closer shooting, can be evidenced in these records.

The edited versions, in this case "The Hula of Old Hawaii," can more clearly illustrate the decisions, allusions, and editing interventions of the filmmakers, progressing from production to finished product.

55. Travelers' representations and contacts with the people of the South Pacific have recently engaged anthropologists investigating the intricate nature of colonial encounters. Recent work in this area includes Bob Connally and Robin Anderson, *First Contact: New Guinea Highlanders Encounter the Outside World* (New York: Penguin, 1988); James L. Peacock, *The Anthropological Lens: Harsh Light, Soft Focus* (Cambridge: Cambridge University Press, 1986); Mary Helms, *Ulysses' Sail: An Ethnographic Odyssey of Power, Knowledge and Geographical Distance* (Princeton: Princeton University Press, 1988); and Marshall Sahlins, *Islands of History* (Chicago: University of Chicago Press, 1985).

56. W. R. McGee, "Cinematography Goes to War," *Journal of the Society of Motion Picture Engineers* (February 1944): 104.

57. R. Jester, "Operation of Army Air Force Combat Units in Theaters of War," *Journal of the Society of Motion Picture Engineers* (August 1943): 136–40.

58. Reed Haythorne, A.S.C., "The Air Corps' Newest Camera Gun," *American Cinematographer*, January 1942, 11.

59. William Stull, A.S.C., "The First Real Combat Camera," *American Cinematographer*, November 1942, 474.

60. "Aerial Photography First Step to Battle," *American Cinematographer*, December 1943, 435.

61. Wilton Stott, "Amateur Movie Gadget Contributes to War Effort," *American Cinematographer*, April 1942, 142.

62. Claude DeVinna, "Field Hints for Military Cinematographers," *American Cinematographer*, May 1942, 198.

63. Thompson et al., *The Test*, 104.

64. McGee, "Cinematography Goes to War," 105; Thompson et al., *The Test*, 401.

65. See, for example, Hal Hall, "Fighting with Film," 324–25, 346; Wilma Madden, "Shooting the War in New Guinea," *American Cinematographer*, June 1943, 209; Harry Perry, A.S.C., "Camerawork on a Convoy," *American Cinematographer*, January 1943, 12, 26; Alvin Wyckoff, A.S.C., "Fighting Cameramen," *American Cinematographer*, February 1944, 444–45; Burr McGregor, "Cameramen At War," *American Cinematographer*, May 1944, 150–51.

66. Lieutenant Arthur Arling, U.S.N.R., A.S.C., "Cameramen in Uniform," *American Cinematographer*, January 1944, 32.

67. James Wong Howe, "The Documentary Technique and Hollywood," *American Cinematographer*, January 1944, 32.

68. For a discussion of the work of the Society of Motion Picture Engineers War Standards Committee, see D. E. Hundman, "War Standards for Motion Picture Equipment and Processes," *Journal of the Society of Motion Picture Engineers* (April 1944): 211–19; J. M. Whittenton, "Report of Subcommittee G on Exposure Meters," *Journal of the Society of Motion Picture Engineers* (July 1944): 250–59; Paul Hyndman, "Report of Engineering V.P. on Standardization," *Journal of the Society of Motion Picture Engineers* (July 1944): 1–4.

69. Northeast Historic Film in Blue Hill, Maine, has initiated a long-term project to archive amateur and semiprofessional films shot in Maine as local history of daily life. It has extensive and continually growing holdings of these films.

70. "Hopi Horizons" is archived in the Human Studies Film Archive of the Smithsonian Institution, interestingly, as an ethnographic film on North American Indians.

71. Ezra Goodman, "Post War Motion Pictures," *American Cinematographer*, May 1945, 160.

72. "What's New in Equipment, Accessories, Service," *American Cinematographer*, November 1945, 371. For a good overview of documentary uses in commercial and industrial film, see Herb A. Lightman, "New Horizons for the Documentary Film," *American Cinematographer*, December 1945, 418, 422.

73. Herb A. Lightman, "The Techniques of the Documentary Film," *American Cinematographer*, November 1945, 371.

74. Irving Browning, "The Documentary Film," *American Cinematographer*, February 1945, 45, 64–65.

75. Goodman, "Post War Motion Pictures," 160, 176.

76. "Academy War Film Library," *American Cinematographer*, April 1945, 46.

77. Howe, "The Documentary Technique and Hollywood," 32.

5. Do-It-Yourself: 1950–1962

1. Marty Jezer, *The Dark Ages: Life in the United States, 1945–1960* (Boston: South End, 1982), 118–53.

2. Dero A. Saunders and Sanford S. Parket, "30 Billion for Fun," in *Mass Leisure*, ed. Eric Larrabee and Rolf Meyersohn (Glencoe, Ill.: Free Press, 1958), 162.

3. See, for example, Alfred C. Clarke, "Leisure and Occupational Prestige," in *Mass Leisure*, ed. Larrabee and Meyersohn, 205–14.

4. "Leisured Masses," *Business Week*, 12 September 1953, 142–43.

5. Ibid., 145.

6. Jezer, *The Dark Ages*, 192–234.

7. "Leisured Masses," *Business Week*, 145.

8. Joseph S. Zeisel, "The Workweek in American Industry," in *Mass Leisure*, ed. Larrabee and Meyersohn, 149.

9. Arthur D. Little, 1956 audit of Bell and Howell Corporation, 22, Table IV, Bell and Howell Corporate Archive.

10. Ibid., 33.

11. 1949 Bell and Howell Annual Report, 10; see also 1946, 1947, and 1948 Annual Reports, Bell and Howell Corporate Archive.

12. 1952 Bell and Howell Annual Report, 18–19, Bell and Howell Corporate Archive.

13. 1952 Bell and Howell Annual Report, 4–5.

14. Ibid., 12.

15. Little, 1956 audit of Bell and Howell Corporation, 34, Table X.

16. 1952 Bell and Howell Annual Report, 6; Robinson, *Bell and Howell Company*, 84–92.

17. Little, 1956 audit of Bell and Howell Corporation, 2; and 1954 Bell and Howell Annual Report, Bell and Howell Corporate Archive.

18. 1954 Bell and Howell Annual Report, 37.

19. Paul A. Wagner, "What's Past of Prologue," in *Sixty Years of 16mm Film, 1923–1983; A Symposium*, Film Council of America (Des Plaines, Ill.: Film Council of America, 1982), 12. This book contains numerous articles on the use of 16mm for industry, education, churches, community groups, and libraries. For a view of educational films in 16mm generated during the period of the 1950s, see F. Dean McCluskey, "Public Schools," pamphlet (Evanston, Ill.: Film Council of America, 1954).

20. Bell and Howell press release, 27 January 1955, 1–2, Bell and Howell Corporate Archive.

21. See Richard Pollenberg, "The Suburban Nation," chap. 4 in his *One Nation Divisible* (Harmondsworth, England: Penguin, 1980), 127–63. For a very thorough historical study of shifts in housing toward outlying suburban areas that explains the relationship between community, ethnicity, income, and suburbia, see Kenneth T. Jackson, *Crabgrass Frontier: The Suburbanization of the United States* (Oxford: Oxford University Press, 1985).

22. 1954 Bell and Howell Annual Report, 3.

23. "Leisured Masses," *Business Week*, 143.

24. David Reisman, "The Suburban Sadness," in *The Suburban Community*, ed. William M. Dobriner (New York: G. P. Putnam's Sons, 1958), 375–408.

25. United States Department of Commerce, "The Do-It-Yourself Market," in *Mass Leisure*, ed. Larrabee and Meyersohn, 274-81.

26. Dero A. Saunders and Sanford S. Parket, "30 Billion for Fun," *Fortune*, June 1954, 115-19.

27. Little, 1956 Audit of Bell and Howell Corporation, 3,

28. Ibid., 42.

29. Ibid., 43-44. For a discussion of how Bell and Howell saw the introduction of lower-priced equipment as a way to counter increased foreign competition, see 1954 Bell and Howell Annual Report, 3, 9.

30. Little, 1956 audit of Bell and Howell Corporation, 66; "Bell and Howell: A Case Study," *Tide*, 1 July 1949, 23-27.

31. Revere camera ad, *Photography*, August 1953, 97.

32. Bell and Howell camera ad, *Photography*, July 1953, 94.

33. Kodak camera ad, *American Photography*, May 1951, 302.

34. Bell and Howell 70DL ad, *Photography*, August 1953, 86. For further discussion of professionalization in the 1950s and 1960s on the social and economic fronts with a focus on the removal of academics from the public sphere, see Russell Jacoby, "The Decline of American Intellectuals," in *Cultural Politics in Contemporary America*, ed. Ian Argus and Sut Jhally (New York: Routledge and Kegan Paul, 1989).

35. Sklar, *Movie-Made America*, 283.

36. Ibid., 283-85.

37. Ibid., 285.

38. Herbert O. Johansen, "Wide Screen Movies Come to the Home: Filmorama," *Popular Science*, February 1955, 225-28.

39. DeJur camera ad, *Popular Photography*, April 1962, 107.

40. Little, 1956 audit of Bell and Howell Corporation, 74.

41. Ibid.

42. Ibid., 48-54.

43. James D. Tarver, "Suburbanization of Retail Trade in the Standard Metropolitan Areas of the United States, 1948-1954," in *Mass Leisure*, ed. Larrabee and Meyersohn, 195-205.

44. "Percy Profile," TS, December 1959, 12, Bell and Howell Corporate Archive.

45. Ibid., 13.

46. "Investors Forum: WGN-TV Suggested Material for Leisure Time Discussion," TS, November 1961, 3, Bell and Howell Corporate Archive.

47. "Percy Profile," 5.

48. Ibid., 6.

49. "Investors Forum: WGN-TV," 7-10.

50. Ibid., 12-13.

51. *How to Make Good Movies* (Rochester: Eastman Kodak, circa 1950) 28.

52. David Reisman, "Leisure and Work in Post-Industrial Society," in *Mass Leisure*, ed. Larrabee and Meyersohn, 368-79.

53. Wendell Bell, "Social Choice, Life Styles, and Suburban Residence," in *The Suburban Community*, ed. Dobriner, 234.

54. Roy Pinney, "Tell a Story with Your Movie Camera," *Parents Magazine*, September 1956, 139.

55. Bell and Howell internal memo, "Information for Television Magazine," 22 October 1954, 1, Bell and Howell Corporate Archive; and "Investors Forum: WGN-TV," 1-12.

56. "Investors Forum: WGN-TV," 1-12.

57. See Jezer, *The Dark Ages*, 138-46, for a discussion of the transportation industry during the 1950s.

58. Jezer, *The Dark Ages*, 143-44. See also Jackson, *Crabgrass Frontier*.

59. Dean MacCannell, *The Tourist: A New Theory of the Leisure Class* (New York: Schocken, 1976), 34.

60. Francis X. Nolan, "You Need a Plan for Your Movies," *American Photographer*, August 1951, 500.

61. Esther Cooke, "Travel Checklist: Make a Travelog," *Popular Photography*, July 1962, 110.

62. *How to Make Good Movies*, 71–75.

63. For example, see "25 Tips for Sharper Movies," *Popular Photography*, August 1961, 86–87.

64. "Shooting Script for Christmas Time Home Movies," *Better Homes and Gardens*, December 1960, 26.

65. Arvil Ahlers, "Special Effects," *Popular Photography*, September 1962, 88–89.

66. Hugh Bell, "Ringlight Your Next Party Film," *Photography*, November 1954, 105.

67. Ed Corley, "Liberate Your Camera," *Popular Photography*, April 1962, 100.

68. Ibid., 98.

69. *How to Make Good Movies*, 61.

70. James C. Dobyns, "Three C's for Movie Makers," *Photography*, August 1953, 96.

71. Carlyle F. Trevelyan, "Let's Make Movies," *American Photography*, October 1952, 42.

72. Quotation is from Roy Pinney, "Better Home Movies," *Parents Magazine*, May 1955, 126. For additional examples of this emphasis on audience comprehension, see also Payton M. Stallings, "How to Make Your Movies More Interesting," *American Photography*, June 1951, 359–61; and Bob Clouse, "Jerry Lewis, Movie Maker: Hints to Fellow Amateurs," *Photography*, December 1953, 87, 164.

73. Roy Creveling, "How to Sustain Movie Interest," *Photography*, September 1953, 94, 115.

74. Carlyle F. Trevelyan, "Put in a Good Word: Editing and Titling," *American Photography*, January 1952, 51.

75. For example, see Robert B. Rohberton and Arthur Goldman, "Edit Your Movies for Applause," *American Photography*, February 1952, 42–77.

76. Robert Newman, "When Your Film Needs Words," *Popular Photography*, September 1959, 82–88.

77. Harry Kursh and Harold Mehling, "Your Life on Film: Ralph Eno, Amateur Editor," *American Mercury*, November 1956, 69.

78. Chester Burger, "Cover Your Town for TV," *Popular Photography*, October 1955, 68–69. See also John Gilligan, "Television Documentaries Use Amateur Footage," *Popular Photography*, January 1958, 120.

79. Burger, "Cover Your Town for TV," 68–69.

80. For discussions of this second wave of avant-garde film, important secondary sources are Curtis, *Experimental Cinema*, 49–133; LeGrice, *Abstract Film and Beyond*, 74–85; Renan, *An Introduction to the American Underground Film*, 83–103; Sitney, *Visionary Film: The American Avant-Garde, 1943–1978*, 3–172, which describes the films of Maya Deren, James Broughton, Stan Brakhage, and Kenneth Anger during the 1950s; and Lauren Rabinovitz, *Points of Resistance: Women Power and Politics in the New York Avant-Garde Cinema, 1943–1971* (Urbana: University of Illinois Press, 1991).

81. Sklar, *Movie-Made America*, 306–307.

82. Charles Reynolds, "Maya Deren," *Popular Photography*, February 1962, 83.

83. Sitney, *Visionary Film: The American Avant-Garde, 1943–1978*, 40.

84. Ibid., 40–46.

85. Curtis, *Experimental Cinema*, 51.

86. Maya Deren, "Planning by Eye: Notes on 'Individual' and 'Industrial' Film," *Film Culture;* 39 (Winter 1965): 35.

87. Ibid., 35, 37.

88. Maya Deren, "Amateur versus Professional," *Film Culture* 39 (Winter 1965): 45–46.

89. A few examples of these reviews can be found in Barbara Krasne, "Sound Tracks to Art Appreciation," *Independent Woman*, June 1948, 176–78; M. A. Guitar, "Facts on Film," *Nation*, 26 August 1950, 194; Cecile Starr, "Film Forum," *Saturday Review*, 23 September 1950, 28; Starr,

"Film Forum," *Saturday Review of Literature*, 24 February 1951, 37; Starr, "Film Forum: 16mm Sound Films," *Saturday Review*, 28 June 1852, 32; A. Rosenheimer, "Small Screen: 16mm Distribution in Non-theatrical Field," *Theatre Arts*, September 1947, 7. The *Magazine of Art* ran film reviews of art films from 1949–1953.

90. For a discussion of John Whitney and James Whitney, see E. Willis, "Abstract Film Explorations," *Theatre Arts*, February 1947, 52–53; a description of the films shown in the Museum of Modern Art Program of Abstract Film can be found in Cecile Starr, "Dots and Dashes, Circles and Splashes," *Saturday Review*, 8 March 1952, 64, 78–79; a description of Norman McLaren's films is in "Movies without a Camera, Music without Instruments," *Theatre Arts*, October 1952, 16–17; and an essay by experimental filmmaker Hans Richter arguing for film as a plastic art is in "Easel, Scroll, Film," *Magazine of Art*, February 1952, 78–86. A satirical look at low-budget, feature-length art films appears in Paddy Chayesky's "Art Films: Dedicated Insanity," *Saturday Review*, 21 December 1957, 16–17.

91. Arthur Knight, "Self-Expression," *Saturday Review of Literature*, 27 May 1950, 38.

92. Ibid., 40.

93. Cecile Starr, "Animation: Abstract and Concrete," *Saturday Review*, 13 December 1952, 46–48.

94. Reynolds, "Maya Deren," 83.

95. Jezer, *The Dark Ages*, 223–25.

96. Ibid.

97. Ben L. Williams, "Home Movies for a Winter Evening," *House and Garden*, December 1954, 162. Further examples of this promotion of amateur filmmaking as a family endeavor include a number of articles by Cecile Starr in *House Beautiful*: "You Can Make Your Own Movies," April 1954, 113–15; May 1954, 240–43; "You Can Make Your Own Movies: Word Portrait of J. E. Davies," June 1954, 170–72; "Your Child's Own Moviemaking," September 1954, 22.

98. Margaret Mead, "The Pattern of Leisure in Contemporary Culture," in *Mass Leisure*, ed. Larabee and Meyersohn, 14.

99. Ernest Mower, "The Family in Suburbia," in *The Suburban Community*, ed. Dobriner, 157.

100. "How You Can Make the Most of Family Leisure," *Woman's Home Companion*, October 1955, 110–19. For other articles on the family as the subject for amateur films, see also David McLane, "Stories in Close-Up: Film Record of Family Activities," *Photography*, December 1953, 163; David W. DeArmand, "How to Shoot Home Movies," *Parents Magazine*, April 1953, 110; and Roy Pinney, "Make a Motion Picture Record of Your Baby," *Parents Magazine*, October 1955, 146.

101. Virginia C. Rylands, "We Make Movies for Remembering," *Woman's Home Companion*, October 1955, 112.

102. DeArmand, "How to Shoot Home Movies," 110.

103. Vance Packard, "We're in the Movies Now," *American Magazine*, October 1952, 38–39, 111. Quote in text is from page 111.

104. Ibid., 111.

105. Ibid.

106. Martha Wolfenstein, "The Emergence of the Fun Morality," in *Mass Leisure*, ed. Larrabee and Meyersohn, 91.

107. Pinney, "Make a Motion Picture Record of Your Baby," 146.

108. Meryl E. Nelson, "Catch and Keep Your Happiest Moments," *Parents Magazine*, August 1951, 42.

109. Roy Pinney, "Better Vacation Movies," *Parents Magazine*, June 1956, 26.

110. The material on Ethel Cutler Freeman is archived in the Ethel Cutler Freeman Papers, National Anthropology Archive, National Museum of Natural History, Smithsonian Institution. The papers are fairly extensive, including correspondence, field notes, endless drafts of research papers, conference articles, newspaper-clipping files, and diaries. Her films on the Semi-

noles and Africa are housed in the Human Studies Film Archive of the National Museum of Natural History.

111. A sample of the articles in her film file include "Confiscated Film Cleared in New Jersey," *New York Times*, 20 May 1952; Bosley Crowther, "A Lesson in the Cinema," *New York Times*, 5 September 1948; as well as many articles on documentary and amateur filmmaking that were not cited. Her reviews include "Captain John Smith and Pocahontas," *Natural History*, December 1953, 476; and some undated reviews from *Films in Review*.

112. Ethel Cutler Freeman, "Africa 1950," 10 March 1950, 1, Ethel Cutler Freeman Papers.

113. Ibid., 4.

114. Ibid.

115. Ibid., 7.

116. Ibid., 5.

6. Reinventing Amateurism

1. *Nissan Ariana Window* is available from Filmmakers Cooperative, 175 Lexington Avenue, New York, New York 10016. *Peeping Tom* is available from Corinth Films, 34 Gansevoort Street, New York, New York 10014. *Demon Lover Diary* is distributed by Demott/Kreines Films, 5330 Kennedy Avenue, Millbrook, Alabama 36054.

2. For examples of this discarding of amateur film, see William C. Banks, "Taking the Horror Out of Home Movies," *Money*, September 1983, 61–66; Harry Waters, "Personal Historian," *Newsweek*, 30 December 1983, 52–53; William D. Marback, "Video's New Focus," *Newsweek*, 30 December 1985, 56–57; Leendert Drukker, "Video," *Popular Photography*, May 1982, 96–180; "Making a Minor Motion Picture," *Esquire*, March 1982, 26–27; Drukker, "The Video Difference: Taping vs. Filming," *Popular Photography*, May 1981, 90–92, 191; Randall Tierney, "Pieces of 8," *American Film*, December 1990, 50; "Putting Your Home Movies on Tape," *Forbes*, 26 December 1988, 128.

3. Banks, "Taking the Horror Out of Home Movies," 61.

4. See Dawn Gordon, "Buying a Video Camera?" *High Fidelity*, February 1982, 44–45; Edward J. Foster, "A Full Measure of Enjoyment," *High Fidelity*, January 1981, 9–15; *Audio/Video Buyer's Guide*, Spring 1987; *Video*, March 1987; *Video Review*, March 1987; Drukker, "Video," 96; Marback, "Video's New Focus," 56–67; Drukker, "Sony Shows Prototype Video Camera/Recorder," *Popular Photography*, September 1980, 42; Drukker, "Video/Movie Methods," *Popular Photography*, April 1982, 70, 72, 74; "Picture Brightens for Portable Video," *High Fidelity*, July 1983, 45; Georgia Dullea, "Camcorder! Action! Lives Become Roles," *New York Times*, 15 August 1990, A1, sec. C10; Dullea, "Look! Down in the Basement! It's Captain Video of the East Coast Tuning His Ham TV!" *TV Guide*, 27 August–2 September 1988, 30–33; Karen Geller-Shinn, "Make Your Own Still Videos", *Petersen's Photographic Journal* (February 1989): 14; George Schaub, "Beating the Video Boos," *Video*, December 1988, 48, 129, 149; David Hajdu, "How to Shoot Your Own Video," *Seventeen*, December 1988, 71–72; Brent Butterworth, "New Gadgets Glamorize Home Shooting," *Video*, 1 April 1990, 18–19.

5. Leendert Drukker, "Shoot Home Movies Like a Pro: Al Maysles Says Attitude Is the Key," *Popular Photography*, December 1982, 44–46, 64. For another example of an article on handheld shooting, see Benjamin C. Pratt, Jr., "Video Vignettes," *High Fidelity*, May 1982, 38–39.

6. Drukker, "Shoot Home Movies Like a Pro," 46.

7. See "Making a Minor Motion Picture," *Esquire*, 26–27; Michele A. Frank, "The Gadgeteria," *Popular Photography*, May 1982, 22, 62. Frank discusses how amateur video is deficient

> when the home user puts his attempts at video "filming" on the television screen, and the results are judged against what he is accustomed to seeing, his work will seem woefully inadequate. The amateur doesn't have sound stages or banks of lights, and he can't easily edit his tapes, add sound, or perform a multitude of professional "tricks." (62)

8. George Kuchar, "Shooting 8mm Video," *Motion Picture* 1 no. 3 (Winter/Spring 1987): 3.

9. The persistence of this ideology of familialism can be evidenced in almost any representation or discussion of home-video usage: for example, Kenneth Korman, "Home Video Contest Winners," *Video*, September 1991, 46–47; Bonnie Remsberg, "I Wish I Could Hold You More," *Reader's Digest*, June 1989, 147–52.

10. For a discussion of Sadie Benning's use of Pixelvision, see Susan Sturgis, "Up from the Underground," *Village Voice*, 7 December 1993, 76. Benning's frank discussions of her own sexuality in the form of autobiography need to be set up within the discourse of home-video pornography; Benning's work represents redefining her own sexuality, while the productions of home porn illustrate how dominant representational systems have colonized the private production of sexual imagery. For example, see Anastasia Toufexis, "Sex, Lives, and Videotape," *Time*, 29 October 1990, 104; and Gerri Hirshey, "Surveillance Sex," *Gentleman's Quarterly*, February 1993, 47–52. According to Hirshey, amateur sex videos are a growing portion of the two-billion-dollar-a-year adult video market. Benning's films are available from Women Make Movies, 225 Lafayette Street, New York, New York 10012.

11. *Silverlake Life: The View from Here* was one of the most widely acclaimed documentaries of 1993. See Arion Berger, "Last Will and Testament," *LA Weekly*, 19 March–25 March 1993, 47; Kenneth Turan, "To Be Young, Vital and Dying of AIDS," *Los Angeles Times*, 19 March 1993, 48; Bruce Mirken, "Life and Death in Silverlake," *Los Angeles Reader*, 19 March 1993, 25. The film is available from Zeitgeizt Films, 247 Center Street, New York, New York 10013.

12. Earl Casey, Managing Editor, Cable News Network, phone interview, 21 September 1987. For discussions of home-video news production, see Jeff Greenfield, "Our Lives, Our World, Our Camcorders—TV in the Video Age Finds the Old Notion of Media Power Turning on Its Head," *TV Guide*, 25–31 July 1992, 17–19; Joanna Elm, "Tonight's Hot Story Is Brought to You . . . by You!" *TV Guide*, 24 February–2 March 1990, 22–27; Stan Pinkwas, "Camcorder Justice," *Video*, October 1991, 4; News on the March," *Video*, February 1991, 12–13; "Handy Cam," *Discover*, January 1992, 64; Greg Luft, "Camcorders: When Amateurs Go after the News," *Columbia Journalism Review* (September 1991): 35–37.

13. Marbach, "Vidoe's New Focus," 57.

14. Drukker, "Video/Movie Methods," 16, 36.

Index

Patricia R. Zimmermann is associate professor in the Department of Cinema and Photography at Ithaca College. Her articles on the history of amateur film, documentary, and feminist film and video have appeared in *Screen*, *Afterimage*, *Journal of Film and Video*, *Cinema Journal*, *The Independent*, *Genders*, *Wide Angle*, and *Current Research in Film*.

LaVergne, TN USA
23 January 2011
213564LV00002B/7/A

9 780253 209443